Other Penny Whistle Books:

The Penny Whistle Party Planner
The Penny Whistle Lunch Box Book
The Penny Whistle Halloween Book
The Penny Whistle Christmas Party Book

The Penny Whistle™
BIRTHDAY
PARTY BOOK

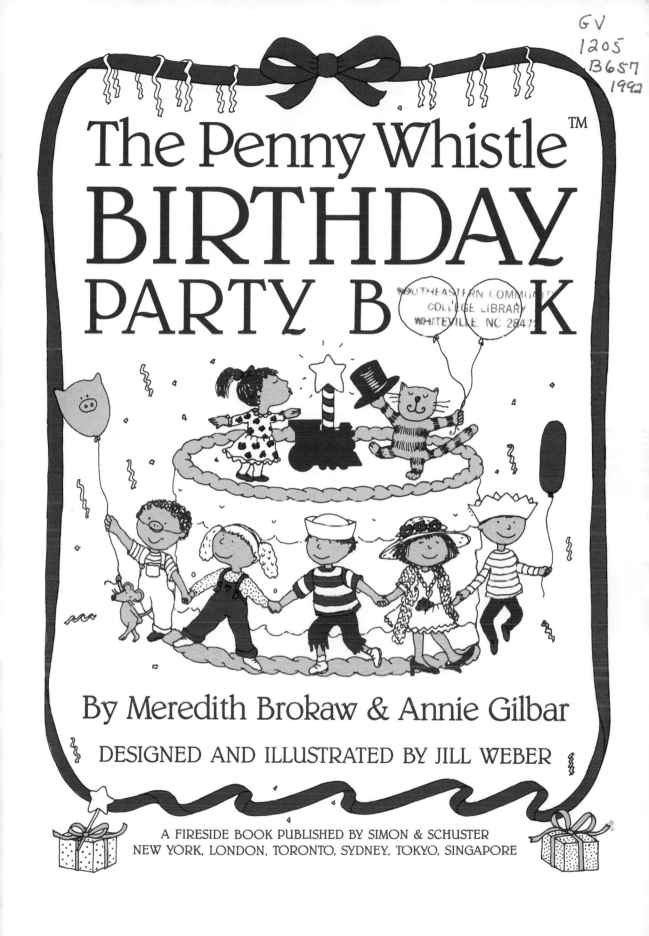

By Meredith Brokaw & Annie Gilbar

DESIGNED AND ILLUSTRATED BY JILL WEBER

A FIRESIDE BOOK PUBLISHED BY SIMON & SCHUSTER
NEW YORK, LONDON, TORONTO, SYDNEY, TOKYO, SINGAPORE

SIMON & SCHUSTER/FIRESIDE

Rockefeller Center
1230 Avenue of the Americas
New York, New York 10020

Designed by Jill Weber
Manufactured in the United States of America

10 9 8 7 6 5 4 3 2 1
10 9   Pbk.

Library of Congress Cataloging in Publication Data

Brokaw, Meredith.
  The Penny Whistle birthday party book / by Meredith Brokaw
& Annie Gilbar; designed & illustrated by Jill Weber.
     p.   cm.
  "A Fireside book."
  Includes index.
  1. Children's parties. 2. Birthdays. 3. Games. I. Gilbar, Annie.
II. Title.
GV1205.B657 1992   92-3771
793.2'1—dc20   CIP

ISBN 0-671-77853-6
     0-671-73795-3 Pbk.

To JENNIFER BROKAW,

the eldest of the Brokaw and Gilbar clans,
whose ingenious creativity inspired
many of the parties in this book.

ACKNOWLEDGMENTS

Thank you, Thank you, Thank you:

• To Lisa and Marc Gilbar, Andrea and Sarah Brokaw, and Remy Weber, for continuing to patiently tell us your ideas, opinions, and experiences whenever we ask—which is often!

• To Tom Brokaw, Gary Gilbar, and Frank Weber, for everything.

• To all our readers who take the time to write us, recounting your experiences with our books and especially generously sharing your own creations and ideas. Keep them coming!

• To Suzanne Donahue, Bonni Leon, Caroline Cunningham, Jackie Seow, and Fletcher Typesetting—for all your help; Kathy Robbins, Elizabeth Mackey, and everyone at The Robbins Agency for *unequaled* patience, not to mention expertise with a smile.

• To Sydny Miner, our favorite editor (and mother).

• And to our many friends who still answer our phone calls, knowing full well we'll be asking you to share yet another recipe or memory.

Aileen Adams
Susan McRee Adams
Jill and Cindy Anderson
Maureen Barum
Brittany Bell
Candace Block
Karen Blumberg
Evan Bogart
Louanne Bond
Jean Brokaw
Amos, Sophie, Jeff, and
    Suzanne Buhai
Inez Burgen
Patricia and Eve Bushouse
Colette, Jim, and
    Nancy Chuda
Gabriel Cowan
Melissa, Cassie, and
    Adam Dabilis
Emily Deschanel
Cynthia and Michael Doyle
Kacey and Ellen Fields
Erin Fischer
Chana Leah Friedman
Tim Green
Jane Hait
Mrs. William Hart
Betty and Matt Kerpen
Margie Hollingsworth
Sonia, Andy, Sarah, and
    David Israel
Adam and Miki Jaeger
Alix Kantor
Jon Kasdan

The Kassans
Janey and Lou Klein
Suzy Kreiser
Pam, Lind, and
    Bobby Krenzke
Sharon Krost
The Lallis
Penny Landreth
Chris Landry
Tracy Large
Matt Lattanzi and Chloe
Debbie Lingrey
Dale, Matthew, and
    Joanna Mallory
Betsy Mallow
Jennifer, Jerry, and
    Erin Mann
Nancy and Andrew Marks
Ellen, Jennifer, and
    Sarah Meyer
Cindy Molnar
Natalie and Françoise
    Morison
The Nathansons
Cherie Nelson
Peter Nikolaidis
Charlene Ochs
Nell Otto
Katherine and Nicholas Page
Dee Ann Pallais
Betty and Eric Pearson
Sandy and Bob Pittman
Jan, Richie, and
    David Platt

Matthew Randall
Vicki Reynolds
Nancy Rubin
Mary Ann Rush
Dr. Lee Salk
Heidi Schulman
Andrew, Christian, Wesley,
    and Reid Schwartz
Lew Schwartz
Abby Shafran
Nancy Shockman
Brenda Simmons and Dawn
Karen Simms and
    Amanda Lee
Suzanne Slessin
Thea Sprecher
Jake and Lucie Steinberg
Susan Strauss
Donna Swift
Steve, Molly, and Mary
    Tallitsch
Cele Theisen
Jenna and Joyce Bogart
    Trabulus
Janice Treadwell
Maggie Moss, Jonathan,
    Paul, and Jennie Tucker
Mary Unterbrunner
    and Jason
Eric Warner
The Wilsons
Phyllis Wolfe
The Librarians at the
    Whipple Free Library

CONTENTS

INTRODUCTION

It has been nearly six years since our first book, *The Penny Whistle Party Planner*, was published. Almost immediately following publication there were requests for a follow-up book but we were busy creating and testing parties and recipes for other books in the intervening years: *The Penny Whistle Lunch Box Book*, *The Penny Whistle Halloween Party Book*, and *The Penny Whistle Christmas Party Book (including Hanukkah)*. We knew we had more party ideas to share, and we also knew, as a result of the hundreds of letters we have received over the last few years from parents and children all over the country, that there were many children out there wanting still more birthday party inspirations.

At first, the challenge seemed somewhat intimidating. After all, there are over 75 complete party plans in all the books. How many more could we come up with? How many more new cakes, games, activities, invitations, and themes could we write about? The answer turned out to be—many, many more.

The reasons are interesting. First, our "birthday" lives had changed. Meredith's girls, who were 14, 16, and 18 when we started, are now 21, 23, and 25. Naturally, she's not hosting many birthday parties nowadays! But her years of experience in giving parties (at Sarah's count, over 42 birthday parties and countless holiday parties), and from talking and listening to many friends and customers in the Penny Whistle stores in New York, insured that birthday parties and party giving have remained part of her life.

Annie's kids, who were 5 and 9 when *The Penny Whistle Party Planner* was written, are now 11 and 16. She is still in the thick of it, additionally acting as a consultant for all her friends. Last year's party for Marc was a soccer party (see page 163), and the year before that was an overnight camp-out. Lisa had a carousel Sweet-Sixteen party this year and Jill Weber's son Remy, who is now 17, is still talking about the version of the "Kidnapped" party that was thrown for his 16th birthday.

We're also tickled that our offspring have been so interested in all of the *Penny Whistle* books and have often added their creative ideas to the mix. Jennifer Brokaw, now a medical student, was the inspiration for several of the themes in this book. She recommended astronomy, photography, and a sixties philosophy as excellent teenage interests. "Cloud 9" was her answer to Annie's plea for a preteen fantasy celebration, and the "It's a Dog's Life" party was Jennifer's response to her mother's newfound preoccupation with a yellow lab named Sage. Lisa Gilbar recommended a "This Is Your Life" production since she and some school friends gave such a party for an unsuspecting classmate with great success.

What pleases us most about this involvement with our children is that we can see they are determined to carry on some of these traditions. Planning, sharing, and giving parties with their friends and, in the future, their own children will be as rewarding for them as it has been for us.

The other reason we have been able to continue to write about children and parties is because we remain delighted and encouraged by the response of our readers. We have been collecting letters from readers, written by both parents and kids, since 1987. The parents write of their own delight at how enjoyable and unforgettable the process of creating a party with their children has become; they write about our ideas they used, the ones they were inspired to come up with themselves, the ones they loved, and the ones that did not turn out so well.

The children write about their own ideas for parties we missed, what they thought worked and what didn't, games they liked, and games they thought they could improve. The letters are thoughtful and detailed, but most of all, and what has so cheered us on, they are full of the joy and pleasure that parents and children feel and remember about the birthdays they have shared. As you read through this book, you will find these stories they have shared.

So to all our readers, we say thanks—for the ideas, for the advice, for the reactions to things that worked (and those that didn't), and for taking the time to tell us that you have taken our thoughts to heart. As we are sure you know, nothing is more rewarding than to hear that parents and children are indeed sharing and loving the experience of birthdays.

Party Principles

THE PENNY WHISTLE PRINCIPLES OF PARTY PLANNING

IT'S WORTH IT!

Believe it or not, almost every child we've ever talked to claims his or her best birthday parties have been the ones held at home. This doesn't mean spending a lot of money or planning a lavishly, overly produced party, but rather spending your time and energy with your child. The dividends of this investment will last far beyond the actual party day.

DO IT YOURSELF

This is *your* child's party, and it should be as uniquely and personally his or hers as you can make it. Anyone can hire a party planner to "do" a party. There's nothing personal about it, and there will be another two dozen just like it.

Child psychologist (and parent) Dr. Lee Salk says: "There is an attitude nowadays in our society that other people can do things better for your children. That's just not true. There is nothing personally creative about hiring someone else to put together your party. And the messages to the child are: I can't be bothered with doing it myself. I don't have the time to do this for you. I can't wait for this to be over. I don't want to mess up my house. I don't want to be involved so I'll give you this prepackaged (and often expensive) party."

By delegating the creating, planning, and giving of your child's party to an outsider you will find that you are missing a great opportunity for your family to share a special experience together. Half the work of party giving is in the planning and organizing stage; the *Penny Whistle Birthday Party Book* gives you 32 complete party plans, from invitations to games to refreshments. Just follow the guidelines and suggestions, add a few of your own twists, and you'll have a success on your hands.

PLAN THE PARTY WITH YOUR CHILD

This is your child's party, and not yours. He or she should share in all aspects of the planning and decision making involved in the birthday party. Even two-year-olds will let you know that they love superheroes or puppies or dressing up. You just have to listen.

Dr. Lee Salk comments: "Your child's birthday is such an important social event in his or her life. It is a great opportunity for the family to come together and discuss things, for a child to participate actively in the decision-making process. Kids need choices, and this is a great time to give them the chance to make some."

Consider what your child loves: What are his current passions? Who is her favorite hero? What games does he love to play? Ask what kind of party she wants and listen to the answers. Even if they present added problems or greater difficulties (you found a terrific puppeteer, but your son wants to have a scavenger hunt; he dreams of having an Olympics party with the entire class, while you had hoped to get by with a pizza party for six), try to compromise and fulfill your child's party dreams. And *don't* try to talk your child into having a party you would like—chances are pretty good it will backfire! Several years ago Annie's son Marc dreamed of having a ghost party. Annie and her husband had planned a magic party and convinced Marc that it would be terrific. It was a good party, and Marc and his friends had a fine time, but several weeks later, Marc mentioned quietly, "Magic was fun, but I really wish I'd had a ghost party." Next year, he had a ghost party!

Sharing the party planning process with your child will make him feel as if he is the most special child in the world. If you can arrange it, choose and make the invitations, decorations, and favors together. Choose the games together, and when you contemplate the menu, talk over the choices with your child.

This does not mean that your child must have the final word on *all* the decisions, but if you consult him you'll be surprised how much more all of you will enjoy the planning process.

Turn your child's birthday into a day where everything revolves around him. Let him be "boss" for a day (he can make up the menu; he can tell *you* what to wear; he can remind you to clear the table). You get the picture—it will be your child's version of "King" or "Queen" for a day!

Our friend Mary Tallitsch writes about a tradition at her children's birthday parties: As the birthday child opens a gift, the giver of that gift gets to choose a gift for himself from a basket of favors.

BOTH PARENTS SHOULD BE AT THE PARTY

On this special day it is important for both parents to be there, if at all possible. Parties with both parents present always work better.

TEMPER YOUR EXPECTATIONS

It's so easy to get carried away planning a party, but it's important to keep the process and the event in perspective. This is, after all, only a party, not an international summit meeting. If the unexpected happens, you will handle it. If a game is a bust, it's not a tragedy. Remember—children just want to have a good time and don't need total perfection to be happy.

PLAN FOR EVERY MOMENT

A party is theater. Planning it is just like constructing a play: You have a beginning, a middle, and an end.

Act One—the Beginning

Children do not arrive at the party all at one time, so you will need to keep the children busy as they arrive. You will find that each of our parties has a game that can be played by those prompt arrivals, and some have tasks designated for the early comers so they will feel welcome and at ease.

Act Two—the Middle

SCENE ONE: This is when the activities take place. We have suggested games and activities in each party to fill *at least* two hours (depending on the party and the ages of the children). Planning more games than you think you'll need will give you the flexibility to move on from a game that the children don't like, or to add a game if they finish one sooner than you had planned. By building in these contingencies, you will never find yourself with children who have nothing to keep them occupied.

SCENE TWO: At this point, the children will need to calm down. This is a good time to serve the food. They'll be seated, they'll devour the food, they'll sing the birthday songs, and will slowly begin to unwind from the more hectic activities. At some of our parties we have suggested several quiet table games the children can play.

Act Three—the Denouement

When they are done eating, you can gather the children around and involve them in the final activities, including opening the gifts, if you choose to do so. If you have made a videotape of the party, you can show it at this time. You can also help your child distribute the party favors. By this time the parents should be arriving to collect their children. If there are some children still waiting for their parents, gather this small group and let them help you put the gifts away.

OPENING GIFTS

We have our own opinions on whether or not to have your child open his gifts at the birthday party, but the decision is yours. We've found that children like to open gifts in front of their friends, and their guests take pleasure in seeing the birthday child's reaction to the gift each of them has brought. After all, half the fun of giving a gift is seeing the recipient enjoy it!

Since even the most polite children can forget a "thank you" in the rush and excitement of a birthday party, it might be appropriate to spend some time before the party going over some obvious yet important thoughts about gifts. It's a good opportunity to teach your child to be as thoughtful and kind about a small gift as a large one. (This is difficult for a lot of kids because "bigger" is usually synonymous with "better.")

You might discuss the problem of the duplicate present. The gift a guest has brought is important to him, and he will be anxious to see a reaction. If your child already has the gift, a kind thing to say might be, "Thanks so much! I love this toy so much that I already have it!" If it is something he really doesn't like, suggest that he can be polite and say something simple like, "Thank you for your thoughtfulness," or "Thank you for this gift."

Then there is the matter of thank you notes. If your child cannot write, make sure he thanks the guest at the time of the party—and that's it. If your child can write, the thank you note is a very nice way of his letting his guests know that he really appreciated the gift.

Thank you notes are always treasured by the receiver, and are a good way to teach your child to show appreciation for those friends who took the time to choose a gift just for him. If your child is very young, a thank you in person should suffice. But as a child reaches the age where he can write, a simple "Thank you for the gift. I love it!" will be appreciated. As kids get older and can use computers, they may like composing personal thank you notes and printing them with various designs (they will also love how fast they will be able to get the task done!).

Here's a trick from Maggie Moss Tucker: "When we handed out prizes at the end of the activities at Jonathan's party last year, we wanted to make sure that everyone got rewarded. So, as each child got his award, all the children shouted out something terrific about that child. You should have seen the looks on those kids' faces!"

THAT PERSONAL TOUCH IS IMPORTANT

You'll find that in our parties we make a lot of things at our parties because the personal touch is simply more meaningful. In each party we have combined items that you can buy with those that you and your child can make. Take the time to try these; they are simple, and it will mean a lot to everyone that you took the trouble. Use our ideas or let them trigger your own imagination.

FORGET COMPETITION!

The idea is not to outdo anybody else but rather to personalize your own party. Don't overdo; spending a lot of money may send the wrong message to your child. This is a child's party—don't give it the feeling of a lavish adult extravaganza. Forget the fireworks; make a birthday banner yourself and your child will remember it forever.

DEALING WITH SIBLINGS

This is the birthday child's day, but that does not mean that his sister or brother must be ignored. Parent after parent we talked with told how they always included the siblings. (If he or she does not want to be there, it's easy to have him spend that time at a friend's house. But it seems that more often than not, siblings hate to miss out on any action going on at home.) Have the brother or sister invite his or her special friend over for that day. They can either play apart from the party or they can be helpers. You can also have the birthday child assign special duties to his brother or sister—he or she could be in charge of a game, greeting guests, or collecting presents.

TAKE AN ACTIVE PART IN THE PARTY

Taking an active part in the party means not only being there at all times but participating in the activities. If the children are on the floor, get down there with them. If they are participating in a race or in the scavenger hunt, go along. You've already cooked the food and set the table; now share in the fun!

Our friend Susan Strauss is a wonderful example of a mother who truly gets involved in her son Jonathan's parties. Many of her friends have been surprised when Susan, who normally dresses very fashionably, greeted them and their children at the door in full costume (she's been Supergirl, in red and blue tights, a handmade satin cape, and headband for a superheroes party and Tinker Bell for a Peter Pan party). When anyone asks Jonathan about his birthday parties, he always mentions that his mom "always dresses up just like me!" With such personal gestures, Susan has made his parties memorable and made Jonathan very proud.

PLAN AHEAD

Give yourself enough time to plan a party. At the beginning of each party in this book you will find a "Get Ready" list that will help you prepare ahead of time for all the things you need to buy and make. If you can, begin about six weeks ahead. But if you find that you must begin to plan your party two weeks ahead, just follow our guidelines and everything will fall into place.

GUEST LISTS

You will make up the guest list for a pre-schooler. After the age of three or four, your child needs to be consulted.

First, how many children do you invite? A rule of thumb that some people use is to invite as many children as the child's age (a five-year-old, for example, would invite five children). The benefit of having a small group is that it's easier to handle the guests and give each child the attention he needs.

If your child's teacher has asked that no children be left out of a party, this means that the entire class must be invited. Relax. *Don't* panic! Most of our parties are flexible and can easily accommodate 20 kids or so.

Some parties lend themselves to inviting neighbors, relatives, and friends outside of school. If you would rather limit the number of children at the birthday party, you could have a separate family dinner to celebrate the birthday.

Almost all the *Penny Whistle* parties can be enjoyed by boys and girls (although you may feel some, like the "Doll Shower," are more appropriate for girls alone). Before age five and after age ten, boys and girls like to attend parties together (in between they often profess to not being able to stand each other). The choice of inviting girls or boys or both is up to you and your child.

Tim "Pied Piper" Green is now 31, although there are those who think he's still going on 10. Even though he is a fitness expert by training, Tim's true love is playing with children. No game is too silly, no chase too long, no contest too hard for this "kid," which is why every child Tim meets invites him to his or her birthday party—which just goes to show how important it is for all adults to really get involved in their children's birthday parties!

19

GET HELP

You do not have to give a party alone. Get help if the size of your party demands it. Ask your neighbors, relatives, or friends to help the day of the party. Hire some high school students to help organize or to entertain the children (see our suggestions under each party for using high school kids).

AGE-APPROPRIATE PARTIES

Since you know your child best, you should decide whether a particular theme is right or not; *The Penny Whistle Birthday Party Book* will guide you to the suggested age range for each party. While we have included a section totally devoted to parties appropriate to children ages 2, 3, and 4, there are also several parties suggested for older children that will also work for many four-year-olds ("Chocolate Factory," "Doll Shower," "Giant-land," "Gone Fishin'," "It's a Dog's Life," and "Under the Big Top").

Don't assume that 11- or 12-year-olds don't like games. They may try to act older and more sophisticated but playing games also takes the pressure off trying to be cool and so grown up. Chances are they'll participate with enthusiasm!

Children don't need to be urged to grow up any faster. If other mothers are urging girls to have boys at their parties or giving makeup parties for eight-year-olds and this seems inappropriate for your child (and your child is uncomfortable with such plans), buck the trend and stick to your guns. Knowing your own values and the personality of your child will guide you in making the decisions that will make you and your child happy.

BE FLEXIBLE

One of the best things about the *Penny Whistle* parties is that they afford as much flexibility as you want and need. We have designed and organized complete parties, but many of their parts are interchangeable. If your child is planning a "Stargazing" party but also can't wait to play one of the games included in the "Camp-out," just add it to your "Stargazing" party. The same is true for our suggestions for favors and menus. It is our hope that the ideas you read about here will trigger your own imagination.

KEEP THE COST DOWN

Really successful parties do not need to be expensive. That's why you will find that we list a choice of items you can buy or make according to your time and your budget.

This is a party for your child and his friends. It need not impress other parents; it is not supposed to make headlines or set any records. It should be fun at the time and fun to remember later.

TAKE PICTURES!

Take *lots* of pictures! Both you and your child will want to remember the party. Assign this task to some of your helpers, and start when the guests arrive. Use your video camera if you have one (you can also rent one) and play the tape back at the end of the party—the children will love seeing themselves! Polaroid photographs of each child make wonderful party favors. If you are using 35-mm film, you may want to duplicate special photographs of the guests and send them to the parents after the party.

Four-year-olds begin to show a fascination with money. Here's an easy game for them to play, one that helps them with their small-hand coordination: Give each a stack of pennies and have them stack them up as high as they can. The child who makes the highest stack without its falling wins!

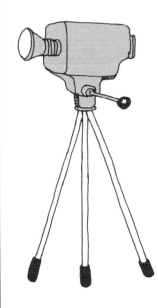

PLANNING THE PARTY

For each party in the book we have provided instructions, suggestions, and ideas for creating invitations, selecting and preparing for the activities, setting and preparing the menu, buying or making the decorations and favors, and selecting and hiring additional entertainment. We have also included an outline of things you need to make and buy, and an actual schedule of party activities.

INVITATIONS

Designing and planning the invitation is an important beginning to planning the party—it sets the stage and gets the guests excited long before the party happens. When your guest receives a folded drinking cup for the "Camp-out" party, a sweepstakes certificate for the "Sweepstakes" party, or a thong in a sand-filled plastic bag for the "Shipwrecked" party, the anticipation begins as the mood for an exciting party is set.

Each party in this book has its own suggested invitation, and each describes everything you will need to create it. We also provide drawings that you can Xerox and use as ready-made invitations. You can always add your own personal touch to these: Choose your own object to send; have your child color in our drawings; or add sequins or feathers or any accessories your child adores.

Stickers are the perfect answer to many decorating needs. They spruce up thematic invitations, are perfect for making envelopes eye catching, and will turn ordinary paper into pretty wrapping paper.

Colored Xeroxes make terrific invitations. Just draw one invitation in color and take it to a printing shop and they will make you as many copies as you need.

Brittany Bell wrote, "I loved my 'Diner' party but two hours is too short. My mother told me to tell you that it was plenty."

LENGTH OF PARTY

Decide on the length of time of your party. You don't have to have a long party; as a matter of fact, a two-hour party that is well planned and chock full of activities is a guaranteed success, while a disorganized gathering for four hours is a sure disaster.

ORGANIZE HELP

Gather your help and let them know the schedule of the party. Acquaint them with the children, the games, and the food. Here's a good rule of thumb: You need one adult for every five young children (up to five years old), and one for every eight older kids.

DECORATIONS

Atmosphere is everything. Once you and your child have chosen the theme, you will find ideas about how to use the most ordinary household gadgets or toys to turn your house into your child's fantasy.

Our suggestions should inspire your own ideas. We urge you not to overdo. You can design the wonderful indoor environment for the "Stargazing" party without asking NASA if you can borrow the Apollo space capsule. You can create a candy wonderland without buying out your local candy store. And you most certainly can plan the "Camp-out" without flying everyone to Yellowstone National Park.

ACTIVITIES

Each of our parties comes with its own suggested activities and games designed to complement the theme of that party. You will find that usually there are more games suggested for each party than you are likely to need. That is because it is better to be prepared with extra activities than to be caught with extra time on your hands. If you don't get to play them all, just save them for the next party.

When making up your own list of games, particularly if you are mixing and matching games from different parties, be sure to keep in mind that rowdy games need to be followed by calming ones.

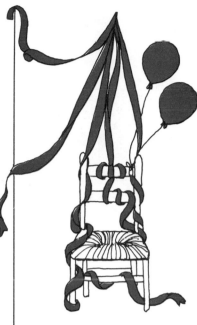

Old-fashioned crepe paper streamers are still perfect when hung from kids' chairs. You can also create a canopy with them by draping them from the ceiling and attaching them to the corners of the table.

ENTERTAINMENT

If you follow our general advice and plan to have your party last for no more than two, possibly three, hours, you will find that time will be amply filled. If, however, you have decided to have a party that lasts longer, you may find that some sort of entertainment is necessary. Or you may simply choose to substitute outside entertainment for a couple of our games.

If you want to hire a clown, a magician, a storyteller, or a puppeteer, go see the performer at another party first. You can simply ask for references and check them out, but if it is at all possible, try to see for yourself. Meredith once hired an animal trainer for a party for five-year-old Sarah—he turned out to be able to handle the children but not the animals. Annie hired a magician that a friend had used who turned out to be a real sourpuss, and who embarrassed the then four-year-old Marc (who ended up in tears), whose jokes were geared toward 20-year-olds, and his magic was, to say the least, mediocre. Apparently, what was okay for Annie's friend did not fit Annie's level of expectation.

We suggest that you hire high school students or other local talent for entertainment. We have found, from our experience and from talking to mothers all over the country, that these so-called "amateurs" are often quite successful as entertainers. First of all, they have not performed at countless parties, so their acts will not be as predictable or as tired. Second, their freshness and eagerness will more than compensate for their relative lack of sophistication or experience.

FOOD

What's a party without food? Not a party, that's what! But elaborate menus don't impress kids. The name of the game is inventiveness, and the most important word is "cake." We have superb recipes for each cake in the recipe section and easy decorating instructions at the end of each party.

While nutrition is important, a birthday party is the perfect time to make some allowances. So if you're inclined to sugar-free goodies and carrot sticks, please don't be upset that our suggestions include recipes with some ingredients that you might ordinarily limit.

Since it's the birthday kid's special day, Abby Shafran feels that the food served should be whatever the child's favorite food is—no matter what it is. That's why one year when Abby wanted sushi, she was the only one who ate her birthday dinner.

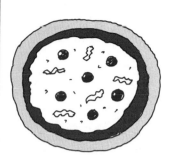

You will also find that you can switch the dishes between parties. If you're intrigued by the mystery menu in the "Secret Agents" party but have another theme in mind—so what! Make it and use it in your party. Note that some dishes can be made either the day before or that morning. You'll find that the menus are simple, easy to prepare, and pretty to boot.

An added note: If you find yourself overloaded with things to do, remember that you can always order a pizza!

PARTY FAVORS

At the end of each party, you will find a list of suggested favors. They were chosen with the theme of the party in mind, with the cost kept at a minimum (although we have given you a choice), and with the appropriate age of the children in mind.

For innovative and inexpensive favors, try The Oriental Trading Company. See Resources, page 249.

You will also find that we suggest you choose the favors at least a couple of weeks ahead of time in the party schedule so you will have time to order, make, or buy the ones you really want instead of settling for last-minute replacements.

Children don't consider the cost, but they do believe that taking something special home with them is crucial to the success of the party. And they're no fools! You can be sure that a party favor that has already been given out at all the other parties or one that falls apart before your guest gets in the car will be discussed and disparaged at a pow-wow in the school yard the next day.

We strongly advocate *not* spending a lot of money on favors. It is the *unusual* party favor, the one that relates to the theme of the party, that is the memorable one, especially if the kids have made it themselves. As often as possible, we use craft projects that everyone works on during the party as the favors.

THE UNEXPECTED

Something unexpected happens at every party, and there is not too much you can do about it, unless you know the number of a reliable fortune-teller. What you can do is the following:

A. Have a lot of help around the house so each child will have the proper amount of supervision. That will usually take care of a tearful moment or an unruly child.

B. Be prepared to deal with a child who is cranky, unruly, and/or refuses to listen.

Abby Shafran, from Malibu, California, remembers her favorite party activity when she was a kid (she's already sixteen). Each guest got a sticker book when they arrived and they got stickers as prizes whenever they won a game. The stickers then went into the books.

25

Here's a tip from Mary Ann Rush in Calabasas Hills, California: For guests who are reluctant to dress up in costume, keep a hat collection in a basket by the door to encourage them to get in the mood.

Explains Dr. Lee Salk: "This is not the time to have a public confrontation with a young guest (nor do you want to embarrass him). But it is also unacceptable to let such a child disrupt your child's party. The best method of dealing with a child who refuses to listen is to take him aside to another room and make it clear that you have rules of behavior in your home and you expect everyone to respect them."

Dr. Salk suggests dealing with the child in the following manner: Say "I'm glad you are here to be part of the party but we have certain rules here and you have to obey them." And, he adds, "You may be surprised at how effective the simple words 'Stop it!' are."

If you can, calm such a child as you would your own; with a lot of patience and some adult guile (bribery works—don't pooh-pooh offering an unhappy child an extra candy or a special chore to do) such a problem will be resolved easily.

There is yet another kind of child—the observer. Such a child is often uncomfortable participating in a lot of games and is content to watch. Again, Dr. Salk: "Not everyone has to participate—some children prefer to be on the sidelines. It's best not to make this child uncomfortable, nor to pressure him to join the group (and this is definitely not the time to try any therapy!). Make sure the child knows you are happy to see him, and let him join the activities at his own pace."

C. Be sure that you have some rudimentary first aid available (Band-Aids, ice cubes, etc.).

D. If your weatherman was wrong (again), and the weather has turned on you, know that most of our parties can be held outdoors or indoors. The "Under the Big Top" party and the "Camp-out" can only take place outdoors, and should be planned only in the summer months when the chance of rain is minimal. The weather messed up the Gilbars' plans twice—once when they gave an "Olympics" party (it's in *The Penny Whistle Party Planner*) and another time when they planned the "Camp-out" with their friends the Buhais (see page 51). In both instances, the parties were postponed a week, and it all worked out fine!

E. Each menu calls for a certain amount of extra food, so you should never run out of anything! It is easy to have extra sandwiches, frozen pizza, cookies, or drinks on hand as additional insurance.

F. We have provided you with extra games for every party. If you find that one game is not popular, you will be able to quit it immediately and start another. If you somehow play all the games you planned for and still have more time, having that extra game or two at your fingertips will avoid having restless children becoming unhappy and causing a disturbance.

G. Plan for the uninvited guest by having more food, favors, balloons, prizes, etc., than you need. You don't want to be caught in a bind if an extra child arrives (some parents may bring a guest's sibling without telling you) or if something breaks. Be sure to have a favor and balloon for your child—sometimes we forget that the birthday child also gets a favor even though he stays home after the party.

Now for the parties!

Here's how you play musical chairs so nobody loses: Have the same number of chairs as participants. The goal is to be the one to get to sit on the "king's throne" (a special chair). Thus, whenever the music stops, someone feels special every time rather than being the one left out.

FIRST PARTIES

Birthday parties for one-year-olds are fun, but that day of your child's first-ever birthday celebration is really for the parents, your family, and friends. A child of a year does not know what a birthday is, nor is he old enough to realize the significance of this day in the lives of those around him. He may love the sight of balloons tied to his high chair, and he'll probably smile and clap his hands when everybody sings, but there can also be tears, especially if there are too many people and too much noise and confusion. A cupcake with a candle and lots of hugs and kisses will be more than enough to have an impact on your "guest of honor."

Do take pictures, have a birthday cake, and make a scrapbook of your child's "firsts." These memories will last a lifetime. And as your child grows up, even just a little, he'll be fascinated with these early photos (the birthday books in our houses were all dog-eared by the time the kids were five!).

The next birthdays are a different story. A child of three or four (and sometimes two) is a social being, capable of making decisions and choices, and eager to voice his opinions. He can interact with other children, and celebrations will be both meaningful and memorable for him. He loves being the center of attention and can enjoy a party that is his very own.

The party principles that we talk about for older children certainly apply here as well (see pages 30–40) and remember to include your child in the decision-making process. It is *his* party (see Plan the Party with Your Child, page 15).

We have a friend, Brenda Simmons, who made a crown for her daughter Dawn's first birthday. Every year Dawn got to add another object (a sticker, a bead, a design) to the crown and continued to wear it, all day, at every birthday (this lasted, believe it or not, until she was eight).

KEEP IT SIMPLE AND SMALL!

Children under four are still very young, and for them, simple is best. Elaborate decorations, a crowd of people, and a lot of noise will almost always end up with a child who is overwhelmed by the chaos and in tears. Scale the party to the age. At these ages, a little cake and a few children playing a few simple games will make for a memorable party.

KEEP IT SHORT AND SWEET!

A party of one to one-and-a-half hours is fine for these ages. Try to plan the party around the children's nap times and ask the parents of two- and three-year-olds to stay at the party. If it fits into your theme, ask the children to bring their favorite toys as it will make them feel comfortable. (For instance, if you are having a "Bear Bash," invite the kids to come with their favorite teddy bears.)

MAKE IT EASY!

Use paper tablecloths, cups, and plates (you can even have crayons on the table so the children can draw while they eat). Children at these ages aren't impressed with a lot of food. Make finger foods (tiny sandwiches, cut-up fruit, cupcakes instead of huge cakes) that are easy to serve and to eat. If your party is in the spring or summer, consider making it a picnic in the backyard. It's always a treat for youngsters to eat on the grass, and you'll all appreciate having the room to run around freely.

GAMES AND ACTIVITIES

Children of these ages don't need as many games and activities as older children. Too many rules, too much commotion, and too many people will result in upset and tearful children (for some youngsters, even a visiting clown or magician can be scary). Try the following:

- Simple hunts (treasure hunts using pictures instead of words are perfect)
- Hiding and finding things (and people)
- Games to music that consist of running, jumping, and dancing; sing-a-longs (tape the kids and play it back and watch their faces as they hear their own voices!)
- Simple costumes (hand out hats, plastic noses, glasses, boas, and jewelry, and you'll have a happy crew).

KEEP GIFT GIVING SIMPLE!

Opening gifts at two, three, and four is very exciting, but it can also be confusing and stressful. We have found that two alternatives work best: Either have a child open a gift as he gets it (so the giver can share in the excitement and your child does not have to wait), or have him open all the gifts at a later time with the gift givers opening their favors at the same time.

When Alex Kassan was two, his parents were getting ready to rebuild their home, so a graffiti party seemed like a great idea! What could be more perfect than to have a dozen two-year-olds draw and paint all over their walls? The kids were in heaven, and smart mom, Ronnie, has the pictures to prove it, and a good thing, too, because the house was demolished the very next day.

Young Parties

These are parties for two-, three-, and four-year-olds. In our first book, *The Penny Whistle Party Planner*, we suggested themes such as your child's favorite cartoon character, his or her favorite color (or rainbow), treasure hunts, a painting and coloring party, one for tool maniacs, parties with your child's favorite pretend animals, car-related festivities, and more. You will also find that some of the other parties in the body of this book will also work for your four-year-old (for example, the "Doll Shower," "Pig-out," "Giantland," "Chocolate Factory," "It's a Dog's Life," and "Stegosaurus & Friends"). But the following parties are geared for really young children. They are simpler in scope, but the fun quotient is enormous!

THE ALPHABET PARTY

Young children are very excited about learning to read, and letters are high on their list of "things I can do and aren't you proud of me?" In these early years, they are beginning to identify letters, sing the alphabet, and spell their names. A party around the theme of letters or your child's favorite letter or letters (such as his initials) is a lot of fun.

Pam Krenzke, of Worthington, Ohio, gave a "Bobby's Big B Birthday Bash" on her son's third birthday. They cut out large "B's" out of tagboard that Bobby decorated with stickers of things that begin with "B"—boats, bears, Big Bird, butterflies, balloons, etc. Pam wrote the invitation on the cutout "B's" and hand delivered them to five families.

Came the birthday day and Bobby couldn't wait to get going! Naturally Bobby wore *blue*, including his *Ball State* T-shirt and *blue* pants. He decorated the house with stuffed *bears*, *bunnies*, and *birds*. He planned the menu, which included *barbecue beef* sandwiches, *barbecue* potato chips, *bananas* in *berry* Jell-O, *birthday* cake with *bears* and *balloons* on it, cheese *balls*, and *baby bagel* pizzas (which Bobby decided to serve in *baskets*). The children strung *beads*, they *built* with *bricks*, they *blew big bubbles*, and sailed *boats* in the wading pool in the *backyard*— and how about a *bowl* full of alphabet letter macaroni so each guest could try to find as many "*B*'s" as possible? After the games, the children made *brownie bears*. And if that's not enough, they took home favors that were *buckets* with a *bottle of bubbles*, a *book*, a *baby* in a *blanket* with a *bottle*.

And we're not done! Even the presents Bobby got were "B's"—a *baseball*, small *bears*, *bubbles*, and an Ohio State "*Buckeye*" shirt. And to top it all, Pam says, "we have the whole affair on '*bideo*' tape!"

Use a white tablecloth to cover a child's table and write kids' names either with rubber stamps or with alphabet stickers. For kids who can read and write, you can place the stickers in the center of the table and let them write their own names, or make up their own words.

Natalie Morison had a Sleeping Beauty Party for her fourth birthday. Françoise, her mother, made tutus for all the girls and wrapped them each in a different paper. She hid their tutus and handed them each a sample of the wrapping paper. They had to find their own tutus by matching the wrapping. They danced to the *Sleeping Beauty* ballet, had cake with ballerinas on it, and took home their tutus and candy kisses from Prince Charming as party favors.

THE BEAR BASH

If there were a designated national stuffed animal, it would have to be the teddy bear. We've met many (including some very big) children who collect anything having to do with the little cuddlies. Marc Gilbar, who is 11, had a "Bear Bash" when he was 3. He still remembers displaying every teddy bear he owned. His dad Gary drew little bears all over a huge piece of foam board and cut out holes for heads so the kids could have their pictures taken as the little bears. Many bear games were played—and a huge bear cake was devoured!

Patricia Bushouse, of Holland, Michigan, gave a bear party for her daughter Eve. Patricia and Eve made all the invitations; they stenciled a bear on each, and wrote a note to ask each guest to bring his or her favorite bear to the party. As each guest arrived, they got to draw on a white sweatshirt which had bears all over it (that stencil came in very handy—Eve had colored in all the bears with puff paints the day before). When the guests entered the party room, they were surprised to see all of Eve's 37 bears sitting around the table! By the time the guests added their bears to the procession, the room was indeed a bear heaven. Balloons with bears on them completed the decor.

In another room, Patricia and Eve had set out a line of small wooden bears, one for each guest, and paints. The guests then got to paint each bear themselves. Later, they played "Musical Bears," passing around Eve's favorite bear until the music stopped, and the one caught "bear handed" was out. The next game was "Hide the Bear"—the guests had to try to find the bear, with the adult yelling "hot" or "cold" as the kids got closer or farther away from the bear.

The cake had bears all over it. Paper cups were decorated by Eve with bear stickers. And on each plate, there were chocolate bears (white and brown) that Eve and her mom had made the day before. After dinner, the children watched a tape of "Corduroy Bear," and just before they went home Eve gave out prizes for all the different kinds of bears (the biggest bear, the best dressed bear, the softest bear, the oldest bear, the newest bear, etc.). The kids left with goodie bags full of pencils with bears on them, the bears they had painted, a bear book mark, the bear award, Gummy Bears, and a wonderful bear coloring book that Patricia had made with Eve's brother Seth (he drew all the bears, Xeroxed the pages, and put together the coloring books). And before they left, Patricia took each kid's picture with Eve and their bears (one for Eve to put in her memory book, and a copy to send to each guest).

Eve's party is still being talked about—not only by the lucky guests, but by Eve and her mom, who both have unforgettable memories of the fun they had planning and giving her bear party.

Donna Swift, from Omaha, Nebraska, and her son planned and gave a medieval party for his fourth birthday. The birthday boy was a knight and the girls, princesses. Donna borrowed a suit or armor, decorated the whole party room in the royal colors red and purple, and hung flags everywhere. The kids played a game of Dragon's Tail.

Cynthia Doyle, from West Milford, New Jersey, had a "Tool Party" for her son Michael when he was three. Michael lives for his hammer, and his daily itinerary consists of fixing things—any things. So when Michael wanted a "Tool Party" for his birthday, he, his sister, and his mom wrote new words for his favorite songs. And here they are (to the tune of "The Wheels on the Bus"):

"The hammers on the nail go bang, bang, bang . . .
The wrenches on the bolts go turn, turn, turn . . .
The saws on the wood go zzzzz, zzzzz, zzzzz . . .
The screwdrivers on the screws go twist, twist, twist . . ."

To the tune of "I'm a Little Teapot," they sang,

"I'm a little hammer, short and strong,
here is my handle and this is my song.
When you get all ready then I sing,
just hold me tight and bang, bang, bang . . ."

FIRE FIGHTERS PARTY

"What do you want to be when you grow up?" Ask that question of a group of little boys and you're guaranteed to hear at least one "Fireman" answer. Riding in a big red fire engine (with a dalmatian hanging off the back), wearing a fireman's hat and slickers, fighting fires (or just operating a water hose), and saving people's lives—just the thought makes children's eyes light up.

On his third birthday, Eric Warner was determined to dress up as a fireman—boots and all—so his invitation (attached to a tiny red fire engine) asked the other kids to wear their slickers to the party. The kids played "Find the Firehouse Dog" (a simple hunt for Eric's stuffed dalmatian) and various water games with his garden hose.

Andrew Marks, who lives for seeing fire trucks whizzing by his house, also chose to have a fire fighter's party for his third birthday. His mom Nancy bought fire hats at the local stationery store and gave each child his own as he came through the door. Unbeknownst to Andrew, Nancy had called the local fire department in Los Angeles and asked if they could come by the house if they weren't on a call. Suddenly, in the middle of Andrew's party, an enormous, block-long, red fire engine, complete with fire fighters (and dog), drove up in front of Andrew's home. When Andrew expressed concern that there would be no one guarding the firehouse in case of a fire, the fire chief explained that another engine was on duty, and in case of an emergency, this fire engine could be on its way in a few seconds. The fire fighters let the kids climb on the truck, and explained all about fire safety and how children can participate in caring for their homes and watching out for fires. As they left, there were real tears of amazement and happiness in all the children's eyes.

When Gabriel Cowan was three, his mom Aileen Adams took him and his friends to the local firehouse. They were given a complete tour of the facility, including the fire trucks. The L.A. Fire Department personnel then gave each child a coloring book about fires and fire fighting, a bunch of stickers (some of which the kids learned they could put on the windows of their rooms so in case of an emergency their rooms would be visible to the fire fighters), and comic books about fire trucks and their importance during earthquakes. The kids had a grand old time, and Aileen must have as well, for not too many years later she became the first woman fire commissioner in Los Angeles!

Dale Mallory also had a fire fighting party for her son Matthew. She bought a red fire hydrant sprinkler at her local toy store and let the children play in the water. Her favors were also great hits: Miniature fire hydrants filled with candy, water pistols, and miniature fire trucks were found in red bags decorated with fire alert stickers; plastic firemen's hats were put on each little head.

TRAINS, CARS, AIRPLANES, ETC.

Cindy Molnar, from Iowa City, Iowa, celebrated her son Christopher's birthday with a car theme. Cindy put cars as place marks at the table and made sandwiches in the shape of cars (the kids ended up having a sandwich race). The highlight of the party was making vanity car plates out of construction paper (Cindy had bought stickers in the shape of letters; you can also make your own with stencils and contact paper), and the guests got to make their names for their own license plates. The boys then rode in the cardboard cars that Cindy and Christopher made from cardboard boxes (remove the top of a TV-sized cardboard box, tape or staple paper plates to the sides for wheels, and use jar caps for headlights and ice cream sticks or wooden chopsticks for windshield wipers). Cindy's touch: The children's vanity license plates were put on their cars as well as yellow "Toddler on Board" signs.

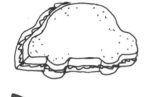

When Ben Matthew Wilson was four, he and his mom and dad invited ten friends and their parents to take a train trip. They packed their lunches, went down to the railway station, boarded the train, and went for a ride for four stops to a nearby town. There they had ice cream and then turned around and came back on the very next train.

MERMAIDS

The legends of mermaids and the images they create—starfish, blue waters, glitter, fantasy—mesmerize little girls. Karen Simms, from Belzidere, New Jersey, created a mermaid party for her daughter Amanda Lee's fourth birthday. She kept the party small—six girls in all, ranging from three and a half to five years old. Karen moved the furniture out of the party room and left a table in the center surrounded by hanging blue and green streamers with pink and lavender balloons. The guests played musical chairs (the winners received mermaid pouches that were decorated with gold glitter). They also dove for pearls (Karen hid some large plastic pearls in a pot of cooked macaroni that had been cooled); each person took a turn reaching into the bowl to try to find a pearl. At first, some of the children were reluctant to stick their hands into a bowl of squishy macaroni, but after the first guest had such a good time, everyone followed eagerly. Then the kids played a game of blowing starfish made out of gold foil across the floor to a designated point.

Karen made a sheet cake with blue icing and edible blue and green glitter and a mermaid with red hair (made from bright red icing). Macaroni and cheese made from seashell-shaped pasta was served with star-shaped sandwiches. Favors were bubbles, mermaid lollipops, mermaid coloring books, and necklaces made from shells hanging on ribbons. Karen's extra tip: At one point, when the kids got too loud, she became a "Sea Witch" and took away their voices!

If your child has a favorite character from a book, build a party around that story. *Peter Pan* is an old favorite—have an all-green cake with tiny figures on it; ask the kids to dress as their favorite character from that story; give out plastic swords and hats when they arrive; have a noisy clock ticking away near the front door; give out eye patches for fans of Captain Hook—and you can even show the movie!

GRANDMA'S ATTIC

This party is a delight for little ones because it revolves around imaginative play—dressing up in old grown-up clothes, something young children love to do! You can send out an invitation in the shape of an old hat, or send a pair of inexpensive granny glasses. On the invitation, invite the children to "Grandma's Attic" (they can even come dressed as their own grandma). When they arrive, have them choose from a variety of old clothes that sit in a trunk (or large basket or box) in the front hall. Include large shirts, hats, shoes, feather boas, costume jewelry, and maybe even some makeup. Be sure to take pictures of the kids in their various disguises; Polaroids are especially effective because the kids can instantly see what they look like, and then take the photos home to share with others.

When Lisa Gilbar was only four, she wanted to tie-dye just like the older kids. Annie thought that was a little too messy and complicated for Lisa's age, but she and Lisa did come up with a terrific version of tie-dye for younger kids. Put a few drops of food coloring in a muffin tin filled with water (a different color in each cup). Now fold a piece of paper towel over again and again like an accordion and dip the corners in the dyes. When you're done, unfold the towel and place flat on the counter to dry. You'll have an instant tie-dye drawing that little kids can easily make!

MINI-CHEFS PARTY

Even two-, three-, and four-year-olds can actually make things in the kitchen, with adult help and supervision. Many youngsters love watching dough turn into a real pizza (as opposed to a pizza appearing out of a box), or mixing up a batch of gooey brownies. Dress up each of your cooks with a paper toque (chef's hat) and an apron. Then to familiarize the youngsters with the kitchen materials they'll be using, let them play for a while with large stainless mixing bowls, plastic measuring cups and spoons, wooden mixing spoons, and kitchen timers.

Remember that the recipes you use need to be geared to the children's ages, and that there is a real difference between what a two-year-old and what a four-year-old can cook. There is also a difference between *your* four-year-old and someone else's. Annie didn't start cooking until she was 21; Carla and Nina Lalli, daughters of great chef and food editor Carole Lalli, were both baking fruit pies and making fresh marinara sauce (Nina could even make homemade pasta) before the age of three. Regardless of how comfortable your children are in the kitchen, when you're inviting other people's children to cook at your house, always assume that they must be watched carefully and that they need supervision at every moment.

For an added treat, show your guests how to make their own play dough.

With your help, they can also make microwave popcorn, lemonade, and Microwave Fudge (see "Doll Shower" recipes, page 234). Chocolate chip cookies are also great favorites of little ones; they can easily mix the dough and spoon the cookies onto the cookie sheets (and you put the dough in the oven). For an instant pizza, give them some pizza dough or pita bread, show them how to spread some tomato sauce and cheese slices on top, place in the toaster oven—and ten minutes later they'll have their very own pizza!

PLAY DOUGH
(Not for eating!!)
4 cups all-purpose flour
1 cup salt
1½ cups cold water

Place all ingredients in a large bowl. Stir until well blended. Turn out onto a lightly floured board and knead for 5 minutes, or until dough is smooth and pliable. It should not be sticky; you can add more flour if necessary.

When Maureen Barum's daughter had her friends over to cook in their kitchen, they personalized their aprons with puff paints. But the kids didn't think that looked too authentic— they thought that putting pizza sauce on the aprons was a much better idea.

WIZARD OF OZ

Dee Ann Pallais, from Richmond, Virginia, gave her daughter Mandy a "Wizard of Oz" party for her fourth birthday. The invitation was a drawing of a yellow brick road. When the children arrived at the party, they had to come up a yellow brick road leading to the front door while the tape of the song "Follow the Yellow Brick Road" played. Each child received a basket of four hats, one for each of the major characters in the story: Dorothy, the Scarecrow, the Tinman, and the Cowardly Lion.

Any popular games can be adapted to your party theme. Dee Ann, Mandy, and their guests played "Melt the Witch," "Glenda Sends Dorothy Home," "Toto, Toto, Where's Your Bone?" "Treasure Hunt in Oz," and "Pin the Heart on the Tinman." A local bakery made a "Wizard of Oz" cake complete with its own yellow brick road.

Says Dee Ann, "One of the best things about the party was that making the hats, planning the games, and decorating the house was something my daughter and I could plan and do together. I feel we had as much fun getting ready for the party as at the party itself!"

Of course, any of your children's favorite stories can be used as the basis for a party. *Alice in Wonderland, Peter Pan* (you can adapt the "Pirate Treasure Hunt" party from *The Penny Whistle Party Planner*), and "Goldilocks and the Three Bears" are three easily planned examples.

How about a "What a Character" party: Invite everyone to come as a character from literature. Each child has to talk and act as that character throughout the party. The sixth grade at Montecito Union School did this as a school project and then had a party to celebrate. Examples include: Willie Wonka, Alice in Wonderland, Peter Pan, Captain Hook, the Wizard of Oz, Tom Sawyer, Heidi, Cinderella, Seven Dwarfs, Little Women, Three Musketeers, Robinson Crusoe, Robin Hood, Oliver Twist, Ramona Quigley, the Mad Hatter, Popeye. Most students even came in costume!

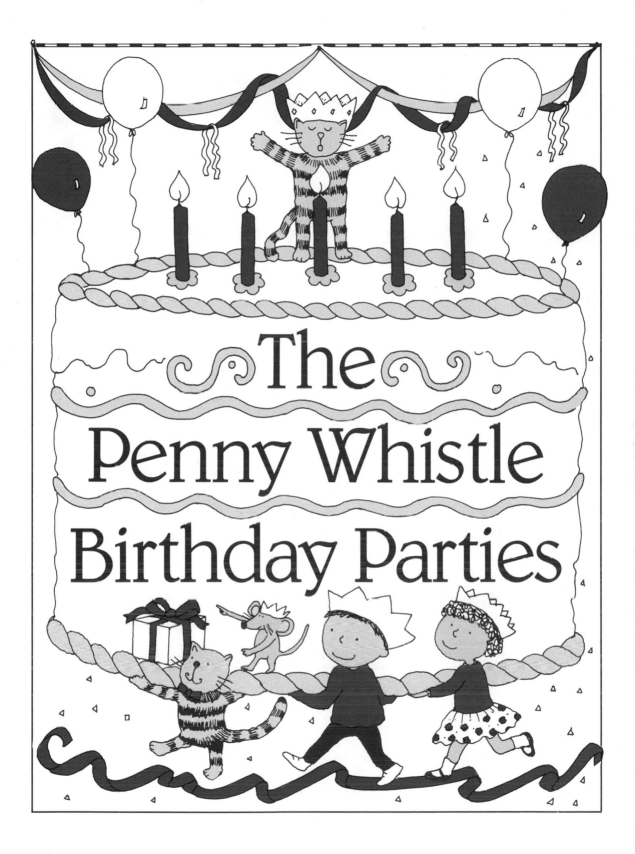

The Penny Whistle Birthday Parties

ART
ATTACK

(Ages 5–12)

$\boxed{K}$ ids often have art attacks—you know, when they must suddenly find the paint set, crayons, drawing paper, and where's the easel? Turn this creative frenzy for art into some birthday party fun. We have been inspired by some of Marc's art projects at his school, the Center for Early Education in Los Angeles, under the direction of his long-time art teacher, Penny Landreth.

INVITATION

Write this copy on the backs of postcards of paintings (all art museums carry them). Choose recognizable, more contemporary paintings that are likely to appeal to kids—ones they admire and could try to copy. Paintings by such artists as David Hockney, Keith Haring, Pablo Picasso, Henri Matisse, Vincent van Gogh, are all possibilities.

Acetate or gel paper can be painted with water-based paints. The effect is very special! You can buy acetate in any art store.

DECORATIONS

Arrange four separate areas for the different activities and decorate with posters of paintings. Arrange the materials on tables that have been covered with plastic tablecloths or old sheets. Multiples of equipment are handy for the children and give the room the look of a real "art studio." Place lots of brushes in empty cans. Line up paints of different colors, as well as lots of markers, crayons, chalk, scissors, and any other materials.

Libraries have slides on file. If your kids really *love* art, borrow slides and show them.

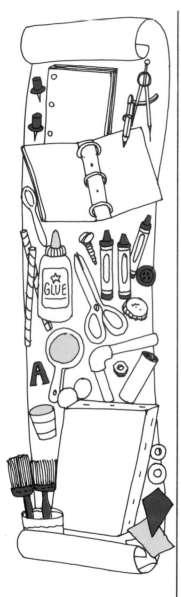

GET READY!

1. Buy white construction paper; white paper and black pens; push pins; compass; pencils for cartooning.

2. Order posters and the postcards for the invitations from the Metropolitan Museum of Art or your local museum for painting.

3. Invite any artists, architects, or cartoonists you may know, or students of the above, to participate in the party. They can bring their works to add to the exhibit.

4. Buy all the materials in quantity: brushes (place in empty cans), crayons, pastels, Craypas, paints (watercolors, spray, and acrylic), canvasses (inexpensive ones, two per person, just in case), foam board, white glue, tagboard in various colors, glue, scissors, straws, and pencils. Set up two to three tables covered with plastic tablecloths or old sheets for artists' materials; for landscape painting, buy packages of tissue paper in various colors (tear into small and medium elongated pieces of paper).

5. Get clay, tagboard, shoe boxes, all kinds of "junk" for the sculpture and collages (see page 47).

6. Find a couple of hand mirrors for self-portraits.

7. Prepare a tape of a collection of different songs for "Painting to Music."

8. Buy favors.

Acrylics are hard to wash off of hands and clothes. Use watercolor or tempera paints which come in easy-to-use large squeeze bottles.

ACTIVITIES

PAINTING

Encourage the children to paint not only with brushes but with unusual materials and combinations (they can use the objects they brought that are not paintbrushes). Give each a canvas.

The following guidelines will encourage the children to use their imaginations freely to create their own masterpieces.

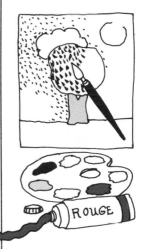

- They can make paintings inspired by the artists whose posters you have hanging around the room. We suggest artists that the kids seem to enjoy, including Henri Matisse (especially the *Jazz* series whose images kids love); David Hockney (any of the swimming pools are a big hit); Pablo Picasso, Vincent van Gogh (the sunflowers are familiar and the kids love to draw their own versions); Keith Haring (the atomic baby); Georges Seurat (the pointillism style is especially intriguing to kids); Red Grooms (the taxi cab, the enchanting people).

  Let each child choose a painting that he or she particularly responds to and have them paint their own version. Marc's two favorite inspirations hanging in his room are of van Gogh's *Sunflowers* and Matisse's *Jazz* series. His friend David Meadows's favorite was inspired by Georgia O'Keeffe's desert landscapes.

- The paintings of Georges Seurat are especially fascinating to children as they are made by the technique called "pointillism," where an image is made by drawing hundreds of tiny dots. Here the kids can design an image on paper, lightly outline it in pencil, and fill it in with tiny dots of paint or markers. They can also make colors by combining dots of different colors—for example, green grass can be made by dots of blue and yellow.

Variation on an art theme: Give out graph paper and pencils. See what kind of drawings the kids can make using the grid.

- Show the children self-portraits done by famous artists and encourage them to try their hand at painting their own images. Give each a hand mirror and let them create their own visions of themselves. Explain that a self-portrait does not have to be a totally realistic reproduction of themselves; instead it is their interpretation of what they look like. This should ease any intimidation of making themselves look "funny."

Lew Schwartz, a cartoonist, and Jill's father, entertained at all of the kids' birthday parties by making a special drawing for each child using the letters of their names. Everyone got to take their drawings home as favors.

When using pastels, chalk, or charcoal, do it outside—it's messy!

Chalk, charcoal, and pastels should be sprayed with a fixing spray or hair spray, preferably outdoors.

- Abstract painting is perfect for children to try because they can do no wrong. Let them know that it is okay to draw upside down and backwards because there is no *correct* way to make art. Show them a reproduction of a Picasso for an example of how contemporary art breaks the rules. Invite them to experiment with different mediums, to combine traditional materials in nontraditional and imaginative ways: They can mix paint and sand and apply this as they would paint; they can glue objects to the painted canvas and paint over them; they can use watercolors over crayons for an unusual effect (first color the paper with crayons, leaving some white space, and then brush watercolors over the crayons and the white sections) and layer paints over glued paper cutouts for texture.

- Making paintings by moving the paint in untraditional ways is another way to understand the wonder of art. Give each child a piece of paper and place within reach a muffin tin filled with a different color tempera paint or watercolor in each cup. Have each child choose a color of paint and pour a spoonful at any chosen spot on the paper. Then with a plastic straw, each child gets to gently blow the paint in different directions by moving the straw and/or moving or turning the paper with your hands at the same time. When the first color dries, add another color and repeat the process.

- Landscapes with tissue paper: This technique takes away the intimidation some kids feel when confronted with other artists' realistic landscapes. Spread some watered down white glue or liquid starch on foam board or tagboard with a brush. Take the torn pieces of tissue paper and place them on the board, one at a time horizontally, to look like a landscape. Then spread the liquid over it again (it will be transparent, so don't worry about brushing the paper totally) and add more tissue. The tissues look great when they overlap one another and are placed askew.

- Painting to music: This is more of a game than an activity, but it's a lot of fun and works well after some kids have finished their painting and are ready to try something else. Play the tape you made with different kinds of music as the children paint. Tell them to follow both the tempo and the mood of the music as they create.

ARCHITECTURE

The object is to have the children create a house or a building using abstract shapes. You can show them a book of contemporary architecture for inspiration; they can make a version of their own home or just create the house of their dreams. Use:

- cardboard tubes from gift wrapping and toilet paper (use as is or cut the long way for vaulted shapes)
- pieces of foam board cut into many shapes and sizes
- toothpicks (for window frames)
- flex straws (to make columns)
- pipe cleaners (for connecting pieces)

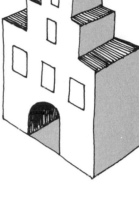

SCULPTURE

Using clay, have the children create a sculpture. They can try to reproduce an animal, make a portrait of someone they know, or concoct an abstract creation with many shapes and a lot of volume. Show the kids how they can add objects to the sculpture. Paper cups, metal pipes, plastic balls, nuts and bolts, toy cars, metal spoons, seashells, and the like all add structure and dimension to a piece of sculpture.

Incorporate "junk" into the sculpture.

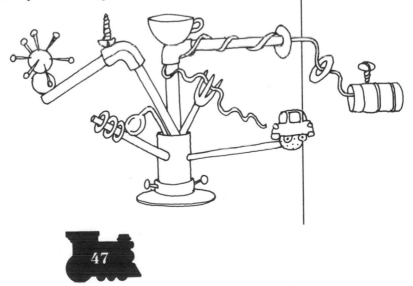

If you are using permanent markers and rubber cement, do so only with adult supervision in a well-ventilated room.

CARTOONING

Cartooning is art, and a favorite of kids and adults alike. Here is a way to make a "phenakistoscope," the first device that gave films the illusion of movement (it goes back to the 1830s and is the forerunner to motion pictures) and the best way to make a "first" cartoon (you'll find another cartooning project in the "Superheroes" party, page 194).

For each child, cut a circle, 8½-inches-round, out of white construction paper. Divide it into 12 equal segments (see drawing). Cut out a slot, 1-inch-long by ³⁄₁₆-inch-wide, at the end of each radius.

Give each child a piece of white paper on which you have drawn (with a template or compass) twelve 1½-inch-round circles. Number each circle with the numbers 1 through 12 written underneath. Then in each circle the child draws an image, in sequence, of what he wants his cartoon figure to do. Urge him to plan his story to make the character or figure move (it can also be a changing abstract shape, an object dropping, etc.). The key is to show change over the course of the 12 different frames.

When the drawing is done, have the child cut out the circles, keeping them in order of sequence. Glue the cutout circles, in order, around the edge of the larger circle, placed between the radius lines (see drawing). Stick a push pin through the center of the circle into the eraser head of a pencil which is on the other side of the cartoon wheel. Make sure that the wheel will spin easily on the pin.

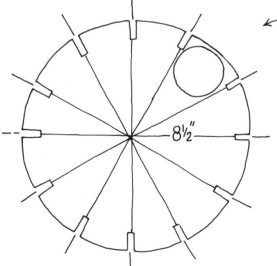

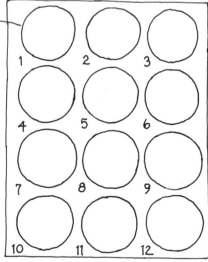

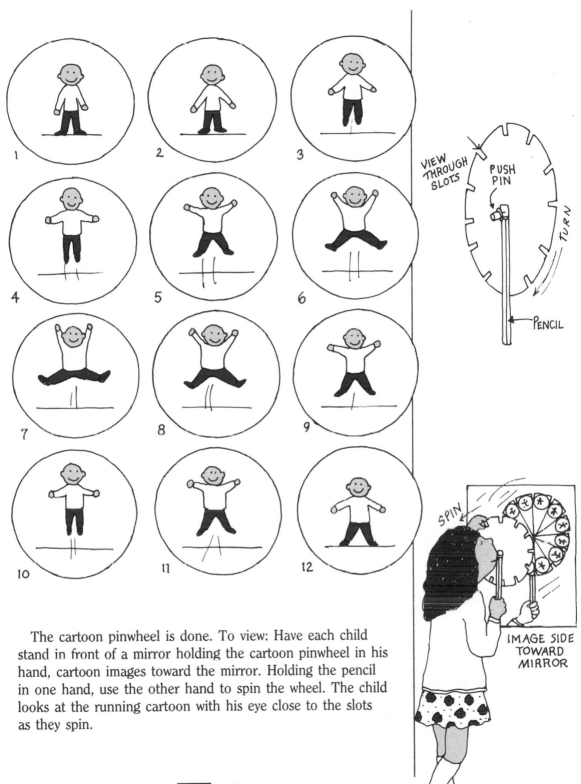

The cartoon pinwheel is done. To view: Have each child stand in front of a mirror holding the cartoon pinwheel in his hand, cartoon images toward the mirror. Holding the pencil in one hand, use the other hand to spin the wheel. The child looks at the running cartoon with his eye close to the slots as they spin.

COLLAGE

Give each child a piece of colored tagboard. Set out separate shoe boxes in which you have collected all kinds of materials that can be painted: paper clips, rulers, old circuit boards, mini cereal boxes, old books, bottle caps, comic strips, plastic fruit, rubber washers, dry flowers, greeting cards, and old miniature toys. Each can be glued to the tagboard. Form mounds of shapes by gluing things one on top of the other. The collage can then be painted in many different colors or all in one color (à la Louise Nevelson, a famous artist who specialized in monotone collages).

FAVORS

Set of paintbrushes, paint sets, books on art or art posters

Peerless Paints makes pads with paper that actually has paint already in it. All you do is wet the brush and paint your design. The pads come in many different colors and make wonderful favors (see Resources, page 250).

MENU

Since the activities in this party take so much time and concentration, it's unlikely that anyone will want to spend much time sitting down to eat. Instead, create three or four "food stations" with finger food that kids can snack on throughout the party. Do keep one area open for a special cake presentation.

STATION #1: Veggies and Peanut-Chili Dip
STATION #2: Sliced Turkey and Small Buns
STATION #3: Fruit: grapes, apples, pears,
                        bananas, strawberries
Lemonade
See recipes on page 229.

MATISSE CAKE

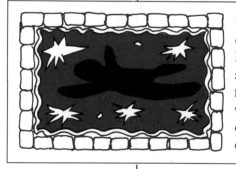

Use **Sylvia's Wonder Cake** recipe, page 227. Bake the cake in a 9 × 11-inch pan. Decorate with **Seven-Minute Frosting** (white is best), page 229. Outline Matisse-like shapes with different colored icings, or cut them out of fruit leathers. Make a frame around the edge of the cake with ladyfingers or any flat cookies. You can serve the cake in the pan or remove it and then serve. Use crayon candles (see Resources, page 249).

CAMP-OUT

(Ages 7 and up)

M arc Gilbar's first camp-out party came about accidentally. Marc, who was then nine, decided to have a party together with his friend Amos Buhai. The boys thought that since their birthdays fell only days apart, and since they were planning to invite the same group of friends, it would be more fun to do it together. The parents loved the idea because they knew it would be more economical and more efficient to give a joint party.

Marc wanted a sleep-over party, but neither the Gilbars' nor the Buhais' homes could accommodate the nearly 40 boys who were to be invited. Amos wanted to camp out in the woods. Marc wanted to have a scavenger hunt in the neighborhood. Annie and Suzanne Buhai wanted the flexibility that being in and around a house brings (lugging equipment and food for this small army of kids seemed like a nightmare). The compromise: the Marc and Amos Birthday Camp-out, held in the Buhais' backyard, complete with tents. The kids slept outdoors, ate dinner under the stars and breakfast in the tents, and the festivities began with a neighborhood scavenger hunt.

If your camp-out party is out in the woods and there is a small pond in the vicinity, you can make a waterscope (a large glass jar that you submerge halfway into the water). Look down through the open top and you may see tiny fish and plants. The glass bottom will magnify everything!

If you have access to a forest or a park, you can do what Bob and Sandy Pittman did for their son Bo's fifth birthday. Their camp-out took place only about 100 yards from their backyard, but to make it seem as if they were hiking to a wilderness, they arranged a winding trail that meandered back and forth so that when everyone finally reached the campsite, it felt as if they were deep in the forest. These campers made a map of the area; they followed animal tracks that an adult "miraculously" discovered (man-made with shoes of various sizes), learned how to mark trails with arrows and stones, and were taught how to use a compass. Several adults slept out in the tents with these youngsters, and everyone made it through the night.

INVITATION

Buy one collapsible plastic cup (available at camping and discount stores) for each invitation. Tracing the bottom of the cup on a piece of white paper, make two circles. Print the invitation copy, arranging the words below so they fit inside both circles. Xerox and cut out the circles. Glue an invitation on the bottom of each cup, with the additional instructions glued to the lid. Collapse the cups and mail in padded envelopes. You can decorate the envelopes by drawing the outline of a tent and writing the address inside the tent.

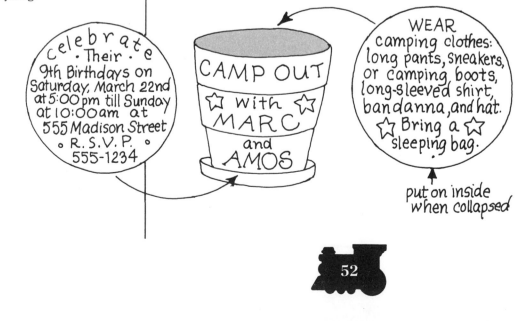

Celebrate
·Their·
9th Birthdays on Saturday, March 22nd at 5:00pm till Sunday at 10:00am at 555 Madison Street
○ R.S.V.P. ○
555-1234

CAMP OUT
☆ with ☆
MARC
and
AMOS

WEAR camping clothes: long pants, sneakers, or camping boots, long-sleeved shirt, bandanna, and hat.
☆ Bring a ☆ sleeping bag.

put on inside when collapsed

DECORATIONS

Since this party is held outdoors, whether it is in the backyard or in the local park or campground, traditional birthday "decorations" are unnecessary.

GET READY!

1. Arrange for rental of tents.
2. Buy large quantities of paper plates, cups, napkins, etc.
3. Buy magnifying glasses and bug catchers (the kids will use these and can take them home as favors).
4. Write the names of as many towns or states as you have kids on slips of paper for the "Town Exchange" game.
5. Type the scavenger lists and make enough copies for each team of two to four guests.
6. Get prizes.
7. Buy rope and cut into 12-inch pieces (one per child).
8. Gather twigs for the twig game.
9. Tagboard or foamboard and glue for the nature collages.
10. Find a copy of *The Pied Piper of Hamelin* by Robert Browning.
11. Set up a large white sheet and have on hand several flashlights for bug watching.
12. Xerox drawings of animal tracks.

If you are having the party in your backyard, it is easy to set up a scarecrow the night before. Use your imagination and give him an outlandish costume!

JAR LID

JAR LID

To make your own bug catchers for your guests, place a piece of screening inside and in between two jar lids and tape closed or use glass jars with holes punched in the lids.

At Sandy and Bob Pittman's camp-out for Bo's fifth birthday, tents were set up about 100 yards from their house in the woods, but everyone hiked by a circuitous route to get to the camp, so it seemed like they were miles from home and deep in the woods.

ACTIVITIES

Give out magnifying glasses, flashlights, water bottles, and bug catchers. Be sure to bring along insect repellent just in case. Tell everybody about the plans for the next two days.

PUTTING UP THE TENTS

At Marc and Amos' party, Amos' dad, Jeff, took on the task of renting the tents (look in your local yellow pages under "Camping"). For 40 children and 6 adults (it was easy to convince some other parents to join in the sleepover), he rented four tents that slept 6 children each and one tent that slept 10. One guest brought his own tent.

Arriving campers should be given directions about where to put their bedrolls and bags, and then asked to help put up tents as the first activity of the party. It will be helpful to have a proficient adult as a director who knows the tents you are using.

FOUR-LEAF CLOVER HUNT

If another activity is needed while you're waiting for everyone to arrive, send the kids out to look for "good luck" four-leaf clovers (you can give them magnifying glasses to add to the fun).

SCAVENGER HUNT

Divide the kids into groups of two to four, hand each team a slip of paper listing the items they must search for and retrieve, and send them off to return with as many of the following items as they can. Always send one adult or teenager with each group.

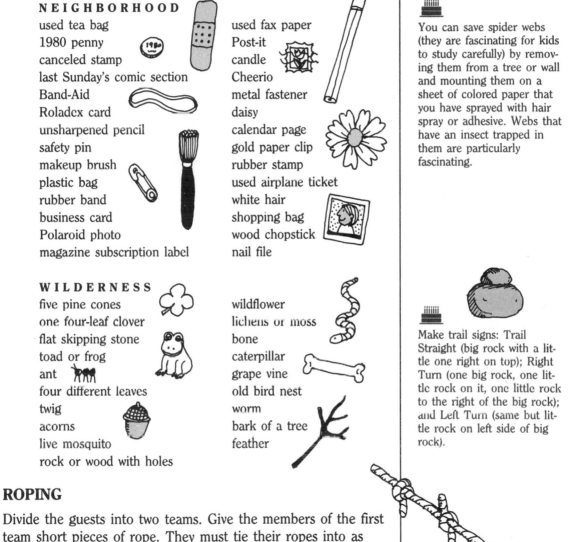

NEIGHBORHOOD
used tea bag
1980 penny
canceled stamp
last Sunday's comic section
Band-Aid
Roladex card
unsharpened pencil
safety pin
makeup brush
plastic bag
rubber band
business card
Polaroid photo
magazine subscription label

used fax paper
Post-it
candle
Cheerio
metal fastener
daisy
calendar page
gold paper clip
rubber stamp
used airplane ticket
white hair
shopping bag
wood chopstick
nail file

WILDERNESS
five pine cones
one four-leaf clover
flat skipping stone
toad or frog
ant
four different leaves
twig
acorns
live mosquito
rock or wood with holes

wildflower
lichens or moss
bone
caterpillar
grape vine
old bird nest
worm
bark of a tree
feather

You can save spider webs (they are fascinating for kids to study carefully) by removing them from a tree or wall and mounting them on a sheet of colored paper that you have sprayed with hair spray or adhesive. Webs that have an insect trapped in them are particularly fascinating.

Make trail signs: Trail Straight (big rock with a little one right on top); Right Turn (one big rock, one little rock on it, one little rock to the right of the big rock); and Left Turn (same but little rock on left side of big rock).

ROPING

Divide the guests into two teams. Give the members of the first team short pieces of rope. They must tie their ropes into as many knots as they can in two minutes. Now the other team must untie the knots in the shortest possible amount of time. Reverse the order. The winner is the team whose members untied the knots in the quickest time.

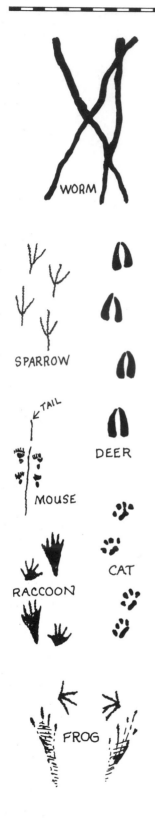

PIED PIPER

If you have younger campers at your party, this is an alternative to the scavenger hunt. You or a friend (preferably one who reads well and can play a kazoo, harmonica, or any other mouth instrument) can read *The Pied Piper of Hamelin* by Browning to the children. Then let your guests, following each other hand in hand, line up and follow the "Pied Piper," who performs funny antics as he leads the group. Each person must do what the leader does; whoever does not is eliminated. Obviously the Pied Piper must do strange and sometimes more difficult things so the kids get confused and silly.

ANIMAL TRACKS

Give each child a Xerox copy of our animal track drawings and see how many of them the children can find. If you have a camera, you can take pictures of them or have the children draw the tracks they see.

TOWN EXCHANGE

The birthday child is chosen to be the first Postman in the town. The other guests sit in a circle on the ground and the Postman stands in the middle. The Postman has a list of the towns or states in his pocket. He passes around a plastic bowl full of slips of paper, each of which has the name of a different town or state written on it. Every guest picks out a name and keeps it secret.

The game begins when the Postman calls out the names of any two towns or states on his list. Those two "residents" must quickly exchange seats in the circle. *The point is for the Postman to try to get one of those seats before one of the residents.* When one citizen loses his seat, he becomes the Postman.

INDIAN SIGNS

This is a memory game. The guests stand or sit in a circle and each, in turn, demonstrates and explains his "Indian Sign." These signs are hand and finger portrayals of some phase of Indian life such as bow-and-arrow shooting, wearing a feather headdress, creating a war whoop, making the peace sign, smoking the peace pipe, waving a tomahawk, and so on. The kids must try to memorize as many of the signs as they can. One child is made the Chief.

When the game begins, the Chief makes his own sign and then the sign of another player who in turn makes the Chief's sign, a third player's sign, and then his own sign. The third Indian makes the Chief's sign, the second Indian's sign, a fourth player's sign, then his own, and so on. The first person to mess up gets assigned a point. After ten minutes, the winner is the player with the fewest points.

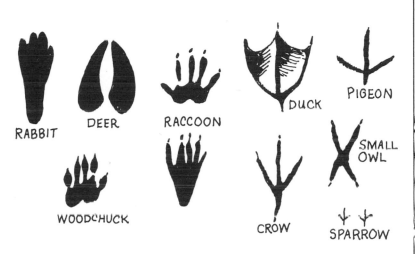

RABBIT DEER RACCOON DUCK PIGEON

WOODCHUCK CROW SMALL OWL SPARROW

FLY BY NIGHT

Insects love light; a great way to see them up close is to attract them to light. Take a white sheet and hang it from a tree branch or against a fence. Have the kids shine their flashlights on the sheet; flying insects will start to congregate on the sheet and will probably stay on the sheet for some time. You will be able to walk right up to them and use your magnifying glasses to get a closer look. Let the children take turns looking at the different insects and shining the lights. You can then try to catch some of the bugs.

If you see any fireflies at your camp-out, gather the troops and try to catch them. You can do that with a little butterfly net or with your bug catchers.

When Phyllis Wolfe's kids have slumber parties, she goes around changing all the clocks to a later time. Sometimes it works!

Have a watermelon-eating contest. It's loads of fun, and the kids can be as messy as they like out in the wilderness!

TEAM TWIG MATCHING

Gather several kinds and sizes of twigs in different lengths. Break each into two parts (try to make each break distinct from the others). Place one set of halves on one table or blanket and the other set on another table or blanket. At a given signal, a guest gets to look closely at one set for 30 seconds; he then runs to the other set and finds one matching twig, runs back to the first set, and holds the matching halves together. If he matches correctly, he gets a prize. If you have time, you can keep going so the players get more than one chance each.

You can also play this game with leaves.

GHOST STORIES

Gather round in a circle and either have an adult read or tell some ghost stories or have each child tell one.

NEXT MORNING

Early risers can make collages from nature materials that you have placed on a large table. Give each a 2-foot-square piece of tagboard or foam board and let them go to town.

An alternative activity is to collect as many different kinds of leaves as you can find to put into a leaf scrapbook.

FAVORS

Bug boxes, magnifying glasses

MENU

DINNER

Dinner can be served in between the games or at the end of the scavenger hunt.

Sandwiches wrapped in bandannas and
attached to bamboo sticks
(have everyone carry them on the way to the campsite)
Campground Stew
S'mores
Lemonade or boxed drinks

CATERPILLAR CAKE (CUPCAKES)

Use the **Piglet Cupcakes** recipe, page 228. The recipe will make 10–12 balls. Bake the cupcakes in a mini ball pan (see Resources, page 249) or a basic muffin tin. Use **Orange Cream Frosting,** page 229, tinted with orange food coloring. Frost each cupcake or mini ball to cover the rounded portion. Cover with shredded coconut, colored or white. Arrange the cakes in the shape of a caterpillar on a long piece of cardboard covered with freezer paper. For the head: Use two colored candy wafers; for eyes: attach a raisin on each wafer with frosting. Use shoelace licorice for antennae, legs, and a smile. Add candles. If you want to write "Happy Birthday," write it with frosting on the board.

LICORICE

NECCO WAFER

CHOCOLATE CHIP

CORN CANDY OR LICORICE

BREAKFAST

Breakfast Cheese Pizza
Bran Muffins
Orange juice with bananas

See recipes on pages 230–231.

Try a breakfast pizza with scrambled eggs, ham, or sausage on top.

CANDID CAMERA

(Ages 10 and up)

"C" ount to three and then say cheese!" Young party-goers, used to responding to that command, will really get a kick out of being on the other side of the camera. Armed with load-and-shoots, Polaroids, disposables, or whatever cameras you can collect, your guests will learn how to shoot photos and have a great time in the process. With or without a photo expert as a guide, you are sure to end up with some unusual and memorable results and a bunch of satisfied photographers. And for those kids who prefer the front of the camera, there's still a chance for some artistic posing.

INVITATION

This unusual invitation was inspired by the one made by Joyce Bogart Trabulus for the birthdays of her children Evan and Jenna. It is a simple process using film developed on a proof sheet (you will need to find a custom film lab to do this; check your yellow pages). First, shoot the whole roll of film featuring the birthday child in various poses. He or she should wear light-colored clothes, perhaps covered by a darker jacket so that the pictures can be partially tinted later. Use props such as sunglasses, hats, an umbrella, a soccer ball, and other things that reflect his or her life and personality.

Take the film to the lab to be developed. From the proof sheets, select 8 to 12 photos. Cut these out (leave the numbers under the proofs and the name of the film company to make it look more professional) and tape them together in strips to form a square (the copy will go in the blank space in the center). Write the copy once on a white piece of paper and then Xerox and tape in the center of the "photo frame." Now take this sheet back to the lab to be printed on the glossy paper that looks just like proof sheet paper (print as many as you need invitations). Hand-color some frames with colored pencils.

DECORATIONS

Lights, fan, props, and a blank wall are the essentials. Transform any room in your house to be a photographer's studio.

GET READY!

1. Alert your local one-hour photo lab as to the day and time of your party. Tell the manager that you will be bringing lots of film to be developed on the selected day and that you are going to need speedy (and hopefully, cheap) service.

2. Buy film in bulk at discount store.

3. Collect cameras.

4. Use a spotlight to help the modeling session photos look more professional.

5. Get out your electric fan for blowing hair and clothing for the "special effects" department.

6. Gather any costumes and makeup you will need for the "models."

7. Prepare a separate area for the "Modeling Session" with a white backdrop (use a white sheet or drop cloth).

8. Buy some inexpensive photo albums that the kids can decorate, and/or poster board for photo collages.

9. Arrange for a "professional" photographer (a friend who is a hobbyist) to come to talk to the kids.

10. Collect all kinds of white items to hide for the "Color-Blind" game. White shoelaces, sneakers, cotton balls, sugar cubes, tissues, rolls of adding machine tape, china cups, plastic spoons, are some suggestions.

11. Organize materials (silk flowers, lace, buttons, beads, and other assorted decorations, as well as markers, paint and glitter pens, glue guns) for decorating photo albums.

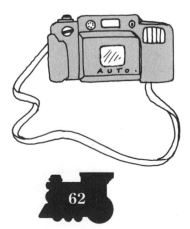

ACTIVITIES

The party is basically divided into two photo sessions with some games to be played toward the end. You can plan a trip to the one-hour photo shop either between the sessions (in which case you'll be going twice) or after both, depending on how convenient this is for you. You can assign this task to a friend or relative helping with the party.

MODELING SESSION

In your "photo studio" the "photographers" prepare for a full-fledged photo shoot with guest "models." A hair and makeup "expert" can prepare the "models" while the photographers set up the lights, fan, and all other costumes or props that are needed. Have one photographer take Polaroid shots of the models to show them what the actual shots will look like. Remind the photographers to direct their subjects to pose so that the photos will show different attitudes and personalities. When everyone has had a turn at being a model, you can run these films to the lab. While you are waiting for photos to come back, you can play the following games and have lunch.

Sonia Israel makes earrings out of old film strips. Just snip off a piece of film and hang from an earring back.

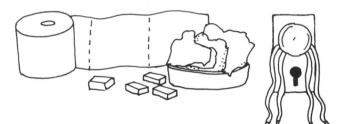

CANDID CAMERA

Send each guest, armed with a camera, on a mission to shoot "candid camera" shots. Instruct them to find unusual, unposed, and possibly funny situations. Make sure, before everyone begins, that each guest takes the first shot of a card with his name on it. It will identify which film belongs to whom.

When the children return from this mission (30 minutes should be enough time), you may choose to run all this film to the one-hour lab while they participate in the next event.

COLOR-BLIND

The game is to find as many white things inappropriately placed around the house as possible (for example, a roll of white paper towels set on top of a mantel, some tissue paper in ashtrays, shoelaces tied around doorknobs, sugar cubes by the telephone, etc.). Each player makes a list of all the white things he sees. The one with the longest list wins.

CLICK, SNAP, AND FLASH

One person starts and claps his hands. The second person must clap his hands and then choose another motion to perform, like winking. The third person then claps his hands, winks, and then might choose to sneeze. The game continues until everybody has had a chance. Whenever somebody misses, they're out.

PARTING SHOTS

As everyone waits for the film to return, have the kids decorate their photo albums using the materials you assembled. When all the photos are returned, give prizes for the most creative, silliest, most unusual, and so on, and have the kids put their photos in the photo albums for permanent memories of this party. They can also make photo collages.

Tracy Large's grandmother, Charlene Ochs, invited her granddaughter and her friends to a dress-up birthday "Tea Party" with a special treat. Grandma Charlene gave each girl a blank book. She then took photographs of each guest, of pairs of girls, and then a group shot. She had someone take the film to a one-hour photo studio. Meanwhile, each girl had to write in each of the other girls' books, composing her thoughts about what she predicted for each girl for that following year. When the photos came back, each girl pasted a photo of herself in the front of the book, and then other photos (including the group shot) inside the book, with appropriate matching shots going with the predictions. The girls who were invited still treasure the books and reread them often. The photos are reminders of a wonderful day!

SHOW AND TELL

There are so many photography hobbyists around that you won't have any trouble finding one to come by to provide hints on taking pictures (lighting, distance, framing, focus) and also to share stories of photography experiences.

FAVORS

Photo albums that the children made and the pictures they took

MENU

Tortilla chips
Chicken Enchiladas
Mexican Bean Dip
Spanish Rice
Green Salad
Crusty French bread
Punch

See recipes on pages 231–232.

FILM STRIP CAKE

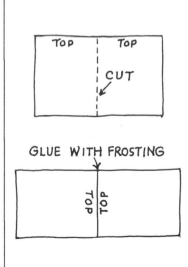

TOP | TOP

CUT

GLUE WITH FROSTING

TOP | TOP

Use the **Perfect Chocolate Cake** recipe, page 224. Bake the cake in a 9 × 11-inch pan. Cut the cake in half lengthwise; place the halves end to end on a large piece of stiff cardboard or foam board. (You can use a little frosting to cement the halves together.) Frost the cake with **Chocolate Frosting**, page 224. Place white butter mints 1 inch apart along the top and bottom of the cake to make film sprockets. Use any white icing to write on the cake.

The perfect birthday gift: At a party for her friend Ellen Meyer, Candace Block brought the best gift. She took photographs throughout the party of all the guests with her instant camera. Then, just as Ellen opened her gifts, Candace inserted each Polaroid shot into a small album she had brought. She then presented the completed album to Ellen as her birthday gift—instant memories that all the guests could share, right there, together!

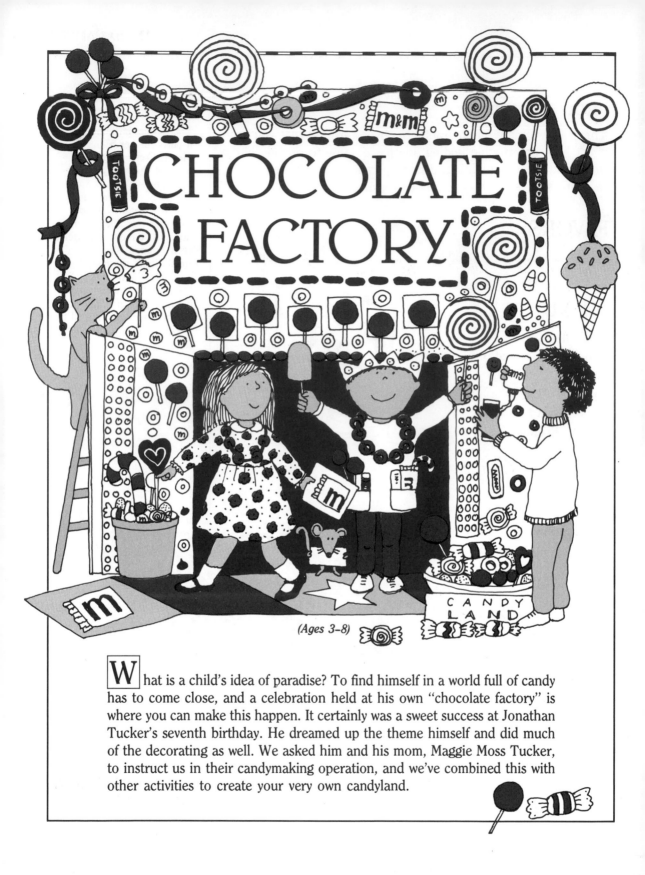

CHOCOLATE FACTORY

(Ages 3–8)

W hat is a child's idea of paradise? To find himself in a world full of candy has to come close, and a celebration held at his own "chocolate factory" is where you can make this happen. It certainly was a sweet success at Jonathan Tucker's seventh birthday. He dreamed up the theme himself and did much of the decorating as well. We asked him and his mom, Maggie Moss Tucker, to instruct us in their candymaking operation, and we've combined this with other activities to create your very own candyland.

INVITATION

A chocolate bar wrapped with your own candy wrapping is the invitation. On the outside of the wrapper write the following:

Jonathan's
7 • 7
CHOCOLATE FACTORY

Come play and eat sweets to celebrate Jonathan's 7th Birthday

Sunday, January 8th
◆ 555 Palm Tree Lane ◆
R. S. V. P. 555-1234

Paint hair, eyes, nose, and mouth
RED HOTS
NECCO WAFERS

Photo of Child's Head or NECCO WAFER
Aluminum Foil
COVER: Xerox-cutout and fold over candy bar. Glue or tape the back.

LIFESAVER
TOOTSIE ROLL
m&m

DECORATIONS

Jonathan had as much fun *before* the party as during it. Together with his mom, his sister Jennie, and his dad, Paul, Jonathan built a giant candy house that served as the entryway to the party. Here's how to make one:

Paint a large appliance box (the kind refrigerators come in) the day before the party. Cut out two door flaps opposite each other through which the kids can enter and exit. Glue candy all over it, but leave some room for the guests to glue some on as they arrive. You can use Life Savers, peppermints, chocolates of all kinds, hard candies, lollipops, cookies, Tootsie Rolls, candy canes, and candy bars.

To add to the candyland atmosphere, Maggie and Jonathan hung strips of lollipops all around the house, especially in front of windows, across tabletops, and from doorways. Maggie then decorated all her chandeliers and lamps with candies hanging from multicolored ribbons.

GET READY!

1. Find a refrigerator box for the candy house. Buy large squeeze bottles of glue and bags of candy.

2. Locate a lid from a gift box and a blindfold for the "Lollipop Drop."

3. Buy several packages of colored construction paper, 8½ × 11 inches, for "Follow the Candy Road." You will also need one huge lollipop, a plastic bucket wrapped in gold foil, and bags of candy bars and hard candy in wrappers—lots of it! You will use some of the wrappers in the "Follow the Candy Road" game and the candy will be part of other games or the decor.

4. Prepare the life-size "Follow the Candy Road" game. Make 3 × 5-inch cards and glue candy wrappers on some "stops."

5. Buy semisweet chocolate chips, candy molds, and chocolate (all available at any baking or candy supply store) for making chocolate lollipops.

6. Gather candy and cereal for making edible jewelry: licorice, Life Savers, Fruit Loops, Cheerios, etc.

7. Buy, borrow, or rent a cotton candy machine.

8. Buy two pounds of miniature marshmallows for the "Marshmallow Move."

9. Gather cellophane corsage bags or plastic bags and ribbons for wrapping and storing favors.

ACTIVITIES

DECORATING THE CANDY HOUSE

Since guests often appear at different times, it is important that the first activity engage each child upon arrival. For this, place the giant candy house by the front door so the guests see it immediately. Set bowls of candies and squeeze-bottles of glue next to the house and ask everyone to help finish its construction.

MAKING CHOCOLATE LOLLIPOPS

This is an easy way to make chocolate lollipops with all the children participating in the fun. Microwave about one ounce of chocolate per child for one to three minutes until melted. Stir well with a wooden spoon. Now, squeeze or spoon the chocolate into the molds. Stick one ice cream stick in each and freeze for five minutes. After the lollipop has hardened, remove from the mold, wrap in plastic, and tie a ribbon around the stick.

FLAVOR TAG

Make a list of colors, giving each color the name of a flavor. For example: green would be lime, red would be cherry, yellow would be lemon or banana, purple would be grape, and orange would be tangerine or orange.

Have the birthday child be the first "Candy Tagger." As he shouts out a flavor, everyone else scatters about to find something of the chosen flavor to touch to be safe. Whoever isn't touching the right flavor gets caught by the "Candy Tagger," and he then becomes the "Candy Tagger." Every time you play this game, you must choose a different color.

Mary Tallitsch made a gingerbread house instead of a cake for son Steven's fifth birthday. She filled it with superballs and then let the kids decorate it as part of the activities. The surprise was that when the kids broke the house to eat it, they discovered the balls inside.

FOLLOW THE CANDY ROAD

The board game Candyland is a classic nonreader's, beginner board game that you can play easily if you have only a few preschoolers at this party. They'll have even more fun, though, if you construct a *life-size* Candyland-like game. Here the kids, rather than pawns, actually move along the path to reach the "pot of gold" at the end.

To prepare: Unwrap the packages of colored construction paper and, alternating colors, tape the pieces onto the floor, one after the other, in a serpentine candy road (about 150 pieces of paper will make an interesting winding path). In fact, the road can meander from one room to another if you'd like; however, don't get the contestants too spread out. Each piece of colored paper becomes a potential "stop" on the road.

Create a deck of cards by cutting pieces of construction paper into 3 × 5-inch pieces; make sure the colors of the "candy road" and the cards correspond. You should have at least 40 cards. (They can be shuffled and used again.)

Next, cut some candy wrappers in half, lengthwise; use a variety of candy bars. Randomly tape one half of each wrapper on a "stop" somewhere along the candy route. Tape the other halves onto the corresponding cards.

To play the game: Shuffle the cards you've made. Each child picks the top card and walks to the corresponding "stop" on the road. The next child picks another card and goes to that color "stop." When a card with a candy wrapper is drawn, the player goes to the nearest corresponding wrapper on the floor, whether it is ahead of him or behind him along the road.

To make the game more interesting, you can also draw a black star on a couple of the colored "stops." When a child lands on one of these "stops," he must stay there until he pulls another card of the same color. Also, you can write the number "2" on a few of the cards so that when you pick a card of a certain color with the number "2" on it, the child moves two spaces of that color.

At the end of the candy road, place a plastic bucket full of small lollipops and one large lollipop. (The bucket is wrapped in gold foil so it's easily identified as the "pot of gold.") Whoever gets to the bucket first wins the large lollipop; everyone else gets the others.

Make your own personalized candy bar by painting a design on a slab of white chocolate that comes with a paint brush and four special confectionery colors (see Resources, page 250).

Kacey Fields had an Ice Cream Party for her third birthday. Her mom, Ellen, baked cake batter in ice cream cones and everyone decorated their cake cones with frosting and candies. They made ice cream cone magnets out of felt and played pin-the-cherry on the ice cream cone. Favors included gift certificates to the local ice cream parlor.

MARSHMALLOW MOVE

Place about two pounds of miniature marshmallows in one large bowl on a table at one end of the room and an empty bowl across the room on another table. Each child takes a turn placing his hand, palm down, into the bowl. The object is to bring up as many marshmallows as he can on the back of his hand. He then has to walk to the other end of the room, keeping the marshmallows on his hand and depositing them into the other bowl. The winner is the one who manages to keep the most marshmallows on his hand. Organize this as an individual contest or as a relay team game.

LOLLIPOP DROP

Draw an outline of a clown face with a large open mouth on the lid of a gift box. Cut out the mouth. Fasten the box against the wall with tape so that the mouth is slightly away from the wall. Each child is blindfolded and tries to toss a lollipop into the open mouth. Each child should be given three tries; the one with the most successes wins.

MAKING EDIBLE JEWELRY

Fill plastic containers with long strands of licorice, Life Savers, Fruit Loops, Cheerios, and any other candies with center holes. Make a knot in one end of the licorice and string the candies, one at a time, to make a bracelet or a necklace. First you wear the pretty jewelry and pretty soon, you eat it!

COTTON CANDY

Old-fashioned cotton candy machines are enjoying a renaissance and are available at many toy stores or through a party rental service. It is easy to make cotton candy with these machines, and the fun of watching sugar spin appeals to all ages.

FAVORS

The chocolate lollipops that the children made during the party are perfect favors to take home when wrapped in cellophane corsage bags or plastic bags tied with ribbons. You can also add other candies to the bags. If you are only having a few children at this party, you might consider giving each guest the game Candyland as a favor.

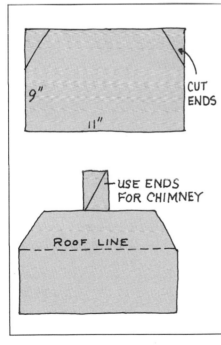

MENU

Oreo Sandwiches

Peppermint Ice Cream Sodas (soda water over a scoop of peppermint ice cream in a tall glass served with a straw)

Carrot lollipops (take the pimentos out of large green olives and place each olive over a carrot stick)

Make-Your-Own-Sundae Bar

See recipes on page 232.

Cele Theisen, who is always creating activities to keep Sarah and David, the children she cares for, busy, remembers this instant, last-minute, just-when-you-ran-out-of-everything puppet. Take a paper cup, turn it upside down, then cut out two holes for the fingers (see drawing). Draw the face: The funnier and sillier, the better. Stick the two fingers through the holes and give that puppet some life!

CHOCOLATE HOUSE BIRTHDAY CAKE

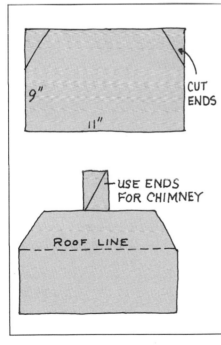

9"

11"

CUT ENDS

USE ENDS FOR CHIMNEY

ROOF LINE

Use **Sylvia's Wonder Cake** recipe, page 227. Bake the cake in a 9 × 11-inch pan. Remove the cake from the pan. Cut off the upper corners to create a roof shape. Cover with **Seven-Minute Frosting**, page 229. Use cookies and candies to create architectural details.

CLOUD 9

(Ages 7–10 ☆ perfect for a nine-year-old)

A "Cloud 9" party is a heavenly fantasy. This is a party that encourages "heads in the clouds" planning. You'll see how much fun this can be when you think about magic stars, stellar rainbows, heavenly wings, and celestial bodies. So get phantasmagorical and allow all your child's secret wishes to surface.

INVITATION

Cut a white cloud out of glossy paper. On it place rainbow stickers with white cotton balls glued around the perimeter of the cloud. Write the copy on the cloud with a silver pen and sprinkle silver glitter glue to the cotton on the clouds.

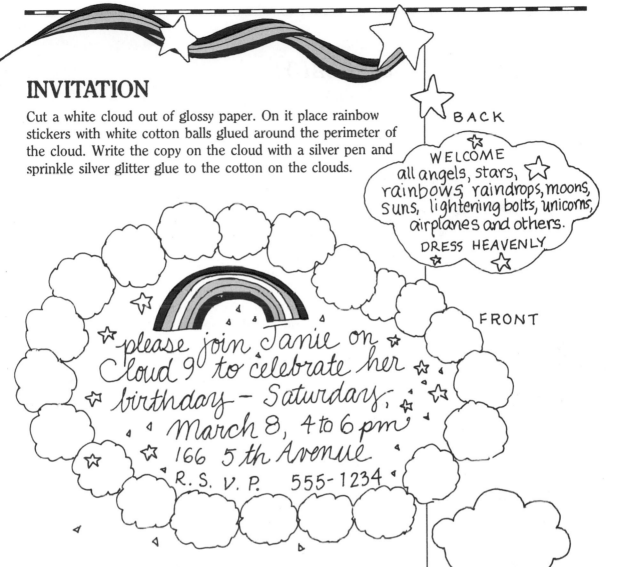

BACK

WELCOME all angels, stars, rainbows, raindrops, moons, suns, lightening bolts, unicorns, airplanes and others. DRESS HEAVENLY

FRONT

please join Janie on Cloud 9 to celebrate her birthday — Saturday, March 8, 4 to 6 pm 166 5th Avenue R. S. V. P. 555-1234

DECORATIONS

Attach balls of cotton to fishing line and hang from the ceiling. Rainbows and silver stars cut out of aluminum foil will add to the decor as well. Hang rainbow streamers and silver Mylar stars. Pillow stuffing or Polyfill is perfect to put all around the floor to give the room an instant feeling of being in the clouds (or use white pillows for an easy alternative).

For your table, tape white cotton clouds at various spots on a blue tablecloth. If a family member is a model airplane hobbyist, hang some models around the room. Attach white inflated balloons to the ceiling. Even a unicorn or two will add to the atmosphere up in this stratosphere.

FLIPBOOK BEGINS HERE!

GET READY!

1. Purchase a *large* supply of cotton balls.

2. Buy bags of Polyfill to put all over the floor.

3. Gather a blue paper or cloth tablecloth, silver stars, and rainbows.

4. Write out the words for the "Celestial Charades" game.

5. When you make the invitations, Xerox a blank white cloud for the "Search for Cloud 9" game and number 20 of them. Or use cotton for the clouds instead.

6. Blow up balloons for the "Cloud Burst" game. Have on hand string or ribbon and kitchen spoons.

7. Buy white and colored cotton balls and plastic spoons for the "Blue Moon" game.

8. Buy a couple of big boxes of Q-tips.

9. Find "sun printing" (light-sensitive) paper, available at art, nature, or hobby shops.

10. Prepare any weather-related song on a cassette.

11. Get prizes and favors.

ACTIVITIES

WIZARDRY

The birthday child or designated guest is the wizard. The wizard chooses an assistant who is in on the secret and sends her out of the room. The wizard asks all the other guests assembled before her to pick out any object in the room for the assistant to guess when she returns. Anything in the room can be chosen. Everyone calls for the assistant to return to begin guessing which object was chosen. The wizard begins by pointing to different things, one after the other, until she points to the chosen object and the assistant guesses it.

How did she know? Before the assistant leaves, you decide that the chosen object will always be pointed to after something pink or another specified color. This is whispered to the assistant before she leaves.

The game is played over and over until someone guesses how it's done, or the guests become bored.

CELESTIAL CHARADES

In a hat, place slips of paper on which you have written words or phrases with "heavenly" associations. Divide the guests into two teams. One team is up at a time. After drawing a word or phrase from the hat, one team member must pantomime that word or phrase and teammates try to guess the word or phrase within a certain amount of time. The team guessing the most words or phrases in the shortest time wins.

Here are some suggestions:

airplane	once in a blue moon
heaven	raining cats and dogs
sky	light-years away
raindrops	fun in the sun
thunder	high as a kite
lightning	under the weather
wind	pie in the sky
angel	head in the clouds
wizard	over the rainbow
cupid	stars in your eyes
rainbow	galaxy
moon	

Peter Nikolaidis, who works at the Montshire Science Museum in Norwich, Vermont, came up with an easy way for kids to make rockets. He puts one regular straw inside a larger straw (the kind you get at fast food restaurants). The tip of the smaller straw has a nose cone and the other end a tail fin (see drawing). When it is done, each child merely blows through the bigger straw and the entire rocket slides out and shoots up into the air.

WAND WORDS

Make one big pile of all your Q-tips. Each child gets to pick 20 out of the pile. The first one to make a word with his, wins. You can repeat the process again and again. If you want to make it harder, ask the children to make words having to do with ethereal heavenly things like "sky," "clouds," "airplane," etc.

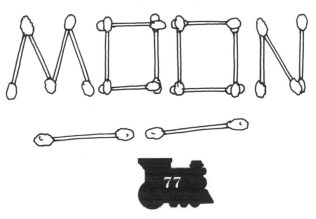

SEARCH FOR CLOUD 9

Hide about 20 white clouds (made of white paper or cotton), each numbered on the back. The one who finds Cloud #9 first, wins. Make Cloud #9 harder to find than the others. For younger children, you can also hide more than one Cloud #9.

CLOUD BURST

Every guest has a "cloud" (a blown-up balloon) tied to his ankle with string or ribbon and a spoon. Divide the guests into couples. The object of the game is to burst your partner's clouds (while protecting your own) with the spoon. Once your cloud bursts, you are out of the game. The person left with his cloud intact is the winner.

SUN PRINTS

The kids may not believe it but the queen of the stars—the sun—can help them make some beautiful prints. Hand out a sheet of light-sensitive paper to each guest. Let them choose whatever items they want to print on their paper. Things like leaves, forks, cutouts, scissors, coins, etc., leave identifiable and pretty prints. Each child places his chosen items on the paper and leaves it in the sun for about eight to ten minutes. Then remove the objects and dip the paper under cold water to permanently set the images.

Meredith's sister, Leslie, had a "Blue Moon Party." The invitation and sign on the door both said, "Friends like you come along once in a blue moon."

BLUE MOON

Have all the guests sit in a circle on the floor. Pile white and colored cotton balls in the center. The blue ones are "blue moons." Each player is holding a plastic spoon. At the signal, the players must pick up as many cotton balls as they can with their spoons and put them in their laps. They have 30 seconds. The player with the most cotton balls in his lap wins. There is a special prize for the player who gets the most blue moons.

WEATHER REPORT

One guest is chosen as the weatherman. The music begins (play "Raindrops Keep Falling on My Head," "Stormy Weather," or any other weather-related tune) for everyone to dance to at the same time. As they dance, the weatherman calls out the weather report. Whenever the weather is sunny, mild, hot, or windy, everyone keeps on dancing. Only when the weatherman calls out a report of any precipitation, such as rain, sleet, or snow or hail, must everyone sit down or freeze. Whoever is last to sit down or forgets to freeze is out.

FAVORS

Glow in the dark stars, sets of rainbow-colored markers, books on stargazing (see Resources, page 251)

MENU

Jenny's Peanut Butter Noodles
Quesadillas with Muenster or Jack cheese
Sliced jicama salad
Lemonade

See recipes on page 233.

Star Writers are glow in the dark paint pens that you can use on sweatshirts, books, etc. (see Resources, page 251).

CLOUD CAKE

Use the **Angel Food Cake** recipe, page 228. Bake in an angel food cake pan. Cool and cover generously with white **Seven-Minute Frosting,** page 229. Sprinkle with candy stars and colored sugar. Add star candle holders and rainbow-colored candles. Serve with rainbow sherbet.

CLUB CASINO

(Ages 8 and up)

D avid Platt loves games of chance, and Jan Platt's creativity made for an inventive and even educational casino party. The kids learned about odds and were totally mesmerized by that little ball on the roulette wheel and its habit of landing on red more often than on black (or was it the other way around?). And, somehow, they managed to pull their math skills together to add up all those different-colored chips at a moment's notice.

This party definitely has David's approval. He has scheduled another casino party for his next birthday, and he can't wait to try out some of these new games. He's also pleased that we included more games than you will need, 'cause he's betting on the chances being good that you'll run out of time before you run out of games.

INVITATION

Xerox play paper money and cut out the face, replacing it with
a photograph of your child's face. Xerox as many of these newly made dollars as you need. Each one becomes an invitation.
On the back, write the following:

EVEN ODDS YOU'LL COME
OUT A WINNER AT
DAVID'S CASINO PARTY
Saturday · Sept. 25th · 12 to 2 pm
AT 555 Las Palmas Drive
R. S. V. P.   555-1234

DECORATIONS

Set up the party room as if it were a casino. The blackjack table
can be a card table covered with green felt; the roulette table
should be large enough for people to stand around it (you can
also rent one at some party supply stores). A bingo table, another
card table, and a "Wheel of Cards" add to the casino atmosphere.

Hang oversize playing cards, slot machines, dice, and other
gambling symbols made from cardboard around the room. Have
the adult and teenage helpers dress in dealer attire: long-sleeved
white shirts with garters on the sleeves, vests, and green plastic
visors. Cover the dining table with green felt and then glue
playing cards all over it.

GET READY!

1. Order or make the decorations (see Resources, page 250).

2. Make three-dimensional dice by creating boxes out of black tagboard (or painting square boxes black) and gluing round white labels to make the dots.

3. Prepare lots of bags of poker chips.

4. Fill a jar with jelly beans. (Buy jelly beans in bags. Count one bag, then multiply by the number of bags you use. You don't want to tediously count each bean!)

5. Rent or make a blackjack table; rent or buy a roulette wheel.

6. Buy ten full decks of cards.

7. Prepare a bingo set.

8. Get tagboard or foam board and large fasteners for the "Wheel of Cards," and make the wheel.

9. Save up several days of classified ads from your local newspaper and have highlighter pens on hand.

10. Prepare the track for the "Horse Race" with masking tape. You will also need plastic horses and dice.

11. Buy candy bars and foam board for "A Sweet Story." Write out the story.

12. Get prizes.

ACTIVITIES

Hand out bags of poker chips to the children as they arrive.

JELLY BEAN JOLLIES

Put a large jar of jelly beans on a table near the front door and have each arrival at the party write down how many beans they think are in the jar. At the end of the day, whoever guesses the closest number wins and gets to take home the jar of jelly beans.

CARD GAMES

Blackjack (Twenty-one)

Station one "dealer" at the blackjack table. Each player, including the dealer, receives two cards, face down; the dealer's second card is turned face up so that everyone can see it. The object of the game is to get more points than the dealer, but less than 22. Each player puts up an "ante," which is the number of chips he decided to bet on each hand. If the player wins, he gets an equal number of chips to add to the ante (the dealer takes the antes of all the losers). In turn, each player tells the dealer whether or not he wants an additional card, called a "hit," until he decides to stop, trying to make 21 but before he reaches 22.

Card Dominos

Deal the deck of cards, face down. Divide equally among the players. Each player sorts the cards in his hand by suit. Whoever has the seven of diamonds starts the game by putting it face up on the table or on the floor. The next person must either put a six of diamonds, an eight of diamonds, or a seven of another suit above or below the card. If that player has none of those cards, he passes. The first player to get rid of all his cards, wins.

Card Memory

Using two decks of cards, take out all the hearts and clubs, and the four jokers, using only these for the game. Set aside the other cards you won't be using. (Save the two sets of spades and diamonds for the "Wheel of Cards" game.) You'll have 56 cards. Shuffle well and lay them upside down on the floor or table. Each player in turn gets to turn up two cards anywhere. If they don't match, he turns them back over and the next player takes his turn. If they match, he keeps those cards and continues until he is unable to make a match. The object is to get as many matches as you can.

Marc Gilbar tried very hard to come up with his very own party for his twelfth birthday. He knew he wanted a sports party, but had already planned and given his most favorites (soccer, tennis, Olympics, baseball...). It didn't take long for him to come up with his latest—pool. With his friend Amos Buhai, and with the help of the Hollywood Athletic Club in Los Angeles, the boys planned a simple pool party that turned into an enormous success! Gary Gilbar drew the invitation—a pool table where the surface looked like a swimming pool (diving board, floats and all). The party plan was simple—the Club rented out five pool tables (for thirty kids) so teams could play at each table. They also made "pool sharks" available to show the kids some tricks. Lunch was hamburgers and hot dogs—"a waste," says Marc, because all the kids wanted to do was return to the pool tables and break away!

I Doubt It

Take two decks of cards and shuffle thoroughly. Hand them out to all the players until there are no cards left. In this game, the colors (or suits) of the cards are not important. The dealer begins by taking from his hand the number 1 (or "ace") card (if he has it). If he doesn't have it, he takes any card and places it face down on the table, calling it a "1" whether it is a "1" or not. Going clockwise, the next player takes a number "2" card and places it on top of the number "1" card, calling it number "2." The game continues with each player placing the next consecutively numbered card down, calling it that number whether or not that number is really the card.

Whenever a player suspects that the card played is not really the card called, he yells, "I doubt it." The player whose play is doubted must show the card he played. If he did indeed play the card he called, the player who doubted him must take all the cards played in the center of the table into his hand. If he was right, the player who was doubted has to take all the cards in the center of the table. The object of the game is to run out of cards.

BINGO

Play a real game of bingo with the children placing their gambling chips of any value as covers for the numbers. The winner of the bingo gets everybody's chips and the losers give up theirs.

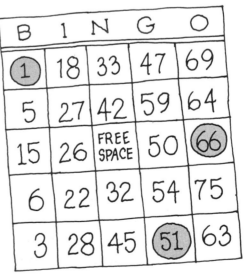

ROULETTE

Set up one roulette wheel. You can teach the children how to bet with odds on the board and to choose how many chips they want to place on the numbers. At the Platts', the children seemed to prefer just betting on the colors red and black, or on even and odd. This simpler version was a huge success because it was easy to tell who won and how much they won. It was also fun to have everybody standing around the table cheering for the different colors.

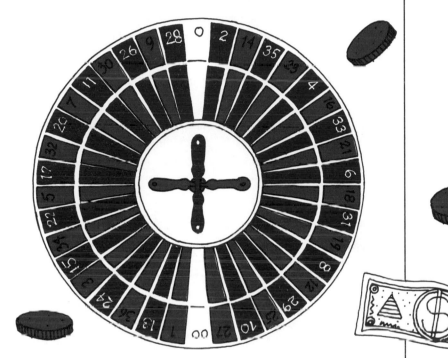

THE WORD IS "MONEY"

Give each player one page of the classified ads from the local newspaper and a highlighter pen. Set a timer to three minutes. The goal is for each player to find the word "money," the symbol "$," the words "rent," "salary," "payment," or any others having to do with money. The one who finds the most words wins a bag of chips.

WHEEL OF CARDS

Cut a circle 24 inches round out of a piece of colored tagboard or foam board. Take the two sets of diamond and spade cards that you set aside from the "Card Lotto" game and separate into two full sets, one each of diamonds and spades. Take one complete set of the two suits and glue the cards down flat all around the outside of the wheel you made, alternating between diamond cards and spades. Make a hole in the center. Stick in a large brass metal fastener and fasten to a larger piece of tagboard that is then hung by a nail on a wall. At the very top, center, which will be behind and above the wheel of cards, stick in another metal fastener which will serve as the pointer. Spin the wheel with your hand; the pointer will stop at different cards every time the wheel stops. At the front of the wheel, place a card table covered with green felt. Place the duplicate set of diamond and spade cards face up on the table.

To play the game: As many children as want to can play by placing their bets (chips) on one or more cards. Whatever card wins, the player who bet on it (whose chips are on that card) gets all the chips. If there are two or more winners, the chips are split evenly.

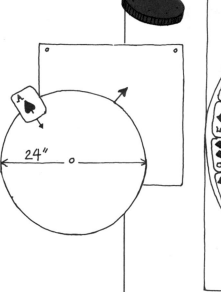

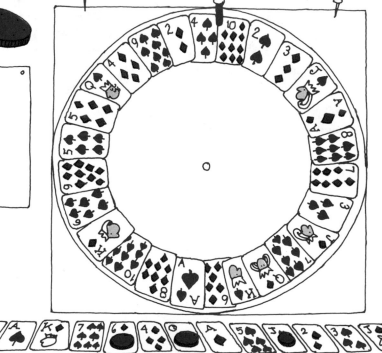

86

A SWEET STORY

This is an after lunch game: Collect as many *different* kinds of candy as you can; their names are used for a fill-in-the-blanks game. You'll stir everyone's imagination with such sweets as: Good 'n' Plenty, Certs, Payday, Mounds, Tootsie Roll, Snicker, Snow Caps, 5th Avenue, Whoppers, Peanuts, Almond Joy, Butterfingers, Baby Ruth, Hot Tamales, M&M's, Mr. Goodbar, Dipps, Milky Way, Sugar Babies, Three Musketeers, and Life Savers.

On a large foam board with a thick black magic marker, write out the following story (or make up your own), leaving some blank spaces. Place all the candy bars on a nearby table. The names of the candy bars are used to fill in the blanks. The game can be hilarious, as the blanks are filled in with some outlandish choices:

This is the story of David Smith a.k.a. [1] _____ who

lived with the [2] _____ on [3] _____. One day,

David invited his friends [4] _____ and some [5] _____

to his house to gamble and [6] _____. Most of his pals

were winners, but they only had [7] _____ to bet because

it was not [8] _____. But for [9] _____, they had

[10] _____ of [11] _____. David's mom, also known

as [12] _____, served the winners a [13] _____

birthday cake which she dropped on the floor. Since there was

no cake to eat, David decided to open his [14] _____ as

the kids yelled [15] _____.

Possible answers:
The options are
"good 'n' plenty"!

[1] DIPPS
[2] THREE MUSKETEERS
[3] 5TH AVENUE
[4] BABY RUTH
[5] HOT TAMALES
[6] SNICKER
[7] PEANUTS
[8] PAYDAY
[9] CERTS
[10] MOUNDS
[11] GOOD 'N' PLENTY
[12] BUTTERFINGERS
[13] WHOPPER
[14] BOUNTY
[15] KUDOS

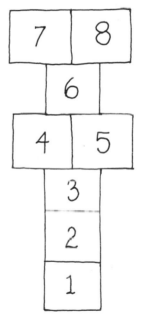

CASINO FLIP

David made up this game for his casino party. He laid out a hopscotch board on the linoleum floor with masking tape and numbered each square just like in hopscotch. He then gave out a handful of chips to each guest, making sure each got chips worth different amounts of money. Each child got a chance to bet on which hopscotch square he could flip his chip into. If he was right, he got to keep that chip and get another in equal amount. If he lost, he also lost the chip.

If you have some straggler children left over at the end of the party, play Yahtzee!

HORSE RACE

Make three to six 2-inch-wide lanes, at least 4 feet long with masking tape along a tabletop. Run additional masking tape along the length of track, creating 24 boxes along each lane. At the starting line, place one plastic horse along each lane. The dealer takes two dice and rolls them for each horse (or each horse owner can roll the dice for his own horse). The number on the dice is the number of squares each horse can move. Other guests can bet on which horse will win using their chips.

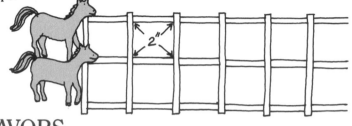

FAVORS

Dice, cards, miniature toys and candy, etc. You can set up a "store" where the kids can "buy" their favors with their chips.

MENU

Focaccio
Assorted sliced fruit
Any juice with sparkling water

See recipes on pages 233–234.

DICE CAKE

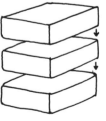

3 TIERS OF CAKES

Use **The Super Chocolate Cake** recipe, page 226. Bake the cake in three 8-inch square pans. Using **Chocolate Frosting**, page 226, cover the tops of the layers and stack to form a cube. Frost the sides of the cake; use large white mint wafers to make the "dots" on the sides of the die. (You can also use white **Seven Minute Frosting**, page 229, and chocolate wafers.) Write "Happy Birthday" on the serving plate.

DOLL SHOWER

(Ages 5–8)

Many little girls love their dolls, and if your daughter happens to be in this stage (eating, sleeping, and talking dolls), organize a doll shower for her next birthday party. Invite her friends to bring their favorite dolls for lunch where the "moms" and their "babies" share the party. And if the little mothers come dressed up like their moms, this role-playing party will be even more fun. We have combined some games that are often played at baby showers with doll-making activities and doll games.

INVITATION

Buy baby rattles, one per invitation. Attach the invitations (written on paper cut in the shape of a bottle) with ribbon to the rattles.

WE'RE HAVING A SHOWER FOR ALL OUR DOLLS TO CELEBRATE LILY'S 6th Birthday Bring Your Favorite Doll COME DRESS AS YOUR MOM June 5, 12to2 at 222 Maple Drive R. S. V. P. 555-1234

DECORATIONS

Use a child-size table and chairs set with doll-size dishes. This is for the guests. Set a separate child-size table just for the dolls. Be sure to include flowers, teapots, pitchers, and other decorations just as you would for an adult party. Cover the tables with colored paper or plastic cloths decorated with paper doilies in different shapes and colors. Place baby bottles filled with candy all around the tables. Fasten a paper parasol or child's umbrella to the back of each chair. Your child's doll collection placed around the room will add to the feeling of doll heaven.

Jill Anderson, of Santa Barbara, California, took a group of friends to a beauty college for her 11th birthday. There they each had their hair done any way they wanted (they all ended up with very dressy, grown-up hairdos, of course). The invitation was wrapped around pink foam curlers. The cake was in the shape of a mirror and had a mirror in the center, so you could look and see "the new you." Favors were combs, mirrors, and makeup bags full of miniature beauty items.

GET READY!

1. Set up two child-size tables surrounded with chairs.
2. Fill the baby bottles with jelly beans.
3. Buy two of each baby toy: rattles, teething rings, pacifiers, etc. Fill a basket with one of each item and place the other matching item at the place settings around the girls' table.
4. Tape small umbrellas or paper parasols to the back of each guest's chair.
5. Buy skeins of yarn in different colors and enough scissors so each child can have her own to make the yarn doll. Also have on hand cardboard, pieces of felt, glue, and buttons.
6. Prepare ½ yard of inexpensive but decorative and colorful fabric and self-adhesive tape for each child.
7. Prepare baskets of Pop-it beads or, for older girls, string, beads of various sizes, and jewelry fasteners.
8. Buy Life Savers and ribbons for the candy necklaces.
9. Find two dolls, two cloth diapers, and a diaper pin for the "Crawling Relay" game.
10. Vaseline and cotton for the "Cotton Relay."
11. Xerox the "Scramble Words" game.
12. Prepare ingredients for the Kiss Cookies.
13. Get prizes and favors.

ACTIVITIES

SEATING BASKET

Have a basket filled with assorted rattles, teething rings, and pacifiers ready for the children to select from the basket as they arrive. To see where she is seated, each must find her match at the table.

CANDY NECKLACES

Give each child a candy necklace or string Life Savers on a ribbon on which she can hang each of her prizes. Every time she wins a game she will get a baby toy as a prize that can be hung from her necklace.

Have a baby pool with as many "rubber duckies" in it as guests. Color code the bottom of the ducks, and match the wrapping colors in the party favors.

Jill Anderson and her mother, Cindy, of Santa Barbara, gave a "Baby Party" when Jill was nine. They invited all the guests to come dressed as babies. The kids crawled through the door to the party room, where each got a corsage made out of a miniature cloth diaper and a colored diaper pin (there was a raisin hidden in one of the diapers and this person got a special prize). They ate at a small table with small chairs, and the birthday girl got to sit in a high chair. The drinks came in baby bottles and the food was baby food (including teething pretzels). All the prizes for games were baby toys.

CRAWLING RELAY

Divide the guests into teams. Each person has to crawl on her hands and knees to a doll and diaper it. When that person has finished, she crawls back and tags her teammate who crawls to the doll to undiaper it. Repeat until all members of each team have had a turn. The first team to finish wins.

COTTON RELAY

Divide the guests into two teams. Put a dab of Vaseline on each person's nose. Each has to crawl to the other side of the room where there is a bowl full of cotton balls. Each player, without using her hands, must get a cotton ball on her nose and crawl back to her team and tag the next person. The first team to finish wins.

SCRAMBLE WORDS

This game is for older girls. Give each person a paper and pencil and have her unscramble the words relating to babies:

1.	DIAPER	PARDEI
2.	BLANKET	KAETBNL
3.	PEDIATRICIAN	TIAIADIPNCER
4.	BOTTLE	TOLETB
5.	SLEEPLESS NIGHTS	LSEPESESL SHNTIG
6.	FORMULA	RLUAOFM
7.	CRIB	RBIC
8.	BABY	YBBA
9.	RATTLE	TAERTL
10.	PACIFIER	CIIRAPEF
11.	TEDDY BEAR	DEDYT ERAB
12.	LOVE	VEOL

DOLL MAKING

Making a doll out of yarn is simple and the best ones are often kept around for years. Doing this together in a group will produce many different and unique variations.

Put the yarn in the center of one table. Have a pair of scissors for each child. Give each child a piece of cardboard (shirt inserts are the perfect size). Wrap the yarn around the board about 100 times, then slip the wound yard off the board. To keep the pieces of yarn together, just tie with a piece of yarn through the top. Now cut the loop at the other end (see drawing). To make the doll's head and neck, tie another length of yarn tightly around the hank. For the arms, divide the hank equally in two and then divide each half in two again. The outside bunches on either side are the arms. Tie each arm at the "wrist" with a length of yarn. Cut off the rest of the yarn with your scissors.

The two bunches of yarn that are left hanging are the body and the legs. Tie a length of yarn at the doll's waist to form the body. For a girl, leave the rest of the yarn hanging; that will be the dress. Cut the bottom off to trim. For a boy, divide the yarn below the waist into two equal bunches at the ankle. Trim off any excess yarn to form the feet. To finish off the doll, make button eyes and glue on felt pieces for facial features and clothing.

TIE WITH PIECE OF YARN

TIE YARN TO MAKE THE HEAD

Margie Hollingsworth, from Irvine, California, suggests a "Pioneer" birthday where everyone dresses in pioneer clothes, the electricity is off, the kids make their own ice cream, churn butter, and make a quilt out of paper (precut squares of construction and wrapping papers work great!). They could also make a corncob button doll.

FOR ARMS, GATHER, TIE, AND TRIM

TIE AT WAIST FOR A GIRL DOLL

TIE AT BOTTOM FOR A BOY DOLL

ADD HAIR & FELT FEATURES

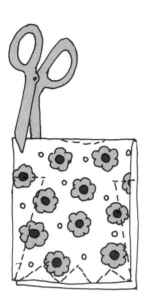

DOLL CLOTHES

Now the children can make clothes for their dolls. Each child should have approximately half a yard of fabric, self-adhesive tape (or a stapler), and a pair of scissors. In a given amount of time (ten minutes is good) each has to make any outfit of some sort for her doll. Award a prize for the prettiest, funniest, most original, and so on, so each child receives one.

DOLL JEWELRY

Pop-it beads make for instant jewelry. If you have baskets of beads in the center of the table, the children can make the necklaces and bracelets for their dolls and for themselves. While these beads are particularly good for younger children, you have other beading options with older girls. For them, collect string and beads of various sizes (include fasteners for necklaces and bracelets) and let the girls create their own jewels.

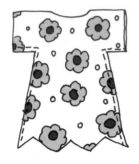

KISS COOKIES

Now that the dolls are made, dressed, and ready to have their lunch, your shower guests can bake some Kiss Cookies for their little charges (although they might want to sample them themselves).

KISS COOKIES DOLL RECIPE

1 pkg (20 oz.) refrigerated
   sugar cookie dough
Food coloring (optional)
Colored sprinkles
Colored crystallized sugar
Foil-wrapped chocolate
   kisses (unwrapped) and
   mint flavored drops

Preheat oven to 350°F. If desired, knead food coloring into the dough. Shape into 1 inch balls and roll in sprinkles or crystallized sugar. Press kiss or mint drop into the center of each ball and flatten slightly. This makes approximately 32 cookies.

Place cookies on an ungreased baking sheet. If the dough is very soft, refrigerate it until firm (about 30 minutes) before baking.

Bake 7–10 minutes or until lightly browned.

FAVORS

Place-card toys, baby bottles filled with jelly beans, other baby or doll toys that can be won as prizes and hung from their necklaces, the dolls and jewelry they made, books of paper dolls

Dale Mallory, from La Grange, Georgia, had a pretend spend-the-night party for daughter Joanna's fifth birthday. "I could never handle having twenty five- and six-year-olds spending the *entire* night," says Dale, so she asked all the girls to wear their "jamas," play many games, and be picked up at 8:00 that night.

MENU

Tea Sandwiches
Peanut Butter Ladyfingers
Fast Ice Cream
Kiss Cookies
Microwave Fudge
Hot chocolate

See recipes on pages 234–235.

DOLL CAKE

Use the **Angel Food Cake** recipe, page 228. Bake in an angel food cake pan. Decorate with pastel-colored **Seven-Minute Frosting,** page 229, as if the whole cake were the bottom of a dress. In the hole in the center, place any 11-inch-tall or taller doll, dressed in a top and hat. If you want to write "Happy Birthday," place the letters along the bottom hem of the dress.

(Ages 9 and up)

W oodstock, here we come! The decade of tie-dye, batik, and macrame is back. Dig out the old Beatles and Peter, Paul, and Mary tunes, dust off the peace signs, tie-dye some T-shirts, make some granola bars, and invite the new generation of flower children for a far-out, mellow, groovy, hip, and very cool birthday.

INVITATION

The fold and dip technique used in creating paper that looks like tie-dye makes the perfect invitation for this party. Using rice paper, cut out a square or T-shirt shape. Pour a cup of water into a shallow soup dish and then add four or five drops of oil and each paint color you want to use. Then, using a dropper, add five drops of vinegar. Take the invitation paper and put it on top of the water; the paper will immediately absorb the paint. Lift the paper off and lay it flat to dry.

You can also use a folding technique to make this invitation. In this method, fold the invitation paper first at the corners and then over once or twice. Dip the corners of the paper into your paint (you can use watercolors for this, each color in a different section of a muffin tin). Open the folds, let the paint dry, then refold (you can fold the corners every time, or you can fold the whole sheet in accordion pleats or in the shape of a fan) in a different pattern and then dip the new corners in either the same paint colors or different ones. Write the copy and draw a peace sign with a marker across the front when dry.

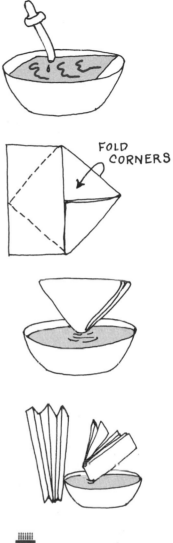

FOLD CORNERS

BE FAR OUT BE COOL
BE A FLOWER CHILD!
WE'RE GROOVIN' ON ANDY'S
BIRTHDAY SATURDAY
FEBRUARY 10th FROM 2-4 pm
AT 555 R.S.V.P.
REYNOLDS 555-1234
LANE
WEAR SANDALS AND 60'S CLOTHES

For the fold and dip technique for the invitation, you can use food coloring instead of paint.

DECORATIONS

Your party room should be adorned with sixties posters, peace and love signs, and slogans from that decade such as "Make Love, Not War," "Never Trust Anyone Over 16," "Peace Will Rule the Planet," and "This Is the Dawning of the Age of Aquarius." Play sixties music, and burn incense to really set the mood.

GET READY!

1. Gather posters, peace signs, and tapes of sixties music. You may want to make some posters yourself.

2. Purchase inexpensive white T-shirts, dyes, plastic gloves, rubber bands, wooden spoons, and plastic buckets for tie-dying.

3. Buy beads, leather laces, belts, earring backs, etc., from a craft shop for jewelry and belt making.

4. Buy embroidery thread in many varieties of colors at a fabric or hobby shop to make the knotted bracelets and hair ornaments. Two skeins per person is plenty. You will also need rubber bands for the hair wrapping.

5. Collect silk, paper, or real fresh flowers and ½-inch ribbons for flower wreaths.

6. Find a double boiler, tracing paper, pencils, scissors, brushes, plastic table covering, rubber gloves, an iron and ironing board, newspaper, waxed paper, fabric (i.e., 12 × 12 inch per child), paraffin and bees wax, fabric dye, and a plastic tub for the batik.

ACTIVITIES

MAKING FLOWER WREATHS FOR YOUR HAIR

Flower children should have a daisy or two to wear to feel authentic, so have everyone make a wreath for their hair to wear throughout the party. Gather your flowers (silk or paper are fine, but fresh—such as stock, baby's breath, and miniature roses—are especially beautiful) and the ribbons. For each guest cut a piece of ribbon 3 feet long. Start by holding one flower by the stem (see drawing) and laying it flat on the ribbon. Wind the ribbon around the stem very tightly and then add another flower. The stems are always lying flat on the ribbon as you wind the ribbon around them and add stem after stem. Continue until you have a wreath long enough to fit the child's head, tie in a knot, and let the rest of the ribbon hang down. You can make this with two ribbons of different colors for a pretty effect.

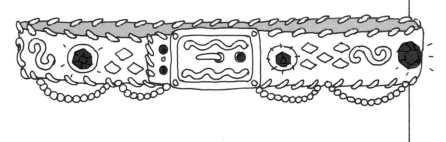

MAKING BELTS

Handcrafted leather belts were also a mark of the sixties. They are still as easy to make and as much fun for the kids to wear. You can buy belts of various sizes at a craft store and then lace them with different colored leather laces, decorate with beads or silver pieces, or paint with puff paints.

For Brett Kassan's eighth birthday, she invited all her friends to come dressed as their favorite rock 'n' roll stars. That night, as rock 'n' roll music was blaring from the stereo, the party room was full of white-gloved Michael Jacksons, purple-haired Princes, scantily clad Madonnas, and long-haired Beatles. Prizes were given out for the best costumes, the best imitations, the best dancers, etc.

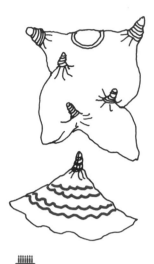

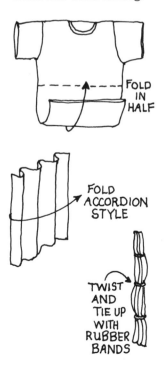

Any packaged dyes (Rit is the one most supermarkets carry) are easy to use. You might try using less water to make the colors stronger. There are also batik and tie-dying dyes available; they cost a little more but they are very fast (they take to fabric well) and retain their colors after much washing.

FOLD IN HALF

FOLD ACCORDION STYLE

TWIST AND TIE UP WITH RUBBER BANDS

TIE-DYE

You can't get more sixties than this! The tie-dye effect happens when fabric is tied together to keep the tied portions of the fabric from absorbing the dye. The amount of dye that penetrates the cloth depends upon how tightly or loosely the fabric has been bound and how long it is left in the dye bath. You can also get a beautiful blending of colors by tying and dipping, then tying new areas and dipping again, as often as you want, from light to dark. Some of the things that can be used for tie-dyeing are T-shirts, scarves, socks, or ties.

Pull up the fabric into your hand wherever you want the pattern to go. Fasten with a rubber band as tightly as possible (the fabric under the tied area will remain unaffected after you've dyed it). You can pull as many areas of the fabric as you like and tie as many times and in as many places as you like. For added designs, you can actually tie objects to the fabric like bottle caps, buttons, etc.

Follow the directions on the dye package to make the different colored dyes, keeping each color in a separate plastic pail or basin. You may want to wet the fabric before dyeing it, but be sure to squeeze out the excess moisture. After tying the fabric, dip it into the dye, always starting with the lightest color first. The color of your dye should be slightly darker than the color you want to end up with because it will dry lighter. To avoid having the colors turn muddy, don't dye red and green or blue and orange together.

This process of tying and dying can be repeated again and again. When done, rinse the fabric in cold water. Squeeze out the excess moisture, roll in a towel, and let dry for about 20 minutes. Now untie and let dry completely before ironing. Drying T-shirts may take as long as a day, so chances are the children may be taking damp T-shirts home with them.

Here are some variations on tie-dyeing techniques:

Mandy Gordon folds her T-shirt in half and then in accordion pleats. She then gives the whole thing a twist and puts rubber bands all along the rolled-up fabric at 4-inch intervals. She dips the different sections between rubber bands into different colors.

Jake Steinberg, 9, loves the spiral shape, so he and his friend Betsy Mallow, 11, made spirals by putting the T-shirt flat on the table, sticking a fork in the middle, and twirling it as if it were spaghetti. Take the fork out and pull the rubber band across one diameter and then across the other, resulting in four sections. Jake's friend Anouck Damaz, who was visiting from France, taught them a "French twist." She took a glassful of dye and poured it on one section of the spiraled T-shirt, and then poured a different color on each of the other three sections. The kids then immediately opened up the shirts and let them dry. The spirals were, and are, spectacular!

Lucie Steinberg, who is six, made a tie-dye minidress. She crumpled it up into a ball and wrapped it in about six to eight rubber bands all the way around (you could actually throw it like a ball, it was that tightly wrapped!). She dipped the whole ball in dye and then untied it. The design was elaborate and dramatic!

Janice Treadwell uses Pentel Fabric Fun Pastel Dye Sticks to add designs to her tie-dye shirts.

Adding a teaspoon of uniodized salt to each quart of dye will help fix the color in the fabric.

glue earring backs on the back

Sharon Krost gave an "Earring" party where the sole activity was to make many different kinds of earrings.

JEWELRY

Making things by hand was a big thing in the sixties, with jewelry at the top of the list. Bead bracelets, made from different colored beads in various sizes, are always a hit and a challenge to the imagination (for example, you can try using beads of unusual textures and sizes in the same piece of jewelry). Necklaces made from leather laces strung with large ceramic and wooden beads are a hit with boys and girls.

Earrings are always popular, and there are many different kinds you can make by hand. One method involves cutting up small pieces of foam board or tagboard in about 1½-inch shapes and decorating with beads, sequins, and glitter glue. Glue earring backs on the backs and you're done! Another entails taking wire and shaping it in the form of a peace sign. Then simply hang on an earring back and that's it!

Sonia and Sarah Israel swear by Friendly Plastic. Available in craft stores, Friendly Plastic is actually a jar full of pieces of plastic in many vibrant colors. With adult supervision, dip the plastic pieces in hot water that is *not* too hot to the touch (you should be able to put your fingers in the water). The pieces are removed with tongs and given to each child to mold and shape, attaching different colors to one another. Beautiful and professional-looking earrings, necklaces, and pins are the result.

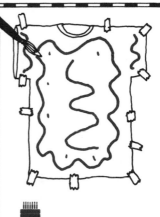

BATIK

The process of batik is said to date back 2,000 years, becoming really popular in Indonesia in the sixteenth century. It is a simple technique that produces designs by applying hot wax to fabric and dying the part of the fabric that isn't covered with the wax. Sometimes the wax is deliberately cracked so that the dye penetrates the fine lines and creates a beautiful pattern. At the end of the process when the wax is removed, the design appears on the fabric where there was no wax.

The first and most important thing to know about batik is that it must be done with adult supervision because hot wax can be dangerous. Also note that it takes time for the fabric to dry before you can peel off the wax, so you may want to start the party with this activity. The first step is to draw a design on tracing paper or write on your fabric. While the children are doing that, have an adult melt paraffin wax in the top of a double boiler at 170 degrees. (For a smooth effect and total coverage, use half beeswax and half paraffin. For a crackle effect, use only beeswax.) Place the fabric on a flat table or the floor and tape the edges at various points to the covered tabletop or floor, stretching the fabric as tight as you can. Dip the brush into the hot wax, and then paint the wax onto the fabric wherever you don't want the fabric to be dyed.

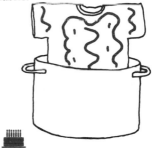

If the paraffin wax starts to solidify as you are working with it, just reheat it. The wax should harden on the fabric.

Now pick up the waxed fabric and dip it into your dye. Leave it there for about 10–15 minutes. If your dye tub is big enough, like a plastic garbage pail, you can put several pieces in at the same time. Now remove the fabric from the dye, rinse under warm water, and hang up to dry (remember, the color will dry lighter than it was in the dye).

When heating the wax remember that it is ready to use when it is dark.

To remove the wax, cover your ironing board with newspaper. Place the fabric on the board and iron both sides of the fabric between waxed paper or paper towels until all the wax melts into the newspaper. When all the wax is off, iron all over the fabric to seal in the color. The finished batik can be framed.

Hot wax will run a little, so use smaller amounts and add more as you need.

Waxed paper

newspaper

HAPPY BIRTHDAY

If you don't have or cannot find a cassette of sixties songs for the "Flower Child" party, make a game out of merely trying to name as many Beatles songs as the kids can remember.

NAME THAT TUNE

Play the traditional game with a new twist—try identifying sixties songs. There are many "golden oldie" cassettes featuring songs from that decade or you can tape your own old favorites. Now divide the guests into two teams. Play the first five seconds of a song and have the teams identify the song. If they can't, you can play an additional five seconds. The team that guesses the most songs in the least amount of time wins.

You can also play different versions of this game. Get a cassette of only Beatles songs (or The Mamas and the Papas, Peter, Paul and Mary, Bob Dylan, Jimi Hendrix, The Doors, Crosby, Stills, Nash & Young, Joan Baez, The Grateful Dead, or any other group) and see how many of those can be identified.

STREAM OF CONSCIOUSNESS

One of Lisa's favorite games, which she learned at camp, is a version of what she used to call the "Symphony of Emotions." Here's how you play: Assign one person to be the conductor, who instructs the members of his orchestra to play a "stream of consciousness" symphony. Each guest is assigned a particular style in which he will speak a statement or make an appropriate sound. These include: documentary, romance, child's story, science fiction, mystery, horror, musical theater, and comedy.

To play, the conductor points to a person and he has to make the appropriate thematic sound or statement. For example, if the first person pointed to is "musical theater," he begins by saying, "I could have danced all night, and still have begged for more" (from *My Fair Lady*). The next person pointed to is "documentary," and he continues the stream of consciousness by saying, "and as he danced, three cars crashed on the freeway and a whole load of watermelons spilled out on the road." The third person the conductor chooses could be "mystery," and he continues the story with, "Meanwhile, in the dead of night, there was a sudden noise coming from the attic." Some players can choose to merely make appropriate sounds, and others can continue the story with a stream of consciousness narrative. Meanwhile, as the conductor chooses his players, he can also "conduct" them to make their sounds louder or softer.

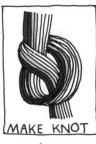

MAKE KNOT

MAKING KNOT BRACELETS

Although the knotted bracelet has recently become the rage again (for both boys and girls), it was in the sixties that "weaving" bracelets was such a popular hobby. Here are some simple instructions (from the DMC Corporation, with Jennifer Brokaw's and Lisa Gilbar's added clarifications) to make such a bracelet. This activity really needs no supervision so several children can make the bracelets at the same time.

From the embroidery thread you bought, have each child choose the colors he or she wants. In the diagram, color X is your first color, color Y is the second, and the Z color doesn't matter because it won't show (it forms the core of the bracelet and will be covered by the other colors).

To make a multicolored bracelet, you will need two 2-yard strands of color X, two 2-yard strands of color Y, and four 15-inch strands of any color Z. Arrange the strands so the two X strands are on the left, followed by the two Y strands, and then the four Z strands. Tie all the strands in a knot, leaving about 2 inches as a tail on top. Tape flat with scotch tape to the edge of a tabletop (or pin with a safety pin to a bedspread, tablecloth, or the clothes you are wearing). Smooth them out so that they are in the correct order.

Now begin making the knots. Wrap one X strand over and then under all the other X, Y, and Z strands to form a knot (see diagram; it looks like a backwards number 4). Pull tight. Continue knotting: You will see that you will be forming a diagonal row of knots slanting down (to make sure, make each knot go under the one above and not on it). Make *six* of these knots. Twist the bracelet slightly to the right so the X strand is again on the right. Now make six knots with the second color strand, Y. When those are done, return to X and then again Y, etc. Repeat these steps until the bracelet is long enough to fit around the wrist. Tie the strands together in a final knot, leaving a tail like you did in the beginning. Tie the tails together around the wrist, cut off the remaining tail, and you are done.

For good luck, this bracelet must be worn at all times and never taken off!

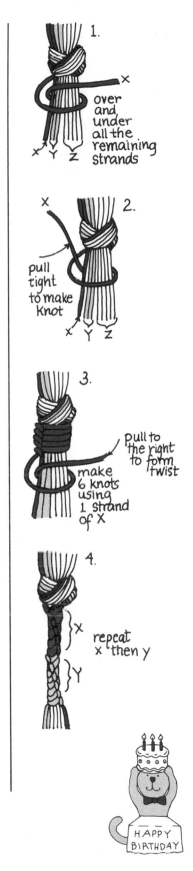

1. over and under all the remaining strands

x Y Z

2. pull tight to make knot

x Y Z

3. pull to the right to form twist

make 6 knots using 1 strand of X

4. } X repeat X then Y } Y

105

HAPPY BIRTHDAY

HAIR WRAP

Another rage that has been reborn is knotting a bracelet around some hair—in effect, wrapping the hair as a hair ornament. You have to do this on a friend's hair, and have them do it on yours.

1. First pick out a bunch of strands of hair about ⅛ inch thick. Make a braid and fasten with a rubber band at the bottom.

2. Next pick out some embroidery thread or crochet strings in three different colors (you can do it in more or less colors, but our instructions here are for three).

3. The length of the strings depends on the length of your hair. For example, for shoulder length hair or shorter, measure 1½ times the length of your arm; if your hair comes down to your chest, measure the string to double your arm length; if your hair is waist length, measure triple your arm length.

4. Line up all the strings evenly and tie in a knot around the top of the braid you made in the hair. Take one of the strings in your right hand and the braid and the other two colors in your left hand. Then place your pointer finger of your left hand under the braid and two colors; with your right hand, put the string that you are holding in your right hand under the tip of your pointer. With the same string, go over the braid and the other two colors (if you look carefully, you have made the design of a backwards number 4). Now with the fingers of your right hand pull that same first color through the loop ("4") you have formed. Take the pointer out and pull that first color all the way up to the top of the braid and then pull it tight (it will be a knot). You have now made your first knot.

Now repeat this again and again with that same first color— 30 knots is fine. Now take the second color and put that in your right hand, putting the other two colors (first and third colors) in your left hand. Do the same thing with this second color—30 knots. Repeat with the third color, and then return to the first. Keep repeating with these three colors until you reach the rubber band at the bottom of the braid. Once you reach it, take the rubber band out and continue making the knots. If you like, you can end the braid there (and still have some hair hanging at the end) or you can continue (even when you run out of hair) and keep tying the knots around the other two strings (rather than the hair). This will give you a kind of knotted tail at the bottom of the braid. Note that you can't see the braid anymore; it has been completely covered by the knots.

To end, tie the strings together in a knot and cut off the extra string.

FAVORS

Things the guests made, and/or crystals, tie-dye shirts, flower wreaths, knot bracelets, Hackysacks, incense

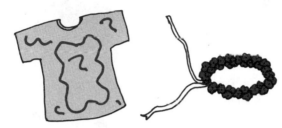

MENU

Cheese Fondue
Rarebit Fondue
Chocolate Fondue
Punch

See recipes on pages 235–236.

PSYCHEDELIC CAKE

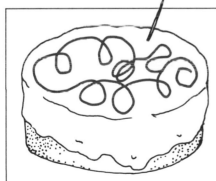

Use the **Carrot Cake** recipe, page 225. Bake the cake in two round 9-inch cake pans. Frost with the **Cream Cheese Frosting,** page 225. Using liquid food coloring, drop three drops of one color right on the frosted cake and, with a toothpick, make swirls on the cake. Add three drops of a second color and repeat to form a psychedelic design. Finish with rainbow candles.

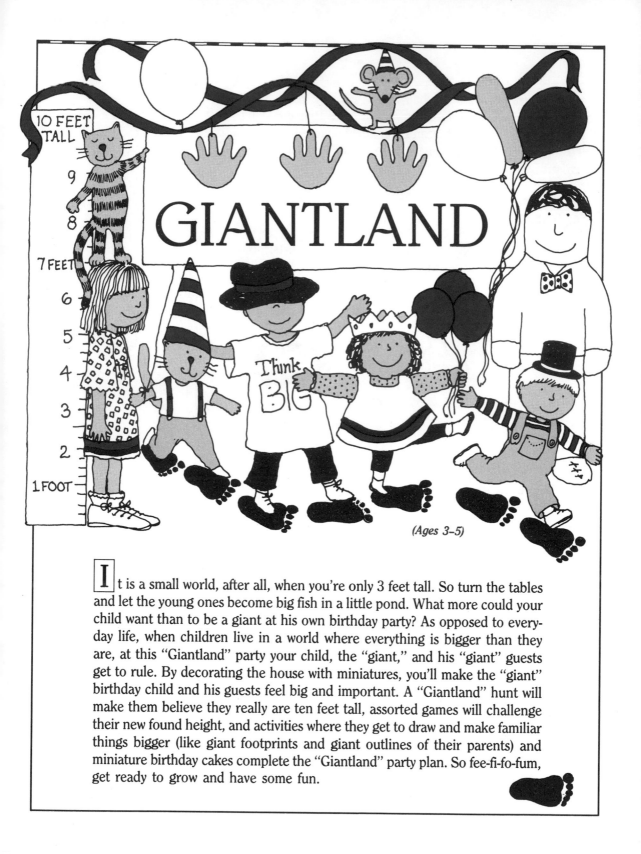

GIANTLAND

10 FEET TALL

9

8

7 FEET

6

5

4

3

2

1 FOOT

(Ages 3–5)

I t is a small world, after all, when you're only 3 feet tall. So turn the tables and let the young ones become big fish in a little pond. What more could your child want than to be a giant at his own birthday party? As opposed to every-day life, when children live in a world where everything is bigger than they are, at this "Giantland" party your child, the "giant," and his "giant" guests get to rule. By decorating the house with miniatures, you'll make the "giant" birthday child and his guests feel big and important. A "Giantland" hunt will make them believe they really are ten feet tall, assorted games will challenge their new found height, and activities where they get to draw and make familiar things bigger (like giant footprints and giant outlines of their parents) and miniature birthday cakes complete the "Giantland" party plan. So fee-fi-fo-fum, get ready to grow and have some fun.

INVITATION

On a long sheet (approximately 36 inches) of white paper (butcher paper wrap or fax paper work well), write the invitation copy in huge letters. You can also stencil the words using large (3-inch) block letters.

YOU ARE

FEE: Karen's **4**TH
BIRTHDAY

FI: Wed. November 4TH

WEAR SOMETHING

INVITED TO BE
GIANTLAND

WAY TOO BIG, WAY TOO

A GIANT IN

FO: 3 to 5PM
555 Bennet Lane
FUM: R.S.V.P.
555-1234

SMALL, OR BOTH!

DECORATIONS

Hang huge outlines of footprints and handprints around the room. Pages from a giant coloring book taped on the wall will also create instant atmosphere. Set a long children's table with doll dishes and child-size chairs.

HAPPY BIRTHDAY

GET READY!

1. Buy one or two giant coloring books and chubby crayons.

2. Collect a set of miniature dishes. Use doll china or be inventive by collecting plastic container tops for plates and demitasse spoons for the utensils. The children will be eating with these.

3. Trace and cut out outlines of an adult shoe or foot or giant handprints out of paper or a plastic tablecloth. You can hang these around the house; cut out about 30 footprints to be used in the "Follow the Giant's Footsteps" game.

4. Buy butcher paper and very wide washable markers.

5. Cut out large pictures from magazines and collect these for "Lost in Giantland." Place three pictures in each envelope (you will need as many envelopes as you have guests). Remember, you will have to hide the matching miniatures before the party.

6. Prepare a tape of a song for "Shrink 'n' Grow."

7. Find two plastic tumblers and extra-large balloons to be blown up for the "Balloon Balance."

8. Prepare the river for "Giant Leapfrog" with masking tape.

9. Collect tubes from toilet paper rolls or paper towel tubing and cut in half (at least two per person) for making binoculars. You will also need colored cellophane and ribbon.

10. Get prizes.

You can have the parents dress in clothes that are too small for them.

ACTIVITIES

MAMMOTH COLORING

As the children arrive, hand out pages from the giant coloring books for the children to color with oversize crayons.

MAKING BINOCULARS

Make binoculars to use when the kids are "Lost in Giantland"; we think the easiest is the way our friend Erin Fischer makes them with her kids. For one pair of binoculars, take two cardboard toilet paper rolls and tape together by winding masking tape around the center (see drawing). Cover the ends on one side with colored cellophane. If you want to have them hang, staple or tape a ribbon from one end to the other.

GIANTS, GIANTS, EVERYWHERE

Have the kids each draw an outline of a parent or another adult on butcher paper using very wide washable markers and place them around the party room for more giant decorations. They'll also probably want to take their artwork home.

FOLLOW THE GIANT'S FOOTSTEPS

Tape the footsteps on the floor meandering from one room to another. The game is played by each child rolling a die and moving as many steps as the number that comes up. The person who gets to the end first, wins. For variety, you can include a couple of feet made out of different colors so that when a child lands on one of these, he has to go back to the beginning. You can also include a few double footprints, which means when a child lands on one of these, he has to stay there until he rolls a "six."

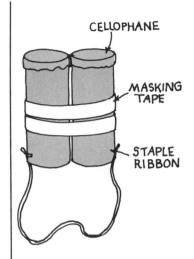

CELLOPHANE

MASKING TAPE

STAPLE RIBBON

To make opening gifts special for everyone, seat the children in a circle on the floor or around the table. Have each child take turns presenting his gift to the birthday child. As the gift is opened, everyone will share in the surprise, and the giver of the gift feels as special as the birthday star.

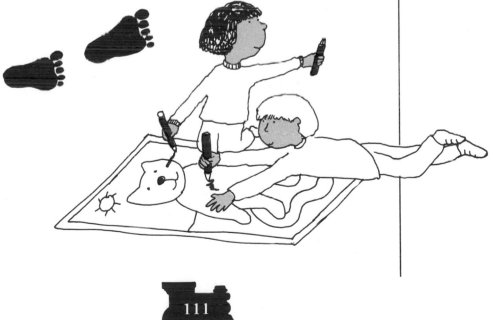

HAPPY BIRTHDAY

LOST IN GIANTLAND

Hand out large pictures cut out from magazines of things you collected in miniature (the miniatures are hidden in the room or yard). Each child gets an envelope with three pictures in it. The goal is to have him find the corresponding miniatures. Examples: For a picture of a car, you hide a toy car; a brush, a minibrush, and so on. The children can use the binoculars they made to help them find these hidden treasures.

TOT PARADE

This is a pantomime game where each child acts out an everyday activity and the other children have to guess what he is doing. He could be brushing his teeth or hair, walking the dog, taking out the garbage, making his bed.

SHRINK 'N' GROW

Play a song (your kid's favorite is fine). The trick is, as the song is played, the leader yells "Grow," meaning the children have to look like giants, or "Shrink," meaning the children have to look like tiny leprechauns. When the music stops, the children must stop in place. Whoever moves is out.

Remy and Adam shared the exact same birthday. Adam lived in New York City and Remy in New Hampshire. They shared their birthdays by alternating something fun in New York one year or something you could only do on Frajil Farms in New Hampshire the next. This way both boys got the best from both worlds and shared many fabulous birthdays.

FEE-FI-FO-FUM

Everyone sits in a circle, and one person is named the giant. He walks around the outside of the circle and taps each person, in turn, on the head, saying one word with each tap: "Fee-fi-fo-fum, watch out, giants, here I come." As soon as he says "come," the person whom he has tapped at that moment has to run around the circle and tag the giant. If the giant gets to the empty seat before he is tagged, that person is the giant.

GIANT LEAPFROG

With some masking tape, tape two straight lines about 6 feet long and 6 inches apart. Tell the children that each line is the bank of a river and what these giants have to do is leap over the river without getting wet (because if they get wet, they shrink and become leprechauns). The children form a long line of giants ready to leapfrog over the river. Each child or "giant" takes turns running or jumping over the river. If the giant falls into the river and turns into a leprechaun, he has to start again at the back of the line.

As soon as all of the children have run over the 6-inch separation, pick up one masking tape strip and place it further away from the other. Sarah Meyer's trick is to throw obstacles into the river. Last time around, her giants had to leapfrog over giant teddy bears, trucks, and a shoe here and there.

Due to popular demand, Nancy Shockman, from Milton Freewater, Oregon, has played the same game at her birthdays from the age of 8 to 13. Everyone is invited to come dressed in their parents' oversized clothes, with their own outfits underneath. When they get to the party, they take off the big clothes and do one of two things: Either Mrs. Shockman piles all the clothes in one huge mountain in the party room and the kids have to dive in and find their parents' clothes, or she hides them in and around the house and everyone goes on a treasure hunt where they must find the outfits they arrived in and put them back on.

HAPPY BIRTHDAY

BALLOON BALANCE

Have the children make two lines. The first player in each line gets a plastic tumbler and an extra-large balloon, blown up. When each of these leaders gets the signal, he has to balance the balloon on the open end of the tumbler and walk to a certain mark on the other side of the room. The rule is that you cannot touch the balloon with your hands once it sits on the tumbler. If it falls, you have to stop, return to the head of the line, and start again. The first team to finish wins.

FAVORS

Drawings they made, books, giant coloring books and markers, copies of *Jack and the Beanstalk*

Instant-grow animals, those mini-sponges in capsules, are great favors for your giants because kids can put them in water right at the party. You can actually make a game out of it—put all kinds of capsules in a bowl and let the kids pick them out, one at a time, at random, and have them guess what each is as it is expanding in the water. We promise great shrieks of excitement at the discoveries!

MENU

Mini Sandwiches
Mini drinks
Peanut Butter Pretzel Snacks
  with Chocolate Glaze

See recipes on pages 236–237.

GIANT COOKIES

Use the **Giant Cookie** recipe, page 237. Stick in candles and score portions with a knife before the cookies harden; they will break easily when hard. Serve with a scoop of ice cream on each plate.

"HIYAMAC!"
"LOBUDDY!"
"BINEARLONG?"
"COPLOURS."

"CETCHENNY?"
"GODDAFEW."
"KINDARTHAY?"

"GODDASALMON."
"THADALL?"
"ATOONATOO."

"ANYTHINELSE?"
"BEARACOODA."
"BEARAWHO?"

"BEARACOODA.
HOWBOUTYOU?"

"NUTABITE!"

"WULL,
GULUCK!"

GONE FISHIN'

(Ages 3–6)

I f this sounds like one of your kids or something your child would long for, this party's for you. This version is for younger kids—those over six or seven might appreciate being taken to a real fishing pond. When Marc went to his friend Jon Nathanson's fishing party at a trout farm in Agoura, California, the kids got to fish using their favors—tackle boxes with bait and lures—and then played games. Almost everyone "Goddafew," and those who caught more than one trout eagerly shared theirs (sweet visions of cleaning the fish did *not* dance in their heads) with those whose luck had run out. The result was a group of happy fishermen and freezers full of fresh trout.

For other fishing devotees, these fishing games and activities will make their day.

INVITATION

Place gummy worms in a plastic bag and seal with a ribbon. Include a message on a fish-shape cutout of paper that says:

GOIN' FISHIN'
Join Us For Tom's Birthday
at the BEST Hole in town
Saturday, April 12th
from 12 to 2 pm at the MILTONS'
555 Arlington Place
R.S.V.P. 555-1234

A variation on a fish mobile: Make an outline of a simple fish shape with household or florist wire. Trace it on white tissue paper. Take markers and color designs inside the fish shape. Cut around the shape, leaving a little overhang (see drawing). Pipe or paint white glue onto the wire. Cover with the tissue paper fish and pinch the edges over the wire. Let it dry—and hang! You and your children can make a dozen of these and hang them from the ceiling or over the table.

DECORATIONS

Hang fish mobiles, blue and green streamers, crepe paper, and fish cutouts all over the house, concentrating on the party room. Cover the table with a plastic blue tablecloth with fish pasted all over it. Plastic or rubber boats 10 to 12 inches long are perfect for lunch plates. With permanent markers write "SS" and the child's name on each. Play the tapes of "fishy" music and place your "boats" all over the house. You can also place rubber worms around the table.

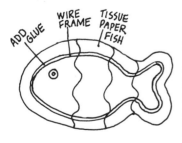

ADD GLUE WIRE FRAME TISSUE PAPER FISH

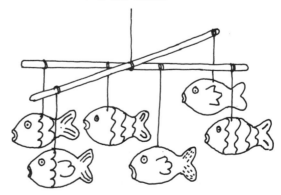

GET READY!

1. Make fish mobiles (see illustration and tip).

2. Buy blue and green streamers and crepe paper to hang down from the ceiling and tables.

3. Buy inexpensive blue plastic tablecloths at your local party supply store. Cut out pictures of fish from coloring books or from magazines and tape to the tablecloth that will cover the party table. You can also make a stencil of a fish shape and cut out colored fish from other plastic fabric or colored paper and glue to the blue tablecloth. If you are using a white paper tablecloth for the table, it's easy to rubber stamp fish shapes all over the cloth. Color in with markers.

4. Prepare tapes of appropriate music like "Under the Sea" or "Row, Row, Row Your Boat" as background music. In large music stores or at the Nature Company, you'll also find interesting tapes with sounds of the ocean, dolphins, and whales. You can play these throughout the party. You will also need these for the "Musical Lily Pads" game.

5. Turn card tables upside down—they become instant boats! Tie twine from leg to leg; buy plastic inflatable tubes at the five-and-dime and throw one over each of the legs (instant life preservers). By placing blue plastic tablecloths on the floor, your upside down tables become "boats" on this "blue ocean." Three to four small kids will fit into each boat. Your sailors can play some of the games aboard ship and eat on deck as well. You will also have a creative background for free play.

6. Collect white cloth admiral hats or white cloth sailor hats, wind-up pool or bath toys, gummy fish and gummy worms, fish stickers, and tackle boxes (plastic makeup boxes work too) for favors. Write each child's name on the outside.

7. Make fishing poles, lily pads, colored tissue paper fish. Make sure you have magnets, wooden dowels, string, green construction paper, a goldfish bowl, and straws. Write the messages for the game "Gone Fishin'" on your little fish.

8. Buy rubber worms.

9. Get a baby wading pool, lots of goldfish, and a minnow net and a plastic bag for each child.

10. Buy small plastic toy boats.

11. Prepare straws and tissue fish for the "Blow, Fish, Blow," game.

12. Find two 8-foot boards, 6 inches wide, for the "Fish Walk."

The Tallitschs decorated their house for Molly's fishing party. The "land" was upstairs. The downstairs was decorated with blue and green streamers to make the kids feel that they were underwater in the sea.

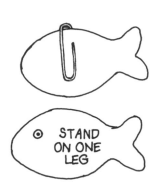

Trish Murphy taped a penny on each paper fish. So every child who caught a fish caught a penny, too.

Debbie Lingrey's fishing party featured a table covered with a blue cloth and sprinkled with silver glitter for waves. Tiny plastic boats with a child's name on each served as place cards.

ACTIVITIES

FISHIN' FOR PAPER FISH

Set up fishing poles with magnets tied on the end of the string. Create a barrier by putting a table on its side or have the children fish into a large cardboard box. In the box or behind the barrier, place your paper fish, each fastened with a paper clip, and with instructions written on it, such as: Stand on one leg and count to ten; make a face of a fish; or sing a song with the word "fish" in it. The object is for each child to fish for little paper fish and when he catches one, to read the message and do what it says.

FISH WALK

Get two 8-foot boards, 6 inches wide. Place them flat on the floor, parallel, several feet apart. Divide the children into two teams. Each team member is assigned a different fish to imitate as he walks down the gangplank. For example, the first two contestants must be jellyfish as they move up and down, back and forth, on the gangplank; the next two must slither like eels; the third couple crawls and snaps like snapping turtles; the fourth swim like sharks; the fifth couple moves like lobsters.

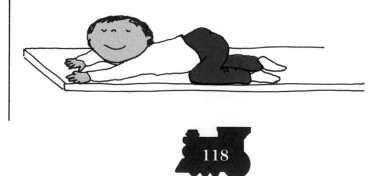

MUSICAL LILY PADS

Susan McRee Adams, from La Porte, Texas, played a version of this game with her youngsters. Cut out lily pads from green construction paper or a green plastic tablecloth, one less than the number of children. Place around the room and tape down with masking or packing tape. Divide the children into two teams of "jumping frogs." Play music and have the "frogs" jump from one lily pad to another. When you stop the music, each "frog" must be on a lily pad. The frog that has no lily pad to perch on is out of the game!

BLOW, FISH, BLOW

This is a relay game using colored tissue paper fish that are scattered on top of a coffee or card table. Nearby, place an empty fish bowl (the younger the children, the nearer the bowl). Divide the group into two teams. Hand out a plastic straw to each child. Each team member, in turn, then inhales through the straw to pick up a paper fish and, holding his breath, keeps the fish at the end of the straw, until he transfers it to the fish bowl. The team that finishes first wins.

FISH, FISH, FOR GOLDFISH

This is the real thing. Fill a baby wading pool halfway with water and add goldfish. Give each child a minnow net and a plastic bag (it's a good idea to have each guest's name written on his bag). Netting these little darters can be a real challenge but also a lot of fun! The caught fish get put into the plastic bag half-filled with water and sealed.

ANCHORS AWAY

A supply of small toy boats to be handed out after all the goldfish have been caught will continue the water play.

FAVORS

Wind-up toys for the bath or pool, gummy fish and gummy worms, fish stickers, tackle boxes, admiral or sailor hats, goldfish the kids caught

MENU

Bowls of Fish Crackers
Tuna Salad in hot-dog bun boats
Boxed drinks
Orange sherbet frozen in a fish mold

See recipes on page 238.

FISH CAKE

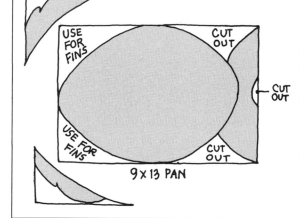

9 × 13 PAN

Use the **All-Around Birthday Cake** recipe, page 226. Bake the cake in a 9 × 13-inch pan. When the cake is done, cut into the shape of a fish (see drawing). Cover with the **Seven-Minute Frosting,** page 229. Use a colored Necco wafer with a raisin attached with frosting for the eye. Using tube icing, pipe scales and fins.

HORSIN' AROUND

(Ages 7–12)

Bring the Wild West to your "Horsin' Around" roundup. Your young cowboys and cowgirls can throw horseshoes, move mustangs, cut down the fence, race horses and barrels, run a steeplechase, square dance, and more. Our versions of these cowboy customs may vary from the more traditional ones you know—when we say horsin' around, we *mean* horsin' around—but they will be at least as much fun, and certainly more manageable. So it's time to gather the hay, saddle up the horses, don your Stetsons, and gather those blue ribbons.

HAPPY BIRTHDAY

INVITATION

In the shape of a horseshoe (tie a colored bandanna to each!).

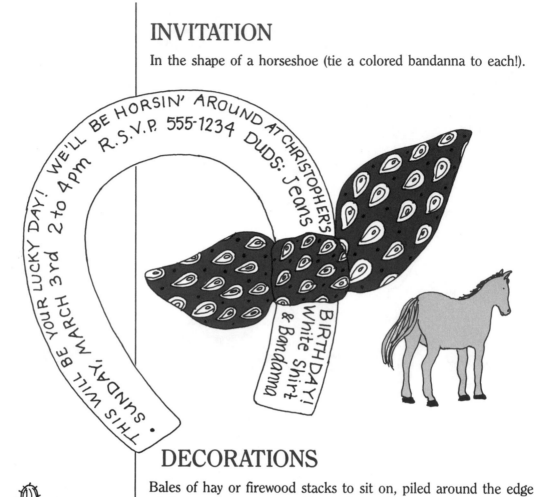

THIS WILL BE YOUR LUCKY DAY! WE'LL BE HORSIN' AROUND AT CHRISTOPHER'S • SUNDAY, MARCH 3rd 2 to 4pm R.S.V.P. 555-1234 DUDS: Jeans BIRTHDAY! White Shirt & Bandanna

DECORATIONS

Bales of hay or firewood stacks to sit on, piled around the edge of the party room or outside in the yard. Any photographs or cutouts of horses, ranches, rodeos, or cow roundups will also add to the atmosphere.

At Alix Kantor's party in Southern California, her mom, Heidi, found that some kids stayed at the party longer than planned and she needed a game to fill up the time. She ran up the hill, cut off a piece of cactus, gathered some rings from an old game, and had the girls play "Toss the Ring on the Cactus."

GET READY!

1. If you have access to a farm, get bales of hay. Logs of wood will also work.

2. Buy large paper plates for the horse race.

3. Find a set of horseshoes and stakes.

4. Purchase leather and cording kits for making leather wallets and key rings, available in craft and hobby stores. Buy puff paints for decorating.

5. Buy cowboy hats and any other items for favors.

6. Organize ribbons and safety scissors for the game "Don't Fence Me In."

7. Collect empty plastic milk bottles.

8. Buy blue ribbons as prizes for the various contests.

9. Locate three barrels or large pots at a local nursery.

10. Prepare a square dancing cassette.

11. Buy 6-foot leather straps for the "Steeplechase."

ACTIVITIES

HORSESHOES

Did you know that horseshoe pitching began in this country in colonial times and has been played for nearly 200 years? There is even a National Horseshoe Pitchers Association of America, which holds national and world championship tournaments every year. The rules for this sport can vary, especially when children are playing. So, read these rules, but feel free to alter them as you like. Divide the guests into two teams. Set up the horseshoe game following the instructions that come with the equipment. Play the game, two people at a time, by throwing the horseshoes, one person at a time. The point is to score a total of 21 points or closest to 21. Scoring is done as follows: You get 1 point for each horseshoe that is closer than your opponent's and 3 points for each "ringer" (that's the horseshoe that actually encloses the stake). If the horseshoes are equally distant from the stake, or if the players get the same number of shoes on the stake, that's a tie and no points are scored.

Thea Sprecher lives for her horse, Topper (and she's got a collection of blue ribbons to prove it!). Thea and her friends at the San Marcos Pass Sporting Life Farm in Santa Barbara vouch for all these games as horse lovin' party pleasers. Thea's only wish is to include a hay ride!

HORSE RACING

In this derby, six "horses" race at a time. Choose six players who will be the horses named Quarterhorse (#1), Palomino (#2), Pinto (#3), Appaloosa (#4), Arabian (#5), and Thoroughbred (#6) (notice that each named horse also gets a number). Place 20 paper plates out on the floor in a straight line (each plate is a "length"). Tape a STARTING LINE at one end and a FINISH LINE at the other. Now line up the horses at the starting gate. Choose one child to be the roller who throws the dice and another to be the announcer who calls the race, and divide the rest of the guests into six teams, each one backing a different horse.

The race begins! The dice is thrown and a number comes up—let's say it's six. The roller then throws the dice again and the number is five. Horse #6 (the Thoroughbred) then moves five "lengths" as the announcer calls, "Thoroughbred is running at five lengths!" The race continues in this way until one horse crosses the finish line. Those guests who backed that horse win and receive a ribbon. You can continue running races with different children acting as different horses backed by the various teams.

MUSTANG MOVE

This tournament pits the guests' strength against each other to "move the mustangs" from one corral to another. Divide the group into couples. Place as many "mustangs" (empty plastic milk bottles) as you have couples between the members of each couple. The couple places their arms on each other's shoulders. The object is to push or pull your partner so he or she will bump over the "mustang" between the two of you. The one who knocks it down loses. All the winners then play each other until only one winner remains.

Thea has a bridle, so this game was easy for her to arrange: Take two English bridles and take them apart. Have two teams of guests put them back together again. The first team to finish and have it exactly right, wins!

DON'T FENCE ME IN

Five contestants at a time play this game. Tie five long streamers of ribbon (at least a yard long) to a post, fence, or chair. Give each player a pair of safety scissors and tell him that he is about to "cut down the fence." At the signal, he must begin to cut up the middle of the ribbon. The object is to get to the goal (the top of the ribbon) as quickly as possible without cutting a piece of ribbon off. Everyone on the sidelines cheers until they get their turn.

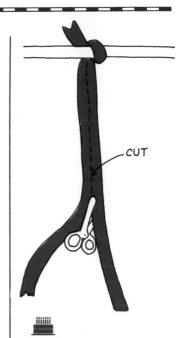

STEEPLECHASE

Divide your guests into "horses" and "riders." Each "horse" gets "reins" (made from leather straps), which are strapped around the shoulders of the "horse." When they run the steeplechase, each "horse" and "rider" will have to run and jump together, which is not always an easy task and requires some coordination and much cooperation.

Set up a course for your "horses" and their "riders" to run the steeplechase. You can have other guests holding sticks at different heights, set up a small wading pool, or use some short bushes, a group of rocks, or a chaise lounge, and the "horses" will have to jump over them.

You can play croquet or miniature golf on the lawn for extra outdoor games.

LEATHER GOODS

At your local hobby shop, buy some kits for making leather wallets and key rings. Get some puff paints and draw horse-related symbols.

At Alix Kantor's "Western" party for her eighth birthday (from *The Penny Whistle Party Planner*), her mother, Heidi Schulman, added a new twist. She hired a square dancing teacher named Maxine Pearl who taught the ins and outs of square dancing. The girls liked the dancing part just fine, but what they really loved were some of Maxine's great calls. Here they were, 25 eight-year-olds, prancing around shouting, "Bull chips, did you step in it? Bull chips, the heck you say!" Heidi isn't sure the girls had any idea what it all meant, but she *is* sure the calls were a big hit because word got back that the school yard has been vibrating with this now-famous chant!

SQUARE DANCING OR THE VIRGINIA REEL

Assign the caller (get someone who knows how to do this or give them a script), set up the music, and get ready to swing! In a square dance, four couples make up a "square" or a "set." The boy traditionally stands to the left of his partner, but this dance is fun whether or not both sexes are represented.

The couples stand forming a square (see drawing). Here are some calls for an old square dance called "Swing Andy Gump" (play any square dancing music):

Jump in the air and come right down,
Swing your honey round and round.
> *[Everyone jumps in the air and when they come down, each takes his own partner in a "waltzing" position and turns around in place twice.]*

Corner left, Partner right,
Grand change eight the whole way round.
> *[Each boy turns the girl on his left with the left hand and continues back to his partner with the right hand, and they make a swing together.]*

First lady out to the right,
And Swing Andy Gump!
> *[Choose a "first lady"; she now leaves her place, goes to the second boy, and swings him around twice.]*

Now that man with the great big bump
> *[The first lady repeats the above swing with the third boy.]*

Now the one with the turned up toes
> *[The first lady swings the fourth boy just as above.]*

Now swing your own with the great big nose!

> *[The first lady returns to the original boy and everyone swings their partners.]*

Corner Left, Partner Right,

Grand change eight the whole way round.

> *[Repeat these calls for the second, third, and fourth partners, calling the "second lady" and so forth where you called the first.]*

BARREL RACING

As in a relay race, set up the barrels or pots as a slalom obstacle course. Divide the group into two teams. Each team's members, in turn, must run around the course and touch the next person on their return. The fastest team wins.

FAVORS

Cowboy hats, leather wallets and key rings

MENU

Spareribs with Barbecue Sauce
Roast Corn on the Cob
Cranberry juice

See recipes on pages 238–239.

CORRAL CAKE

Use **The Super Chocolate Cake** recipe, page 226. Bake the cake in a 9 × 11-inch pan. Place on a large platter or a piece of stiff cardboard. Cover with green **Seven-Minute Frosting,** page 229. Take pretzel rods (not sticks) and stick them standing up into the cake all around the edges. Create a fence with thin licorice strings. Place plastic horses in the corral—even a cowboy, if you have one.

IT'S A DOG'S LIFE

ROSIE

(Ages 3–6)

happy birthday

C ute cuddly puppies are irresistible and when you get together a group of youngsters for some pretend puppy play, you'll all have a yipping good time! Be sure to take lots of pictures of your little darlings acting like puppies—a shot of your child "fetching" the paper in his teeth or attending dog obedience school will be priceless.

INVITATION

Attach a cutout of a dog to a large dog biscuit on which are written the words: "Play dead," "Fetch," "Roll over," "Sit," and "Heel."

IT'S A DOG'S LIFE AT:
JIMMY'S DOG HOUSE
FOR HIS **5**TH BIRTHDAY
Bring your toy puppy.

555 WELLWORTH LANE

R.S.V.P.
555-1234

SUNDAY
Jan. 14th
12 to 2 pm

PLAY DEAD
FETCH
ROLLOVER
·SIT·
HEEL

Meredith's Aunt Inadoll has always believed that having a puppy party should not be limited to youngsters. Indeed, for Uncle Jim's 60th birthday, her invitation said, "Come teach an old dog new tricks."

DECORATIONS

At Molly Tallitsch's "Dog Party," guests found a basket as they entered from which each child could choose dog ears instead of party hats. You can add the following to your decor: a dog house (you can make one from a refrigerator box) that the little "puppies" can run in and out of, stuffed animal dogs everywhere (or you can place all the stuffed dogs in the dog house), dog posters or cutouts hanging on the walls or from the ceiling.

GET READY!

1. Buy or make dog ears (they are easily cut out of felt or fake fur fabric and sewn onto pieces of elastic).

2. Make a dog house out of a large cardboard box (see drawing). Decorate it with a sign that reads: "Spot's Dog House" and attach it to the doorway—the kids will decorate the rest when they arrive. For them, get markers, paints, crayons, glue, and dog biscuits (these can be glued on the box).

3. Collect stuffed dogs and place all around the party room.

4. Buy dog posters or a couple of dog calendars where each month has a picture of a different dog. These can be hung on the walls or on the outside of your dog house.

5. Buy or make dog bone biscuits (they can be used to decorate the dog house).

6. Get whistles for "Snoopy's Hide 'n' Seek."

7. Find a cotton gardening glove for "Catch."

8. Roll up newspaper in plastic wrap.

9. Buy six or seven plastic dog bones and collect plastic wastepaper baskets for the "Throw" game.

ACTIVITIES

As the children arrive, begin decorating the dog house. (If the box has too much writing on it, spray-paint it before the day of the party.) Provide them with paint, markers, and crayons to make windows, doors, and flower boxes. They can also glue the pictures of all kinds of dogs on the outside. Dog biscuits are easy to glue (draw an outline of the door and glue the biscuits to it).

SNOOPY'S HIDE 'N' SEEK

This old classic is still lots of fun: The one who is "it" is Snoopy the dog, who must find all the puppies who are hiding. Snoopy goes into the dog house and counts to 20 while all the children scatter and hide. When Snoopy finishes counting, he whistles to signal the beginning of the hunt and as each puppy is found. The last puppy to be found gets a prize: a dog whistle. Snoopy then chooses his successor.

CATCH

Have Mom or Dad toss a cotton gardening glove in the air for a lucky puppy to catch in his mouth and return (each puppy reaches and whoever catches the glove returns it to the thrower). As Mary Tallitsch says, "No words can adequately describe this game."

FETCH

Roll up two sections of the newspaper and wrap each in plastic wrap. Place them at the other end of the room. Divide the children into two teams, in two rows. The first puppy on each team crawls across the room to fetch the paper in his mouth (his hands may not touch the paper). He then crawls back and drops the paper in front of the next puppy on his team. The first team to finish the relay wins.

Variation on a theme: How about a pet show? Nancy Rubin attended a neighborhood costume party for dogs in Washington, D.C. There was a Hollywood Dog (in sunglasses and top hat), a Surfer Dog (with surfboard on its back), and three dogs came as the Three Little Pigs. You can have the children bring their pets—real or stuffed—to share in the birthday celebration. If you invite live animals, make sure you are prepared to deal with them.

BARK

This is a barking contest where everyone is a winner (a must to video and/or tape record). Any parents present can serve as judges. Each puppy gets a chance to bark his best. Winners include Loudest, Saddest, Squeakiest, Most Real, and Best Howl. Give out the dog bone cookies as prizes.

MIND

The puppies are now going to attend Dog Obedience School, actually "Simple Simon" for dogs. The leader, or Master, gives dog commands. Thus, if Master says "sit up and beg," the "dogs" do it. If the leader fails to say "Master says" before he gives the command, the dogs aren't supposed to obey. Commands include "Roll over," "Sit," "Sit up," "Beg," "Play dead," "Scratch your ear with your hind leg," "Lick your paw," "Bark." If a dog performs the command without the "Master says," he is out of the game. The last "dog" left wins.

Glue small bone-shaped dog biscuits all around a large plastic picture frame. You can pile them one on top of the other, slightly askew. When the glue has dried, insert a photo of your child in his dog costume or a photo of one of your dogs.

THROW

Tape four different dog photos to four waste baskets and assign each basket a value with the farthest having the highest number. Stagger the distance to vary the degree of difficulty. As each child steps up to the mark, he attempts to throw five dog bones into the baskets for the highest score, one at a time. (If you have more than ten children, set a lower number of throws.) The winner is the one with the highest score.

FAVORS

Dog bone cookies, books about dogs, small dog figures (plastic or porcelain)

MENU

To be eaten out of dog dishes:
Turkey dogs
Trail Mix (looks like dog food)
Juice
Chocolate Doggie Bone Cookies

See recipes on pages 239–240.

DOG DISH CAKE

Use the **Rocky Road Cake** recipe, page 225. Bake the cake in a large metal dog dish. Cool in the dish and frost with **Rocky Road Frosting,** page 226. Write "Happy Birthday" with a marker on the outside of the dog dish.

KIDNAPPED ★ PARTY

REMY

(Ages 5 and up)

H ere's a different version of a surprise party—different, but not so new. Friends like Heidi Schulman, of Los Angeles, now a mother herself, recounts stories of having "kidnapped" parties when she was growing up in Seattle (they may not have been a surprise after a while, but they were still as much fun). Heidi's mom would wake her very early in the morning and bundle her into the station wagon while she was still in her pajamas. They would then drive from house to house picking up Heidi's girlfriends (none of whom knew what was up) until there were ten little girls, all in their pj's, huddled in secret delight at the mysterious morning ahead. Although this party reads as if it is for girls only, boys have been known to love being kidnapped too.

INVITATION

No invitation is needed because this is a surprise party to everyone but the birthday child. However, advance warning by phone to the parents of the "kidnappees" is definitely in order.

DECORATIONS

Decorations at this party are minimal, particularly if you end up at a restaurant for breakfast. If, however, you bring everybody to your own home, you might just turn the party room into a festive arena with balloons, ribbons, crepe paper, and paper flowers. Try this: Using a balloon pump, inflate about a hundred long balloons. Tie them together in knots. Each group of six or seven balloons will produce its own abstract design. Tack to the ceiling and/or walls for a great effect.

GET READY!

   1. Prepare balloons, ribbons, crepe paper, and paper flowers.

   2. Cut words out of the newspaper; you will also need 8½ × 11-inch paper and Scotch tape for "The Morning *Times*."

   3. Prepare the anagrams of your guests' names or use ours.

   4. Buy a rubber chicken.

   5. Prepare lined paper with the appropriate words for the game "Kidnapped."

   6. Xerox the drawing for the "Hidden Happy Birthday."

   7. Get prizes and favors.

ACTIVITIES

The first activity is the actual kidnapping. Your child is awakened at 7:00 in the morning, has her picture taken getting out of bed in her pajamas, and immediately gets into a large station wagon or van still in her pajamas. You drive to the first guest's home, where the parents are expecting you, but the child isn't. In fact, she's probably still fast asleep! You wake up that child and while she is also still in her pajamas, load her into the van and take a picture of her (remember to take a picture of each guest with a Polaroid camera as she gets kidnapped). Then you both run to the car to join the birthday girl. By the time the third guest is kidnapped, the three little pajama-clad munchkins in the car eagerly await her appearance.

You continue with this kidnapping activity until all the guests have been rounded up. At this point, you have a couple of choices. You can take all the girls and/or boys to a local diner for breakfast or you can return the children to your house for breakfast and games.

"THE MORNING *TIMES*"

Have a basket full of words that you have cut out of the newspaper. Hand out a piece of 8½ × 11-inch paper to each of the guests as well as a roll of Scotch tape. By picking words out of the basket, each little editor combines words to create his own newspaper headline. Prizes are given for the most outrageous headline, the silliest, the funniest, the most serious, the scariest, the most realistic, and so on.

SHADOW TAG

By the time you finish the rest of the games, the sun should be up just in time for the shadows you need to play shadow tag. The game is played by somebody being "it" who has to step on one of the other players' shadow as each child maneuvers her body to keep her shadow away from "it."

Inez Burgen, from Brookline, Massachusetts, gives her visiting grandchildren unbirthday parties whenever they come to visit. The relatives all bring presents, Inez bakes a special birthday cake, and everyone loves this extra birthday celebration.

WORD ASSOCIATION

In this game, players take turns calling out words that are either closely associated with the previous word or which rhyme with it. The children sit in a circle and the birthday child starts off the game with the word "kidnapped"; the next guest could say "hostage" (which is a word related to "kidnapped"), and the next could say "prisoner." Words that follow in order could be "blindfolded," "surprise," "party," "smarty," "head," "hat," "bat," "wings," "sings," "voice," "mouth," "south," etc. The further you get into the game, the faster you should try to call out the words. If anybody repeats a word that's already been called, they're out of the game. The last player left is the winner.

Older kids can plan parties themselves. The surprise party Jennifer Meyer gave for her friend, Jane Hait, was such a smash! All Jane's 12-year-old friends took up a collection and planned the whole party. They bought the decorations and favors, arranged for a local hamburger cafe to be ready to feed the dozen guests, and organized the games. Not only was the party a huge success, says Jennifer, but the girls had so much fun doing everything together that they plan to surprise another friend soon.

NAME ANAGRAM

Solve the mystery of the kidnappers' names. The following are anagrams of some ordinary names which, when solved, become possible names of the kidnappers. Try to find anagrams of your guests' names.

wander	Andrew
brain	Brian
nailed	Daniel
sinned	Dennis
rice	Eric
lone	Leon
events	Steven
cram	Marc
dangle	Glenda
yak	Kay
soil	Lois
army	Mary
sore	Rose
hurt	Ruth
aimless	Melissa

KIDNAPPED

Give each child a piece of lined paper organized just like the drawing below.

Down the left-hand side, writing downward, write the word "kidnapped" with one letter on each line starting with the letter "k." In the game, each child has to fill in the grid with his own words. So he starts like this: He must think of a color beginning with the letter "k"; this is difficult, so he continues to an animal with the letter "k," which he remembers is "kangaroo"; next, a food with the letter "k," which can be Kellogg's Rice Krispies. He continues down the letters, with "i" being the next. He goes on to "d," where he can easily fill in "dinosaur" for animal, "doughnut" for food, "David" for name, "dungarees" for clothing, and "Dodge" for car.

The object is for each child to fill in as much of the grid as he can with his own choice of words.

Remy Weber had his own version of the kidnapped party for his 16th birthday. One friend was assigned the task of kidnapping Remy and taking him to the local pizza parlor where the rest of his friends were waiting. Favors (tokens for the local video arcade) and specially designed commemorative T-shirts were waiting at the table for each kid. They had a great time and it was a great way to have an "unsupervised" supervised party for teenagers.

	Colors	Animals	Food	Names	Clothing	Cars
K						
I						
D						
N						
A						
P						
P						
E						
D						

HIDDEN HAPPY BIRTHDAY

Make as many copies of the picture below as there are children. In it are hidden the letters spelling "Happy Birthday." The object is for the kids to find the letters; the first child to do so wins.

See answers on page 248.

STEAL THE CHICKEN

Two teams of children line up in two equal lines on opposite sides of the room. Assign numbers to each child on each team. (There will be two children with the number one, two, three, etc.) Place a rubber chicken in the center of the room on the floor. An adult calls out one of the numbers and the two children with that number run to the center of the room. The first one to grab and run with the chicken back to his team wins a point for his team. At the end, the team with the most points wins.

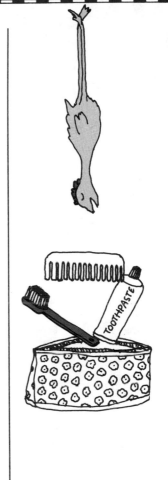

FAVORS

Little makeup or toiletry kits with scented soap, toothbrush, toothpaste, hand lotion, comb, etc., for girls; overnight bags for boys

MENU

If you're planning to entertain the group at a café or diner, pre-ordering will save you time, expense, confusion, and probably the goodwill of the restaurant owner. Likewise, do everything ahead of time if you're returning home. The breakfast menu, unless you have kitchen helpers who can produce the pancakes at the last minute, should be kept simple.

Orange juice blended with bananas

Frozen Yogurts (shake individual fruit yogurts to distribute the fruit, then place in the freezer right before leaving the house to round up your guests; when you return in an hour, the yogurts will be slushy)

Breakfast Banana Splits

Pancakes: Ricotta, Popover, or Gingerbread with Orange-Honey Syrup or Apple Butter

Shortcut Doughnuts (decorate with birthday candles)

See recipes on pages 240–242.

PIG-OUT BIRTHDAY

(Ages 5–10)

The reactions of Matt Kerpen's friends when they received their invitations to his pig-out party for his sixth birthday were revealing. "Awesome!" "Far-out!" "Are you kidding?" "Does your mom know about this?"

The thought of a no-holds-barred party where the kids are actually encouraged to make pigs out of themselves made Matt's friends jump for joy. The kids were able to use the backyard as a "pig sty," which Matt's mom, Betty, covered in bales of hay. Another Betty—Betty Pearson who lives in Provo, Utah—had a pig party for the eighth birthday of her son, Eric, where the highlight was a Water Balloon Toss after which the kids decorated themselves or their partners with shaving cream. Hosing each "pig" off became another giggle-full activity.

So get ready, get set, and go ahead, be a pig.

INVITATION

Written with permanent marker on a plastic bib:

MAKE A PIG OF YOURSELF AT JASON'S PIG-OUT BIRTHDAY PARTY

Dress for the occasion! very messy!

SUNDAY, MARCH 10TH 3 to 5 PM

R.S.V.P. 555-1234

For a wonderful coloring book with pigs, get *Robinson's Racing Pigs* coloring book (see Resources, page 251). They make great favors, too!

DECORATIONS

This party is best held outdoors. Pictures or cutouts of pigs placed in strategic locations will add to the atmosphere. If you can get hold of bales of hay, all the better! You can make a "pig sty" out of a refrigerator box and fill the bottom with hay. This can be where the little pigs eat lunch.

GET READY!

1. Buy plastic bibs for the invitations. Prepare the refrigerator box and hay for the pig sty if you plan to have one.

2. Prepare one bowl of Jell-O per person (make a couple extra). If you like, you can include whipped cream.

3. Collect one sheet of newspaper per guest for "Pig Art."

4. Locate one blindfold and a pillow for "Oink, Oink, Piggy."

5. Find a stopwatch for the "Piggyback Run."

6. Blow up two dozen pink balloons (remember, you always need extras) and draw a snout and tail on each with a black marker for "Swat the Pig." You will also need one fly swatter per guest and masking tape.

7. Prepare several rolls of pennies and a wooden salad bowl for the "Piggy Toss."

8. Get prizes and favors.

ACTIVITIES

JELL-O EATING CONTEST

Make one bowl of Jell-O per person (plus a few extra). Line the bowls in a row on the ground. Each player clasps his hands behind his neck. When the command is given to start, all the contestants begin eating their Jell-O. The first one to clean his bowl completely wins.

PIG ART

Give everyone a large sheet of newspaper. If you are indoors, turn out the lights, darken the room, and ask each guest to tear the paper into the shape of a pig. When the lights are turned back on, the winner is the one whose paper shape most resembles a pig. Use blindfolds if your party is outside.

PIG SNORTING CONTEST

This is just what it says it is: Each guest gets to snort like a pig. Prizes are given for the best snort, the worst, the longest, the shortest, the most obnoxious, the silliest, and so on.

OINK, OINK, PIGGY

Everyone sits in a circle on the ground. In the center is the "Ham," who is blindfolded. Someone turns him around a couple of times and hands him a pillow. He walks around until he finds a person's lap and then sits there on the pillow. The "Ham" says "oink, oink" (like a pig), and the person he is sitting on must repeat the "oink, oink" in a voice that he tries to disguise so that the "Ham" can't guess his identity. If the "Ham" misses, he moves on to another lap. If he is successful, the person whose lap he is sitting on becomes the "Ham." Each time a new pig becomes the "Ham," everyone in the circle should switch places to make it more difficult to guess identities.

PIGGYBACK RUN

In this game the guests compete in pairs. One member of each pair climbs on the other's back. Starting at one end of the yard, the carrier races to the other end, where the rider dismounts and carries his partner back to the starting point. The race is timed and the couple who is the fastest wins.

SWAT THE PIG

Collect about a dozen of the prepared pink "pig" balloons. Divide the guests into two equal teams and line them up behind the starting tape. Mark a goal line with more tape on the other side of the yard. Hand a fly swatter and a pink "pig" balloon to the first person on each team. At the starting signal, each leader places his balloon on the ground and races to the goal line and back, pushing the balloon with the fly swatter the entire way. If a player bursts the balloon, he must return to the starting line and begin again with a new balloon. The team that finishes first wins.

PIGGY TOSS

Give each player five pennies. At a distance of 6 feet (shorter for younger children), place a large wooden salad bowl. The object is to see how many coins each can "feed" into the "Piggy's Trough." The one with the most coins in the trough wins.

143

For children whose birthdays fall on Christmas (Meredith's is one of them), Mary Unterbrunner from Eldridge, Iowa, has an idea: Have a "Rudolph" birthday party like the one Jason had when he was six. As the children arrived, each signed his name with red puff paint on a stocking. After games were played, prizes were found in a hunt, and as each child found his, he got his nose painted red. Making a set of antlers out of brown tagboard (which the kids wore) was next on the list. Then each child finished his Christmas birthday stocking by gluing on a red nose, eyes, and antlers to make it look like Rudolph. They also made Rudolph Christmas tree ornaments and played "Musical Noses" (red noses were taped to the floor and as Mary played "Rudolph the Red-Nosed Reindeer," the kids ran from nose to nose, just as in the old game "musical chairs." As each child was eliminated, he received a Rudolph candy cane. This party sure made up for Jason's sharing his birthday with Christmas festivities!

PIG OUT, PIG STOP

This game is so old, even Meredith and Annie played it when they were kids. It has traditionally been called, "Red Light, Green Light," but we have adapted it here for the little pigs. One person gets to be "it" and the others stand behind the starting line, each guest ready to go at the command. The person who is "it" turns his back to the others, and it is his choice when to call "Pig Out" or "Pig Stop." On "Pig Out" the guests walk on all fours like pigs toward him until he calls "Pig Stop," at which point they must freeze instantly. The person who is "it" then quickly turns around and tries to catch any pig moving. If someone is caught, they must return to the starting line. Remember that as the game goes along, the pigs come closer and closer to "it." At that point, it is wise for "it" to make the "Pig Outs" very short and to call "Pig Stop" more often. If the player who is "it" gets tagged, the player who tagged him gets to be "it" in the next round.

FAVORS

Piggy banks, rubber pigs, pig noses, soap in the shape of pigs

MENU

To be eaten without any utensils:
Spaghetti Marinara
Green salad with fresh peas
Garlic bread
Milk shakes

See recipes on pages 242–243.

PIGLET CUPCAKES

Use the **Party Cupcakes** recipe, page 228. Bake in a mini ball pan (see Resources, page 249) or muffin tin. The recipe will yield 10–12 cupcakes. Frost each cupcake with **Orange Cream Frosting,** page 229. Make the nose with a white miniature marshmallow. Using pink frosting from a tube, pipe two dots on the snout and a swirl for the tail. Make ears with almonds and frost over them with pink frosting.

SECRET AGENTS

(Ages 8 and up)

T here's a reason why the most popular books and movies, cartoons and comic books, have always been mysteries—children of all ages love them! After all, deciphering clandestine codes and cryptic messages, solving puzzles and riddles, unraveling clues that resolve mysteries, are the challenges behind all games, aren't they? But the most fun of all is to pretend to be a secret agent. Your detectives will rub their hands in glee at the challenges that dare them to find the birthday cake, detect the identity of various murderers, uncover clue after clue in daring game after game. Even the birthday lunch is a mystery!

Katherine Page, from Lexington, Massachusetts, is a writer of mystery stories, "so there is always a lot of talk of detectives, crime, etc., in our house." ... So for Nicholas' eighth birthday, he and his mom created an invitation in the shape of a magnifying glass. They had a "whodunit" hunt and a disguised relay race (from *The Penny Whistle Party Planner*). Katherine then wrote a story just for the party called "The Case of Mrs. Throttlebottom's Jewels," which was the starting point of a game to find the missing jewels.

INVITATION

Have your child record a "secret message" in his best Vincent Price voice on a small tape recorder. Find a tape of a Bach fugue or a cantata (any organ or Halloween music works well, too) and play it in the background.

Here's what your secret agent says:

> Your mission (I'm sure you'll choose to accept it!) is to aid Jason Bloom and his fellow agents in solving many mysteries at Jason's birthday. Your reputation as a super secret spy requires your appearance on Saturday, February 4, at 6:00 P.M., at the hidden headquarters of Jason's Interpol Agency, otherwise known as JIA, at 555 Morgan Avenue. You must wear your secret agent attire (trench coats and fedoras are fine). Your code to enter is "D - A - N - G - E - R." Please RSVP to 555-1234 before this tape self-destructs. If it doesn't, you may use it as you wish.

Copy the tape on your machine for as many invitations as you need. Send in a padded envelope, seal with wax, and stamp with your child's initial. Our friend Katherine Page added "Top Secret" on the outside of the envelopes for her son Nicholas' invitations.

DECORATIONS

You can print up wanted posters by taking a photograph of the birthday child (and if you have any photographs of the guests) and blowing them up. You can invent any "crimes" you want, but the sillier, the better.

GET READY!

1. Collect as many short-playing tape recorder cassettes as you have invited guests, sealing wax and seal (available at stationery stores), and padded envelopes for the invitations.

2. Buy colored letter-size files, index cards, a package of white 8½ × 11-inch unlined paper, and one or two black stamp pads for fingerprinting. You will also need some drinking glasses, baby powder, and a brush for dusting the fingerprints.

3. Buy small magnifying glasses, one per guest, for fingerprinting and favors.

4. Buy other favors like detective comic books and mystery paperbacks.

5. Write and hide the clues for the hunt for the birthday cake ("Supersleuths").

6. Make the slips of paper for "Murder, She Winked" and "Is Sherlock Home?"

7. Collect a few extra fedora-like hats, raincoats, and dark sunglasses for "Who's Who."

8. Prepare "The Missing Link" game. A book of tongue twisters will be helpful.

9. Prepare the mystery menu and appropriate accoutrements (in this party, the lunch or dinner is also a game).

ACTIVITIES

FINGERPRINTING

Each secret agent is fingerprinted as he arrives at the party. Make a file for each guest into which his fingerprint record will go. Give each his own magnifying glass.

Fingerprinting is done in this manner: Open a black, well-inked stamp pad. Have each agent press his fingers, one at a time, lightly on the pad, rolling each finger from side to side to make sure it gets covered with ink. Now press each finger down on a sheet of paper with his name on it. Continue the process until all five fingers on his hand have been printed. Have him also make a duplicate set of fingerprints on an index card. Write his name down there as well; this set is one he can take home.

Jill Weber gives each of her nephews a very special present for every birthday—a day with her! For Wesley's tenth birthday Jill bought ten little presents (total cost: less than $10) and hid them throughout her house. The only clue he got was that they were in a basket (Jill has a collection of many, many baskets!). Wesley's brother, Reid, wanted a pajama party for his birthday, so Jill gave him one. She and Reid took ice cream, popcorn, hot chocolate, and two movies to bed. Jill managed to stay awake for the first half of the first movie; she believes Reid when he says he stayed up all night!

Take time to examine the fingerprints under a magnifying glass. Compare each print to see if there are similarities. You can also take prints of both thumbs and compare those. When you compare an agent's with another's fingerprints, you will see that no two people have the same prints (that's what makes them so useful and accurate in identifying people).

Next they'll want to dust for fingerprints. Have a secret agent hold a drinking glass in his hand. Put the glass down and sprinkle the side he touched with some baby powder. Blow away the powder—the part that is left will cover the fingerprints. With a small, clean brush, dust away the rest of the powder and you will see the fingerprints appear.

MURDER, SHE WINKED

All the secret agents sit in a circle on the floor. From a hat or a bowl, they draw pieces of paper, one of which is marked with an "X." That person is the murderer, but he doesn't tell anyone. Instead, he winks slyly at someone whose eye he catches and that person falls over "dead." Thus if he looks at you and winks, you have to fall over "dead." If you see someone winking at someone else, you can immediately identify him as the murderer. Only the murderer is allowed to wink. Once a person is "killed," the guessing begins. As they try to guess, the murderer continues to wink at someone else who then falls over "dead." The game continues until someone guesses who the murderer is.

IS SHERLOCK HOME?

Cut out slips of paper, one for each guest. On one draw a pipe, on another a dagger, and leave the rest blank. Fold them up and mix in a bowl. Have each secret agent pick one slip. The one who gets the pipe is Sherlock, and he tells everyone that's who he is. The one who gets the dagger is the murderer, he must tell no one that's who he is.

Turn off the lights in the house. All the agents scatter throughout the house. The murderer then sneaks around the house until he finds a victim, into whose ear he then whispers "You are dead!" The victim must scream very loudly and fall "dead." Sherlock and the other agents run to where the victim has fallen. He then begins to question all the other agents to try to find out who killed the victim (he asks leading questions, not "Are you the murderer?"). Each agent must answer truthfully, except for the murderer, who can lie unless someone asks him "Are you the murderer?" If Sherlock can't figure out who the murderer is, play again and the murderer gets to claim another victim. Play until Sherlock finds out who the murderer is. You can play again with a new Sherlock.

WHO'S WHO

Divide the agents into two teams. One team of agents leaves the room. They begin to return, one at a time, in this manner: Dressed as the ultimate secret agent, each has on a trench coat with the lapels up to conceal his face and dark sunglasses and a fedora so no one can see him. Disguising his voice, the first agent says, "You're under arrest." The other team gets one guess as to "who's who"—who the secret agent is. If they guess, the next agent appears in the doorway and that team gets a point. If not, the next one appears anyway but the team does not get a point. When everyone has had a turn, the teams switch. Whichever team gets the most guesses right (thereby the most points), wins.

Adam Kassan, on his tenth birthday, had a mystery party at which four carloads of children were driven around town. They picked up clues that Adam's mom, Ronnie, had placed in different public areas. As each clue was found, it led them to the next clue, until all the clues led them to the local pizza parlor for lunch.

SUPERSLEUTHS

Now that you have everyone's fingerprints, you are ready to put your superagents to work finding the birthday cake. The cake is hidden, as are the clues to find it. Each clue has something to do with items used to bake a cake. You give out the first clue to the secret agents and then they have to find all the other clues. As each clue is found, the agents must turn it over and make note of the letter on the back. When all the clues have been collected, the secret agents then must put together all the letters from the backs of the clues and then unscramble them to find out where the cake has been hidden.

CLUE #1
The first clue, the one that is given to the secret agents, says the following:

For your very first clue,
Here's what you do.
To get the right flower,
The garden you must scour.

This clue is found in a sack of *flour* hidden in the garden behind a potted plant; on the back of this clue, write the letter "**i**."
Make sure to mix it,
Or you're gonna have to fix it.
By hand or on auto,
"Do it quick" is our motto.

This clue is written, word by word, on each egg in the refrigerator; one egg has the letter "**z**" written on it.
Tick, Tock,
It's not a clock.
To bake a cake,
Takes time to make!

This clue is inside the bowl of an electric mixer; on the back of this clue is the letter "**f**."
Chickens do make 'em,
Be careful, don't break 'em,
Go look and be bold,
Where it's chilly and cold.

This clue is wrapped around a kitchen timer; on the back is the letter "**h**."
Be careful, be steady,
Because when it's ready,
It's hot to the touch,
But you need it so much!

CLUE #6

This clue is in the oven; on the back is the letter "**e**."
*For cakes, it's a must,
And for birthdays, we trust
You remember it well,
'Cause sweetness is swell.*

CLUE #10

This clue is hidden in the measuring cup in the laundry room; on the back is the letter "**r**."
*Use a stirrer, if you could,
That is made all of wood.
Turn it over; find a clue;
It's so easy for you to do!*

CLUE #7

This clue is in the sugar bowl; on the back is the letter "**r**."
*You mix it and shake it,
And just before you bake it
You pour it in this;
Just be careful, don't miss.*

CLUE #11

This clue is written on the back of a wooden mixing spoon; on the tip is the letter "**t**."
*In the garden, you will find
That I'm covered all in rind.
Peel me first, before you mix me;
The sooner you find me, the closer you'll be.*

CLUE #8

This clue is in the baking pan; on the back it has the letter "**e**."
*No birthday cake
Would you ever make
Without this light
That's in plain sight.*

CLUE #12

This clue is hidden in a bowl of apples in the garden; on the back is the letter "**e**."
*Some are hot; some are cool;
Not all cakes are baked, you fool!
Some have frosting, brown or white;
Others have snowy creamy delight.*

CLUE #9

This clue is hidden among candles; on the back is the letter "**e**."
*For good measure,
Look for treasure;
Not the usual place,
Remember, it's a race!*

CLUE #13

This clue is found taped to the outside of a can of whipped cream; on the back is the letter "**n**."

The final clue says:
*You now have the clues,
Tho' scrambled they be.
Just put them together;
You'll find it, you'll see!*

The children now have all the clues and all the letters; when unscrambled, they will spell "in the freezer." That's where the birthday ice cream cake is waiting!

THE MISSING LINK

Give each player a pencil and paper. To explain the game, write down a four- or five-word sentence, eliminate one letter wherever it appears in the sentence, and copy the remaining letters with no spaces between them that will show the various words. The object is to discover the missing letter and make sense out of the mass of letters. Tongue twisters work great because they repeat the same letter again and again.

For example, write down the following sentence:

"Sally slept in a slippery sleeping bag."

You write the above sentence on your paper. You then eliminate all the "S's" so now you have "ally lept in a lippery leeping bag." Now push these together and have each child write on his paper: "allyleptinalipperyleepingbag." The object is to find the missing letter, in this case an "S." Everyone gets to guess. Then play again.

Arrange a treasure hunt with clues for the guests to find their favors.

FAVORS

Dick Tracy comic books, magnifying glasses, their own fingerprints, and any other mystery paperbacks like *You the Jury* books, *You're the Detective*, and *Super Sleuth* (mini mysteries for you to solve)

MENU

With our "Mystery Menu," eating becomes a game. Prepare seven dishes for this meal and make a list for yourself of these dishes plus seven utensils found at a dinner table.

Examples (this list is not for the kids):

salad	fork
spaghetti	spoon
hot dog	napkin
bun	plate
punch	glass
Jell-O	toothpick
milk	knife

Each item has a code that gives you a clue to what it is (the right side of the list below is the menu you give out to each guest).

Here are some suggestions:

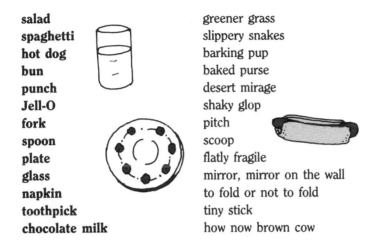

salad	greener grass
spaghetti	slippery snakes
hot dog	barking pup
bun	baked purse
punch	desert mirage
Jell-O	shaky glop
fork	pitch
spoon	scoop
plate	flatly fragile
glass	mirror, mirror on the wall
napkin	to fold or not to fold
toothpick	tiny stick
chocolate milk	how now brown cow

Each secret agent gets to pick six items from this list and that's his dinner. Because he doesn't know what anything is, he might end up with six utensils or six foods with no utensils or spaghetti with a toothpick!

ICE CREAM CAKE

Use a round glass dish with straight sides at least 4 inches deep. Begin by softening one kind of ice cream and spreading into the dish about 1½ inches high. You will need about one pint per flavor. Freeze until firm. Repeat the process with a different flavor for as many layers as will fit into your dish. When the "cake" is frozen, stick miniature magnifying glasses (plastic or glass) into the cake around the border. Write a secret birthday message with candies or frosting in the middle.

SHIPWRECKED

(Ages 7–12)

There is something about the idea of being shipwrecked on an island that has fascinated authors and readers alike. From Robinson Crusoe to The Swiss Family Robinson memorable escapades that illustrate courage, resilience, cleverness, and ingenuity, plus tales of high adventure, continue to enthrall us all. And so we've created a shipwrecked party that combines the aura and mystique of being marooned in an isolated place with the fun and excitement of a birthday party.

INVITATION

S.O.S. We're high and dry,
But we're awfully lonesome, Friday and I.
Please set sail for our little isle,
Pay us a visit, chat for a while.
We'll serve you roast parrot and barbecued goat,
Bread saved ten years from our shipwrecked boat,
Fresh rain water, select native roots,
Nonpoisonous wild vegetables and fruits.
We'll expect you at 12 on next Sunday noon;
If you meet any cannibals, try not to swoon.
Our longitude's 18th and Reed Street, quite near.
We'll light a smoke signal to help guide you here.

June 7th
at the
Reeds
555 Jane St.
12 to 2 pm
555-1234
R.S.V.P.

Fill a Ziploc bag halfway with sand, a few seashells, and one child's thong (Teresa Nathanson bought six pairs of the $.99 variety which made 12 invitations). You can Xerox the poem above (inspired by one a friend found in an attic from an old magazine published in 1936), inserting your place, date, time, and RSVP information and writing a P.S. on the bottom asking the kids to wear tattered clothes and a day's growth of beard. Glue onto a piece of brown paper that you include in the bag.

For Teresa Nathanson's treasure hunt at the beach, she sent invitations with burnt sides to look like they were antique (she dipped white paper in lemon juice and lit a match to the edges). Her treasure was an actual old trunk filled with pounds of candy and buried in the sand.

DECORATIONS

Cover the dining room (or picnic) table with a blue plastic cloth. As the centerpiece, mound the center of the table with sand, seashells, and rocks of various sizes. Make a lighthouse out of boxes (use a tube to make the tower, inserting a small flashlight at the top). Add a plastic galleon sitting on the edge of the sand as if it were in the blue water (the tablecloth). Add plastic palm trees along the edge of the sand.

GET READY!

1. Get a stopwatch.

2. Collect materials for the centerpiece: sand, seashells, rocks, a model galleon, a blue plastic tablecloth, plastic palm trees. Assemble the lighthouse.

3. Buy or borrow a plastic children's tunnel.

4. Find a life jacket.

5. Prepare for the "Survival Course."

6. Buy materials to make lanyards at a craft store.

7. Prepare for the "Shipwrecked Treasure Hunt." You'll need to write out the clues and hide them; also prepare a treasure chest filled with chocolate gold-covered coins and paper play money wrapped for each guest (these will be favors).

8. Prepare the instructions for "Old Salt's Relay."

9. Write the phrases for "Robinson Crusoe's Diary" on slips of paper. Xerox our story or write your own.

10. Use either the letters from a set of "Scrabble" or write letters of the alphabet (omitting "X") on 72 separate slips of paper for the "S.O.S." game.

11. Get prizes and favors.

ACTIVITIES

LANYARDS

1. Secure the key ring for easy weaving. Draw both strands of lace through the loop, making certain all ends are even.

2. Place strand No. 4 **under** strands No. 3 and No. 2 then back **over** No. 2 (under two strands and back over one!).

3. Put the No. 1 strand **under** No. 2 and No. 4, then back **over** No. 4. Pull your braids tight (don't let it twist!).

4. Place strand No. 3 **under** strands No. 4 and No. 1 then back **over** No. 1.

5. Now work on the left side repeating the above instructions.

6. Continue the braid until you have 12 inches of loose strand left. Make a knot at the end of the braid to finish the key ring (you can finish this at home).

S.O.S. MESSAGES TO RESCUERS

In order to get rescued, your survivors will need to send "telegrams." In a paper bag, place those 72 slips of paper with letters of the alphabet (remember, no "X")—or use the wooden letters from your board game "Scrabble" set. Begin by asking each guest to pick out a letter at random from the bag. When there are 12 letters selected, place in a row on the table or floor. Each child has a piece of paper and a pencil and must compose a telegram using words which begin with the letters in the order in which they appear. The word "stop" to mark the end of a thought or sentence can be placed anywhere. If you encourage the players to write telegrams that are funny and unexpected, the results will be memorable. Telegrams should relate to being shipwrecked.

Here's an example: Suppose the 12 letters chosen at random are: L F J U W B S P F L D S
A sample telegram could be:

> Little Freighter Jolted Under Water STOP Busy Staying
> Put STOP Friends Left Deep Suddenly STOP

A sample written by another child could be:

> Left Frisco Journeyed Under STOP Worried Because
> Stranded STOP Please Find Lost Deserters Soon

When everyone is done writing their telegrams, have them read them out loud. You can give the children a time limit to complete the game.

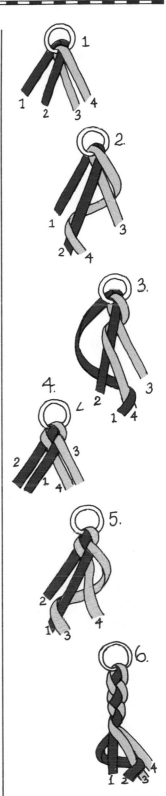

Copy these phrases on slips of paper:

A LOAF OF CORN BREAD
A CUP OF GOAT'S MILK
A TABLE AND CHAIR
A WILD GOAT
A DOVE
MY TENT
A PIECE OF CANVAS
A GOATSKIN
SOME OLD RAGS AND ROPE
A LOUD NOISE
A BIG TREE
MY FIELD GLASSES
A SHIP
30 CANNIBALS
A BONFIRE
DANDELIONS
A CHEST OF GOLD
SOME GUNPOWDER
ALL MY BELONGINGS
A STRONG FENCE
THE TOP OF THE HILL
A PILE OF STRAW

ROBINSON CRUSOE'S DIARY

This is a nonsense game that never fails to crack them up—the sillier, the better! Names of objects are written on slips of paper and dropped into a container. As "Mr. Crusoe" reads his diary, guests take turns drawing from the container to fill in the blanks.

Each "sailor" (or group of sailors) gets a copy of this story with the phrases missing. Each also gets to pick a slip of paper out of a bag. The sailors take turns reading a sentence from the story, and everyone tries to figure out which phrase from the slips of paper best fits that sentence.

Here's the story:

"This morning I woke up early and ate my breakfast, which consisted of _____ and _____. Afterward, I took my saw and hammer and built _____. Since I was shipwrecked and alone, I had to go hunting in the woods to see what I might have for lunch. I forgot my gun, so I had to capture _____ with my bare hands. I also tried to catch _____ but could not run fast enough. I went home to my cave, sat down in _____ and ate my lunch. Since my clothes were all lost at sea, I decided to make myself something to wear. I made a pretty neat hat from _____ and a coat out of _____. I decided to wrap my feet in _____. Suddenly, I heard a _____ and rushed out and climbed into _____. I looked through _____ just in case I might see _____. I didn't, but there on the beach I saw _____ dancing in wild glee around _____. Running up the trail toward my hideout was _____ crying out and looking very frightened. I hid the poor thing behind _____. I then found my gun, loaded it with _____ and stood guard over _____. When it seemed safe, I got busy and built _____ all around _____. Then I finally lay down in my comfortable bed, made of _____, and slept soundly."

OLD SALT'S RELAY

Divide your shipwrecked "sailors" into two groups. The first players in both teams listen for the first command. They must perform it while running across the room (or yard) and back where each must tag the next player. Instruction #1 is for the first "sailor," #2 for the second, and so on.

Instruction #1—Walk with a sailor's roll

#2—Hop on one leg as a one-legged sailor would

#3 & #4—One pushes as the other lies down (it's as if he were pushing a barge across the water)

#5—Blow a foghorn (with cupped hands)

#6—Run for your life jacket and put it on and take it off

#7—Swim for shore

#8—Swim the backstroke

#9—Drag an anchor (pull the left leg along)

#10—Whistle or hum as you row your boat

SHIPWRECKED TREASURE HUNT

Have the whole group of shipwrecked guests look for the treasure together. Write clues that lead the guests from one place to another and place them in accessible areas such as:

- on a bush under a window
- in the end of a drain pipe
- under porch furniture or wrapped around a leg
- in the outdoor grill
- tied to the swing set
- in a tree—you have to climb a few feet
- on a fence post
- in the mailbox
- under the garbage can lid
- tied to the bike
- under the door mat
- under a flower pot

The prize is a treasure chest filled with chocolate gold-covered coins, paper play money, and play jewelry.

Nancy Shockman loves to give surprise parties with this special twist: She invites all the guests but the birthday girl or boy to her house for tea. There the kids decide what each friend will give the birthday child and organize a treasure hunt with clues leading to the different gifts. Come the day of the party, the birthday child must go on a treasure hunt to find those birthday gifts.

SURVIVAL COURSE

Set up a challenge course in the backyard for shipwrecked guests to maneuver. Increase the difficulty of the tasks for older children. At each stop, have a sign post with the name of the challenge. Each part of the course is simple to set up, yet challenging and fun to attempt. Let everyone know that their run through the course will be timed, and assign the stopwatch to an adult.

At the first corner, mark a 5-foot square patch of ground with four wood posts. Run a piece of rope from post to post. Place a sign calling this the "Island Corral" and mark it "Start." Each player must gallop through the corral as if he were a horse and all the way to a nearby tree, on which there is a sign saying, "Hangman's Tree: Run Around Three," meaning that the player must run around the tree three times.

The next stop is a cloth-covered table on which there is a pitcher of lemonade, some small paper cups, and a sign that says, "Nature's Watering Hole: Take One Drink." The player must pour and drink a glass of lemonade (he is not allowed to

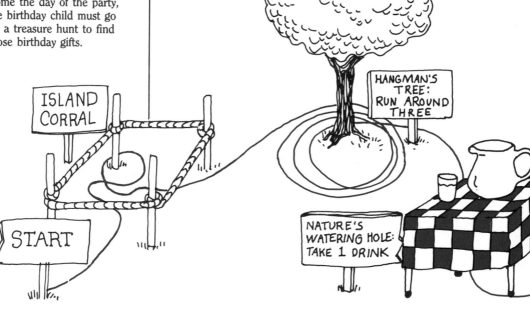

spill any!). At the next stop is a tunnel, which he has to crawl through; this sign says, "Crawl for Your Life."

Next there is a blanket under another tree and a smaller sign that says, "Rest for the Weary: Take a Nap"; the player rests to the count of 10, and then quickly runs to the next stop, which is a barrel (either a wood barrel or a wooden box with both sides cut off). The sign says, "Roll for Your Supper," and the player crawls into the barrel or box and rolls over to the last stop, which is a line of four plastic bowls filled with water set in a row about one foot apart. This sign says, "Hop Just for Fun and You Are Done!" The player must now hop on one foot over the bowls, back and forth, and then make a dash across the finish line.

Since each guest is timed, the winner is the one to finish in the shortest amount of time. You can give out first, second, and third prizes. If you divide your guests into two relay teams, start each team at opposite ends of the course. Player number two on each team starts as number one finishes.

ROLL FOR YOUR SUPPER

REST FOR THE WEARY: TAKE A NAP

FINISH

CRAWL FOR YOUR LIFE

HOP JUST FOR FUN AND YOU ARE DONE!

SING-A-LONG

While lunch is under way, hold a sing-a-long. Either provide the words verbally or on paper to such songs as "Row, Row, Row Your Boat," "Anchors Away," "Blow the Man Down," and other nautical songs.

FAVORS

Lanyards, plastic treasure chests with candy, fake pebble candies, saltwater taffy

MENU

Tuna Salad in cucumber or pineapple boats with pirate flags
Watermelon
Water

See recipes on page 243.

ISLAND CAKE

Use the **Perfect Chocolate Cake** recipe, page 224. You can use a plain round cake pan but, believe it or not, the shape of the superhero pan from Wilton's looks like a rocky island (see Resources, page 249). Place the cake on a large piece of foam board or stiff cardboard. Frost with **Seven-Minute Frosting**, page 229, colored green. Add small candy rocks, walnuts, plastic palm trees, a small plastic boat, and chocolate shells. Surround with blue **Seven-Minute Frosting.**

SOCCER

(Ages 8 and up)

A s you can imagine, Marc Gilbar, at eleven, is pretty much a veteran at creating and giving great birthday parties, but even he was not quite sure how to pull off a soccer party.

Marc invited both boys and girls and, in fact, 36 kids came. This is a hefty number of kids to have at a birthday party, particularly since soccer teams only have 11 players on each team. But here the rules were different. The 36 children were divided into two teams of 17 players each, plus 2 goalies. Each team had both strong and experienced players and kids who just enjoyed the game. (Marc also chose the goalies and during the game other kids tried playing this position.) The point in this massive soccer game was just to score goals. The players had no positions—they just ran around the field attempting to get a goal for their teams.

This party was a smash and has been repeated by many a soccer fanatic!

INVITATION

A soccer cartoon which you Xerox and blow up (you can color on it). Fill in with your own words:

Send the invitation in a large white envelope onto which you can stamp soccer balls with a rubber stamp.

DECORATIONS

This party is held outdoors at a soccer field or in a park, so your decorating skills aren't really needed here. However, you may want to mark the spot with a bunch of balloons. You can turn white balloons into soccer balls by drawing black lines around each in an appropriate pattern.

You will also need to mark the goal areas. Use two plastic garbage cans, 20 feet apart, on each side of your soccer field. The space between them becomes the goal. If you are playing on a regular soccer field, the goals will already be up. However, we have found that during the soccer season the fields always seem to be used for soccer practices or games, so we ended up using a park.

Each team will wear the soccer shirts you ordered or you can choose to assign colors to each team and ask them to wear that color to the party.

GET READY!

1. Buy one plastic sports water bottle for each guest, and write each child's name on it. During the game, they can be filled with water or Gatorade and can be taken home as favors.

2. Order T-shirts for your teams, coaches, and goalies through Offsides, a soccer store in Los Angeles (see Resources, page 251). They will make you T-shirts with an embroidered soccer ball on them for the players (get two different colors, one for each team), matching ones for the coaches (with "Coach" written on them), goalie T-shirts in yellow with a black number "1," and ones for the referees in black with a big soccer ball on them. Call at least a month ahead.

3. Buy or borrow two soccer balls, #4 or #5, and one 24-inch Physio-ball, cones, and large plastic garbage cans for goals.

4. Order posters of soccer players for favors (also from Offsides); ask for close-outs as they often cost only pennies apiece.

5. Buy rubber stamps in the shapes of soccer balls.

6. Use balloons to mark your spot at the park.

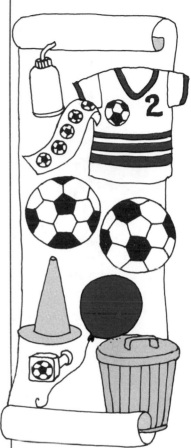

ACTIVITIES

The main activity, obviously, is playing soccer. First give out the water bottles to each child.

Before playing any sport, it is important for the kids to warm up. Kids from local high school or college teams love to participate in young soccer games, and are the most enthusiastic teachers who love to show kids all kinds of tricks of the trade. Start by running around the track and then doing stretches. Then have a *soccer relay*. Divide the group into two teams that line up next to each other; each player dribbles the ball to a cone about 20 yards away and then passes it back to the next player.

For the next exercise, set up the cones on a slalom course and have the kids push the ball with their feet in and around the cones. The third exercise is actually a race where the first player passes the ball over his head to the person behind him, who then passes it under his legs to the person behind him, who then passes it over his head, and so on. The first team to finish this back and forth game wins.

Now everyone should be ready to play soccer. For the first 15 minutes, everyone plays with one soccer ball. Then, throw a second ball into the field. The added challenge of looking for two balls in different areas on the field, and trying to reach them to shoot for a goal, makes for a hilarious game. The second ball somehow makes the game less competitive, the skill level less important, and the entire game more fun. In fact, you can even add a third ball at a later time.

By this time the kids will have been playing for about 30 minutes. You could now replace the two (or three) soccer balls with one large 24-inch rubber Physio-ball. This is a ball originally used in gymnastics and for physical therapy, but because it is so large, it has become a favorite for kids to play with. This surprise element will really get everyone's attention.

Once the kids are done with the Physio-ball, they will have been playing for about an hour. This is a good time to serve lunch. Then, after lunch, they will be anxious to get back to playing soccer. Have them again play with the two soccer balls and then end up with one.

FAVORS

Plastic bottles, T-shirts, posters

MENU

Pizza (have it delivered)
Boxed or canned drinks

Remember how each child, when faced with the prospect of getting a slice of cake, always asks, "Can I get the one with the rose on it?" or "Can I get the one with the balloon on it?" Whatever decorative toys you put on a birthday cake, place enough so each guest can get one.

SOCCER FIELD CAKE

Use **Sylvia's Wonder Cake** recipe, page 227. Bake the cake in a 9 × 11-inch pan. Frost with green-tinted **Orange Cream Frosting**, page 229, and sprinkle with green shredded coconut. Using frosting in a tube, draw a soccer field (see drawing). Add plastic soccer balls and players. You can make goal posts with two straws at each end and some net fabric.

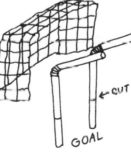

← CUT

GOAL

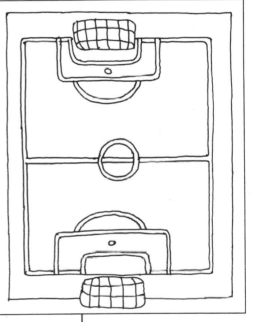

167

SO WHAT'S VS. BIG DEALS

(Ages 9 and up)

C ompetitive sports-minded kids will love this party. It combines physical and mental games with a little "attitude" as the two teams square off against each other. Encourage the players to develop some degree of boastful support for their respective teams. They can even create histories for each team. For example, the "So What's" could be last year's champions who won at the last minute in a hair-raising, nail-biting tie-breaker. This year, the "Big Deals" are out for revenge to rescue their honor. Giving the teams this kind of adversary attitude within a "school spirit" atmosphere will give the party an extra exciting edge.

INVITATION

For this "newspaper" invitation, cut out the name of your town's newspaper and use it as the headline. Then either on a typewriter, computer, or with press on letters, write out the headline "Big Deals Face Off Against So What's." The smaller invitation copy can by typewritten once and then Xeroxed and pasted on the same page. Xerox as many times as you need invitations.

The Birthday Times

JANUARY 12TH, 1992   CIRCULATION 15 ☆

BIG DEALS FACE OFF AGAINST SO WHAT'S

You have been chosen to join the competition between the SO WHAT'S and the BIG DEALS

at a major celebration of LUKE JONES' 11th Birthday on January 12th at 222 Morgan Lane Sign in at 555-1234 at 2 o'clock SHARP!

DECORATIONS

Collect sports posters and pennants, including hockey, baseball, basketball, tennis, soccer, and football, and post around the party room.

GET READY!

1. Buy trophies for award ceremony, and other prizes and favors.

2. Order pencils with the teams' names on them (see Resources, page 249).

3. Order two kinds of hats, enough for each team. Funny ones are great, such as beanies with propellers, skimmers or felt Alpine hats (see Resources, page 249).

4. Type the cheers on pieces of paper so you can give them out to the two teams. If they will make up their own at the party, have paper and pencil so they can write them down.

5. Collect a bunch of paper plates for the "Discus Throw."

6. Buy balloons for the "Windbag Wheelay."

7. Collect two one-gallon plastic milk bottles and a bag of dry white beans.

8. Prepare the sports trivia game "Sports Smarts."

9. Locate a card table and tape a miniature cereal box (with the long end cut out) at each end for "Table Soccer." You will need large straws and Ping-Pong balls. You can draw soccer ball patterns on them with a black marker.

10. Find a shoe box and cut out ten holes big enough for marbles to roll through (see drawing on page 172) for "Mini Bowl." Number the holes with numbers from 1 to 10. You will need at least four dozen marbles (be prepared to lose some).

ACTIVITIES

This party is built around the competition between two teams—the "So What's" and the "Big Deals."

CHEERS

As the guests arrive, make team assignments and teach the team cheers (although the teams might prefer to make up their own).

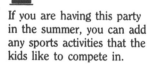

If you are having this party in the summer, you can add any sports activities that the kids like to compete in.

Or

Two bits, four bits,
Six bits, a dollar;
All for Big Deals,
Stand up and holler.

We are the So What's
And we couldn't be prouder,
So you'd better hear us,
And yell a little louder.

DISCUS THROW

Each member of the two teams throws a discus (actually, a paper plate) as far as he can. Mark where it falls. Each player gets three tries and the best one counts. This is the one you measure and record. Calculate how far each team's throws went by adding up its players' best throws. The team with the highest score gets 250 points.

WINDBAG WHEELAY

In this event each player blows a balloon across the room or yard (no hands allowed). As soon as it crosses the finish line, he has to pop it (no pins allowed). Only when the balloon pops can the next player have his turn. The first team to finish gets 100 points.

SHOT PUT

For this event you need two empty one-gallon plastic milk bottles and a bowl of small dry white beans. Each player on each team gets five white beans. Each empty milk bottle is placed on the floor in back of a straight-back chair. A player sits on his knees on the chair, facing the back of the chair with his elbow resting on the top of the back of the chair (if he looks down, he sees the milk bottle). He then tries to drop the beans into the milk bottle. The team with the most beans in their milk bottle after everyone gets a turn receives 100 points.

The Kassan and the Marks children are best friends, so it was no surprise when they decided to give a party together when Alex Kassan and Jane Marks turned 12. What was a surprise was that they invited the boys to come as cheerleaders and the girls to come as football players and proceeded to play games in these exchanged roles!

UP, UP, AND AWAY

One person from each team joins another person from the other team to form a pair. Each pair, in turn, sits on the ground, back to back, arms folded in front of them. The trick is for each player to get up without unfolding his arms. The contestant that makes it up first gets 10 points. Each team then adds its members' points to their total.

TABLE SOCCER

At the indoor soccer table you prepared, have each member of each team play against a member of the other. The trick is to blow the "soccer ball" (the Ping-Pong ball) into the team's goal at the other end of the table, using a straw. If you blow the ball off the table, you must start again from your end. Each couple gets two minutes to score as many goals (one point per goal) as they can. At the end, the team with the most goals wins!

How about a soft drink challenge? Test the kids' taste buds by setting up glasses full of different popular drinks and having them identify what's in what.

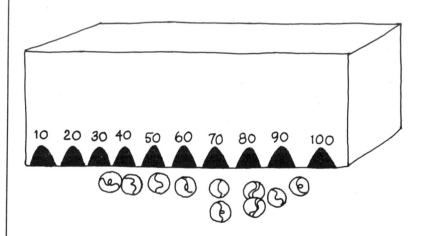

MINI BOWL

Place your shoe box with the holes cut out at the end of a long dining room, card, or picnic table. Tape the back side down so it will be stable. Hand out a dozen marbles to the two players from the opposing teams. Each player takes turns trying to roll as many marbles as he can into the holes. Remember that each hole has a number on top of it so the score will vary, depending on which hole the marble goes into. Have someone adding the scores and keeping careful track. The team with the highest score wins!

SPORTS SMARTS

This is a battle of sports trivia. In order to make this as fair as possible, combine questions about many sports rather than just one or two. Try to include questions about football, baseball, basketball, soccer, tennis, golf, hockey, bowling, boxing, swimming, horse racing, track, fencing (is it possible we forgot one?).

Make a list of 25 questions. Direct the first question towards the Big Deals. If they can't answer it, the So What's get a chance. The second question goes to the So What's first, and the game continues back and forth like this. Each correct answer gets 50 points. Add the total points for each team at the end.

The best way to do this is to make up questions about sports with your child. However, here are some that you can use as guidelines:

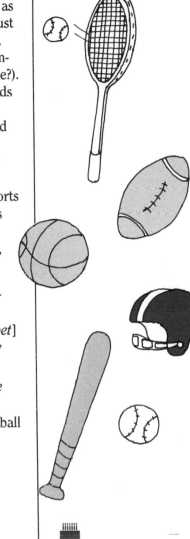

1. In what sport would you say "on guard" and "thrust?" [*fencing*]
2. How many points do you get for a touchdown in football? [*6*]
3. What's a bookie? [*a person with whom you place a bet*]
4. In what sport would you use the term "squeeze play?" [*baseball*]
5. Where is a New Year's Day football game played? [*the Rose Bowl*]
6. What does the umpire call at the beginning of a baseball game? [*play ball*]
7. Who is heavier, a bantam weight or a featherweight? [*featherweight*]
8. For what sport do you get the Curtis Cup? [*golf*]
9. What sport do you play the U.S. Open? [*tennis*]
10. In what sport is "offsides" a common term? [*soccer, football, and hockey*]
11. Where is baseball's Hall of Fame? [*Cooperstown, NY*]
12. "Grounders" was the early form of which of our sports? [*baseball*]
13. Which swimmer won the most gold medals in the 1972 Olympics? [*Mark Spitz*]
14. Which woman tennis player has won the most titles? [*Martina Navratilova*]

If you have access to a swimming pool, have some relay races between the teams in which the swimmers try different strokes.

To create a special award as a prize, Phyllis Wolfe spray-paints empty used Mrs. Butterworth syrup bottles with gold paint.

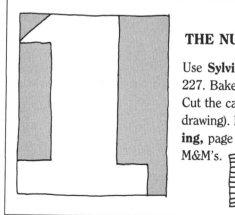

MAJOR DEBATE

Each team retires to a separate room where the members must come up with written reasons as to why they are better than the other team. They must make a speech that takes no longer than three minutes. Then the teams join together to give their speeches in a "debate." After hearing the other team's speech, the teams retire to another room where they have to come up with a rebuttal.

AWARD CEREMONY

Give out prizes and awards to the winning team in a ceremony.

FAVORS

Funny hats for the teams, any sports paraphernalia (posters, pennants, baseball or basketball cards, etc.), personalized team pencils

MENU

The losing team serves the winning team lunch:
Hot Dogs or Peanut Chicken
American Picnic Potato Salad
Corn Muffins
Lemonade

See recipes on pages 243–245.

THE NUMBER ONE CAKE

Use **Sylvia's Wonder Cake** recipe, page 227. Bake the cake in a 9 × 11-inch pan. Cut the cake into a large number one (see drawing). Frost with **Seven-Minute Frosting,** page 229, and cover completely with M&M's.

STARGAZING PARTY

(Ages 10 and up)

J ennifer Brokaw remembers being fascinated with the heavens as a ten-year-old. She suggested stargazing as a party theme and a great way to make your child feel he's the center of the universe. This party combines outdoor meteoric adventures with an indoor, homemade planetarium for fun and games. The first reminder from Jennifer is to carefully choose the date of the party to coincide with a less than full moon (too much moonlight will mask many of the stars). Check with your favorite book on astronomy (one good one is *Find the Constellations* by H. A. Rey, see Resources, page 251) to see what stars should be visible at what times of the year, then hope for a cloudless night. Should the stars be hidden, there will still be plenty to do in your own indoor planetarium. It's bound to be a stellar evening!

INVITATION

On a glossy blue card, draw a constellation (like the Big Dipper, as above) with a silver felt-tip pen and add some star stickers at different points. To the right, write the following, also in the silver pen:

FIND THE BIG DIPPER, ORION'S BELT & MORE AT JOANNA'S PLANETARIUM we are celebrating her eleventh birthday Saturday, February 10th GALAXY TOUR BEGINS AT 8:30 PM RETURN AT 11:00 PM stargazers reply 555-1234

JOANNA 11

DECORATIONS

Stargazing under the stars requires no decorations, but the indoor planetarium should have cutout stars, planets, and moons all over the walls and ceiling. A rotating light will simulate movement in the skies and create an ethereal atmosphere.

GET READY!

1. Order the decorations (see Resources, page 251, for distributors): ★ Glow in the Dark Planetarium (500 self-adhesive stars, planets, comets, and meteors) ★ Glow in the Dark Stargazer Constellation and Solar System (Stick-ems) ★ Glow in the Dark Moon, Earth, Saturn ★ Inflatable Celestial Globe ★ Solar System Mobile ★ Telescopes ★ Super Star Machine (a portable planetarium)

2. Convert a relatively small room into your own planetarium. You can cover the walls with dark blue plastic tablecloths. Then place all those glow-in-the-dark stars, constellations, planets, and moons all over the cloths for an instant feeling of being out under the stars. The Super Star Machine, when plugged in, projects 300 stars, 31 constellations, and 3 exploding star fields, and includes a book, a narrated cassette, and a pointer. You can also hang a mirrored ball from the center of the ceiling for more drama.

3. Contact the Hayden Planetarium in New York or Griffith Park Observatory in Los Angeles and ask for a map for stargazing. They carry poster-size maps to help everyone identify the constellations.

4. Prepare small flashlights with red cellophane (gel) paper covers.

5. Find a hill around your home, either in a park or in a friend's backyard (one where there are no street lights around is best, because they detract from being able to see the stars). The morning of the party, stake out the directions (north, south, east, west) so the spot will be ready for your stargazers.

6. Borrow as many binoculars as you can. Try to have at least one telescope.

7. Organize small notepads and markers for drawing.

8. Find a whistle for the "Apollo Countdown."

9. Prepare pieces of paper with names of stars and planets for the "Star Shuffle" game. You will need safety pins so the kids can pin them on their shirts. You will also need two boards, each approximately 8 feet long by 8 inches wide, for the kids to stand on.

10. Find a scarf for use as a blindfold and a bunch of small items to be used in the "Astronaut IQ" game.

11. Write out the tongue twisters and Xerox so everyone can read them easily for "The Terminator."

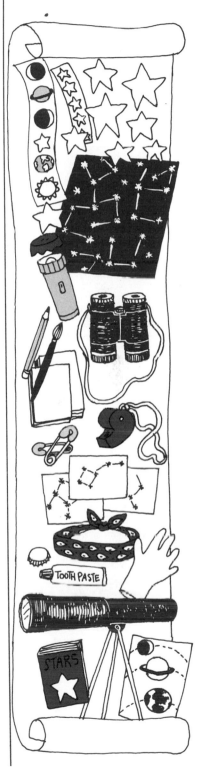

THE BIG DIPPER

ORION

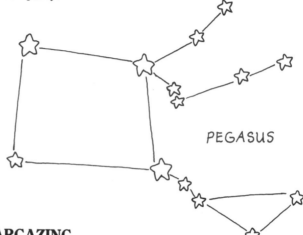

ACTIVITIES

This party is divided into two parts. First, everyone goes to the hill or to the backyard to stargaze and identify the heavens (a hill makes a better observation site because you get a clear view of the sky when you are higher up). This will take about an hour. For the second part, everyone returns home to the "planetarium" for other games and activities and a late-night supper. This party, because it begins at night, also works as a slumber party.

PEGASUS

STARGAZING

Distribute charts or night sky maps to the amateur astronomers as they arrive so they can begin immediately to identify constellations. Have some extra hats, sweaters, and even gloves because it is somehow always chillier than you expect. As you travel to your stargazing destination, have some interesting facts to tell the kids about the heavens (see our tips).

When you arrive at the site, give each child a red-gel-paper-covered flashlight (the red light, as opposed to white light, will not interfere with your newly adjusted night sight). It takes the eyes about 15 minutes to adjust to the darkness, so this is a good time to work on the flashlights and get familiar with their star maps.

Hand out binoculars, pads, and markers. Begin to identify stars, constellations, other planets, and the moon and its craters. If you have one powerful telescope, organize turns for looking at the heavenly bodies up close. Once they begin to actually identify what they are seeing in the sky, they can record or draw their findings in their notepads.

178

Here are some tips for successful stargazing:

- If you're using a telescope, it's worth mounting it on a tripod for a steadier view.
- With good binoculars, you can see about ten times more stars, many details on the moon, and even some of the planets like Jupiter.
- A refractor telescope is easier to use because you don't have to align any mirrors.
- Many stars are seasonal (you will see different ones each month). Check with your astronomical guide.
- It's not as hard to spot shooting stars (which are actually meteors) as you think. So keep on the lookout.
- It's easy to find the planets in the sky: In fact, if you see a bright star which you can't find on your map, you're probably looking at a planet. There are five planets you can easily see through binoculars: Saturn, Venus, Jupiter, Mars, and Mercury.

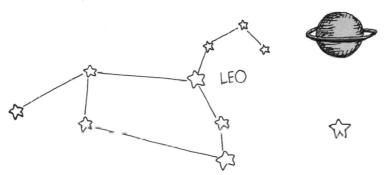

- The moon is the easiest thing to see in the sky. It has no light of its own, reflecting the sun's light, and is so visible because it is our closest neighbor in space. Did you ever wonder about the other side of the moon? Well, you're not going to see it tonight or any other night, because you always see the same side of the moon from the earth (the moon always keeps that same side toward the earth as it rotates around it). You can easily see the craters on the moon as well as the "man in the moon."
- The brightest planet in the sky is Venus.
- Ever wonder why stars twinkle? They only twinkle when you look at them from earth because it is the earth's atmosphere that makes them flicker. That's how you tell a star from a planet: planets don't twinkle.

Any or all of the following books are fascinating for kids to read for a simple understanding of astronomy (see Resources, page 251):

Find the Constellations by H. A. Rey. A wonderful guide with excellent drawings.

Glow in the Dark Constellations: A Field Guide for Young Stargazers by C. E. Thompson. Definitions and explanations of each constellation.

The Young Astronomer by Sheila Snowden. The best all-around primer. This is a superb introduction to astronomy and stargazing which makes the information absolutely mesmerizing. If your guests can look through this book before the party, it will add a whole new dimension to their enjoyment.

Astronomy Activity Book by Dennis Schatz (with a Star Finder Wheel).

Sun, Stars & Planets, by Tom Stacy.

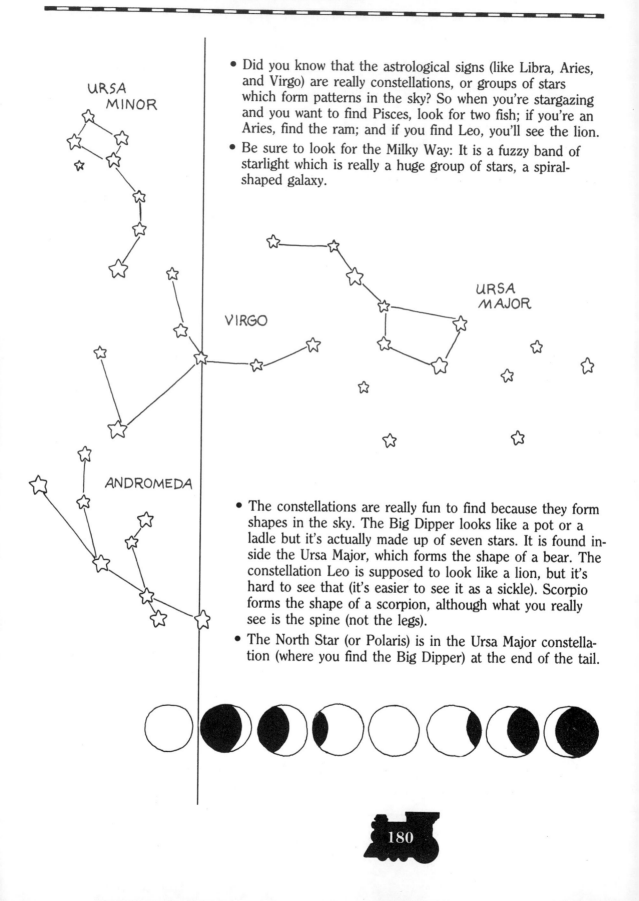

- Did you know that the astrological signs (like Libra, Aries, and Virgo) are really constellations, or groups of stars which form patterns in the sky? So when you're stargazing and you want to find Pisces, look for two fish; if you're an Aries, find the ram; and if you find Leo, you'll see the lion.

- Be sure to look for the Milky Way: It is a fuzzy band of starlight which is really a huge group of stars, a spiral-shaped galaxy.

URSA MINOR

VIRGO

URSA MAJOR

ANDROMEDA

- The constellations are really fun to find because they form shapes in the sky. The Big Dipper looks like a pot or a ladle but it's actually made up of seven stars. It is found inside the Ursa Major, which forms the shape of a bear. The constellation Leo is supposed to look like a lion, but it's hard to see that (it's easier to see it as a sickle). Scorpio forms the shape of a scorpion, although what you really see is the spine (not the legs).

- The North Star (or Polaris) is in the Ursa Major constellation (where you find the Big Dipper) at the end of the tail.

PLANETARIUM FUN

After returning home, you can start playing games in the planetarium that you have created. For some of the games you can keep the lights off so the children feel as if they are sitting under the stars. Other games, however, require that you be able to see.

APOLLO COUNTDOWN

This game originated with our friend Tim Green, who has entertained many a child with this challenge. The leader, who has a whistle, teaches the others a code of commands, which they have to memorize. For example, one blow means they have to stand still; two blows mean stand on one leg; three mean put one hand above your head; four mean jump up and down; five mean sit down; and so on. When the game begins, the leader blows the whistle for any code he desires, and the children must perform what the code means. You're out if you get it wrong!

STAR SHUFFLE

Divide the children into two teams. Each team has to stand on one of the boards you prepared. Give each child a star-related name (Little Dipper, Big Dipper, Leo, Orion, Virgo, Ursa Minor, Ursa Major, Moon, Sun, Pluto, Mars, Jupiter), which you have written on a piece of paper, to pin on their shirts. The trick is to make each team alphabetize its "stars" (thus rearranging the bodies) without stepping off the board.

In celebration of their ninth birthday, Nell Otto's twins made the inevitable lemonade stand where they sold fresh, homemade lemonade and homemade cookies. The difference was that their sign said, "All proceeds go to the Brick Church School." They made a ton of money and had a very happy birthday!

BLACK HOLE

Show the kids a drawing of a simple figure such as a star, a hat, a car. Give each child a piece of paper and a pencil. Now usher them into the planetarium, shut off all the lights, and ask them to draw what they saw in the dark. This game can be repeated again and again.

THE TERMINATOR

You might think this game is called "The Terminator" because it's so hard. That's one explanation, but it also has this name because the "terminator" is actually an existing phenomenon on the moon—it is the line between the sunlit half and the dark half of the moon. The old tongue twister challenge, when performed in the planetarium, rises to new heights! Try these, or make up your own:

Ten terrible twerpy teens told Taurus tales.
Seasonal satellites searched sun scorched skies.
Mystery moon magnified Mercury's meteor mysteriously.
Pluto's purple people painted planets.
Careless comets carve curvy curly craters.

ASTRONAUT IQ

In the planetarium, divide the guests into couples. One couple at a time plays this game. Have each take off their shoes and socks so they are barefoot. Blindfold each member of the couple and have them sit facing each other, toes touching. Give them five objects (such as a bottle cap, toothpaste, a sponge, a rubber glove, an eraser), one at a time, and ask them to identify them with their toes. The person who guesses the most items wins.

FAVORS

Mini flashlights, glow in the dark stars, any books on stargazing and astronomy, star and planet stickers

An easy to handle modeling material, Fimo can be used for crafts, projects, sculpture, or jewelry (see Resources, page 250). Hardened in your kitchen oven, it can then be carved, filed, cut, and painted. It's watertight and washable. Night Glow Fimo glows in the dark.

MENU

Angel Hair Primavera
Stellar Salad

See recipes on page 245.

STAR CAKE

Use **The All-Around Birthday Cake** recipe, page 226. Bake in a star pan (see Resources, page 249). Frost with **Seven-Minute Frosting,** page 229, and sprinkle with colored sugar. Use candles that sparkle (they look like fireworks).

STEGOSAURUS & FRIENDS

(Ages 4–7)

I magine what it was like in prehistoric times when the earth was inhabited by the dinosaurs, lizard-like in appearance and awesome in size. They must have been something, because today, at least 200 million years later, we are still captivated by these extraordinary creatures. Believe it or not, rattling off names like tyrannosaurus, dimetrodon, pterodactyl, and stegosaurus is a cinch for many a six-year-old. For them, and for all the other young paleontologists in their crowd, here is a very do-able dinosaur party.

INVITATION

Xerox the egg and dinosaur and follow the other instructions here.

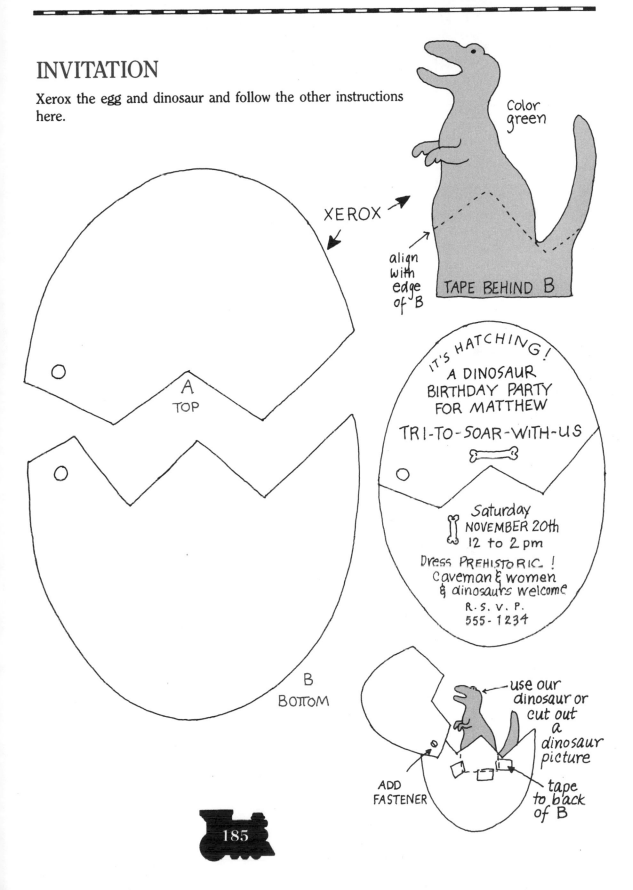

Color green

XEROX

align with edge of B

TAPE BEHIND B

A
TOP

B
BOTTOM

IT'S HATCHING!
A DINOSAUR
BIRTHDAY PARTY
FOR MATTHEW

TRI-TO-SOAR-WITH-US

Saturday
NOVEMBER 20th
12 to 2 pm

Dress PREHISTORIC!
Caveman & women
& dinosaurs welcome
R.S.V.P.
555-1234

use our
dinosaur or
cut out
a
dinosaur
picture

tape
to back
of B

ADD
FASTENER

185

DECORATIONS

You can use the stencils from the dinosaur stencil book in two ways: Take out the cutouts and hang them around or spray paint images of dinosaurs using the stencils. Hang the inflatable dinosaurs around the room. Put tiny plastic dinosaurs all around the table covered with a white tablecloth with large rocks in the center and ferns. Place the dinosaur egg cakes all around the table.

Draw huge dinosaur tracks on paper and tape them going up the walls.

GET READY!

1. Buy large plastic eggs that come apart and a plastic pail for each guest.

2. Buy the *Dinosaurs Punchout Stencils Book* by A. G. Smith (see Resources, page 252; it has 16 different dinosaurs). Place the insides of the stencils on chairs for the game "Extinction." Tape the *Flintstones* theme song.

3. Purchase plywood and tempera paints; cut out a 4-foot × 8-foot × ¼-inch dinosaur shape.

4. Buy T-shirts.

5. Assemble big pieces of clay and/or plaster of paris.

6. Order dinosaur books (see Resources, page 252).

7. Buy plastic dinosaurs. They come in bags of 50 so you can put a couple of hundred on the table.

8. Order inflatable dinosaurs from The Nature Company (see Resources, page 252). You can order inflatable dinosaurs such as tyrannosaurus rex (30 inches high) and pteranodon (with a 96-inch wingspan); they also carry "Make Your Own Dinosaurs" models.

9. Soak big pieces of chalk overnight. You will also need newspaper, sponges, and hair spray for the chalk paintings.

10. Organize large rocks and ferns for the centerpiece. You can also use large pieces of foam rubber sprayed with stone spray that will make them look like boulders.

ACTIVITIES

DINOSAUR EGG HUNT

Get large plastic eggs, fill them with candy and plastic dinosaurs, and hide them all over the house. The guest who finds the most wins. To up the ante, hide one "gold" egg, which yields a special prize. Give each guest a plastic pail to carry the eggs.

PAINT A GIANT DINOSAUR

Jim Chuda, an architect friend who lives in Los Angeles, drew a big dinosaur on a 4-foot × 8-foot × ¼-inch piece of plywood (cut by the lumberyard) for his daughter Colette's third birthday. As guests arrived at the party, they all helped to paint the dinosaur (they used tempera paints, as they are easy to wash off and come in large squeezable bottles) with brushes or sponges. It was an activity that lasted throughout the party as some kids returned again and again to add their extra touches. The many layered result was a masterpiece (which Jim recorded with a Polaroid picture for each child).

There are history and science museums with special dinosaur exhibits in the following cities: Philadelphia and Pittsburgh, PA; New York, Buffalo, and Richfield Springs, NY; New Haven, CT; Princeton, NJ; Chicago, IL; Ft. Worth and Houston, TX; Milwaukee, WI; St. Paul, MN; Iowa City, IA; Ann Arbor, MI; Los Angeles and Berkeley, CA; Bozeman, MT; Ossineke, MI; Cleveland and Cincinnati, OH; Salt Lake City and Provo, UT; Oakley, KS; Kadoka, SD; Carlsbad, NM; Denver, CO; Laramie, WY.

T-SHIRT

Using the dinosaur stencils, paint dinosaurs on T-shirts. You can have each child write his own name on the T-shirt or you can have all the children autograph each shirt.

A great book for favors: *Colossal Fossils: Dinosaur Riddles*, ed. by Charles Keller, Simon & Schuster, Little Simon (see Resources, page 252).

You can show *Flintstones* cartoons or *The Land Before Time*.

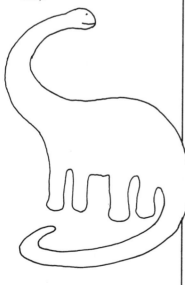

We assume that if your child chooses to have this dinosaur party, then he must be pretty sophisticated in his knowledge of the world of dinosaurs. For those dino-fanatics, here are some games to play at this party that will also teach them more about those times. Dinosaurs and Things is a best-selling board game by Aristoplay; Dinosaurs and Prehistoric Life is called an IQ game; and there is also Dino Dominoes by Ravensburger (see Resources, page 252).

DINOSAUR FOSSILS

Make dinosaur fossils. You can have the kids make imprints with plastic dinosaurs into flats of clay and let dry. You can also make fossils out of plaster of paris. For this method, stir one cup of plaster of paris into ⅔ cup of water. With a wooden spoon, mix it until thick and smooth. You have to work quickly because plaster of paris hardens fast. When the mixture is smooth, take a soup spoon and drop the plaster like cookies onto a cookie sheet covered with waxed paper. After about five minutes, the plaster of paris will harden a little, at which point you can press the plastic dinosaurs into the mixture to make an imprint. If you let it harden, you can then draw a footprint in it with a metal nail.

PLASTER   CLAY

WET DINOS

For another painting game (you can also substitute this for the "Paint a Giant Dinosaur" activity) have the children make wet chalk paintings. Take big pieces of chalk that you have soaked overnight. Put a few in plastic bowls all around the table. Give each child a piece of newspaper and have him wet it with some sponges. The children can then paint the newspaper with the wet chalk for a very pretty picture with lots of texture to it. When it's dry, overlay large stencils of dinosaurs over the painting and cut the dino shapes out. To set the chalk in place, spray the finished product with hair spray.

CAVEMAN'S HIDEAWAY

To play this version of the old favorite "Sardines," the players gather in one room. The birthday child is the first to hide in the secret hideaway or a cave where the cavemen hide from the dinosaurs (this can be a closet, the space under a bed, or a pantry). Each child, one at a time, must find the caveman's hideaway and joins the first child, then the second, third, and so on until all the children are squeezed into the caveman's hideaway. You may admonish the children to keep quiet in their hideaway, but we guarantee many giggles—and in truth, the more giggles, the more fun.

Matt Lattanzi wanted to give his daughter Chloe, and her best friend Colette, a big surprise at Colette's "Dinosaur" party. So Matt dressed as a green tyrannosaurus rex and astonished the guests when he arrived unexpectedly at the party. Everyone agreed he was an unforgettable dinosaur!

EXTINCTION

This is the prehistoric version of musical chairs. Use the insides of the stencils from the stencil book and tape one on each chair (you'll find that the legs of the dino are separate punch-outs, so instead of throwing them away, just tape them to the body of the dino to make it complete). Remember also that there should be one less chair than guests.

While you are playing the tape of the *Flintstones* theme, your guest dinosaurs march around, dinosaurlike, until the music stops. At this point, everybody must find a seat. As the next chair is taken away, that dinosaur becomes extinct.

A great book to read aloud to young dinosaur buffs is *Dinosaur Bob*, by William Joyce (see Resources, page 252).

A great book to read to the kids or give out as favors: *Did the Comets Kill the Dinosaurs* by Isaac Asimov (see Resources, page 252).

FAVORS

Plastic dinosaurs, dinosaur posters, stickers and miniature sponges in capsules, books on dinosaurs, dinosaur soap eggs (when you use them up, there's a little plastic dinosaur in the center), dinosaur T-shirts they made

MENU

Chicken Wings
Egg Bowls
Dinosaur sandwiches (cut with dinosaur cookie cutters)
Peanut Butter Bread (cut with dinosaur cookie cutters)
Lemonade

See recipes on page 246.

DINOSAUR CAKE

Use **The All-Around Birthday Cake** recipe, page 226. Bake the cake in a 9 × 13-inch pan. Cut out the shape of a dinosaur as per drawing. Frost with green **Seven-Minute Frosting,** page 229. Trace the edge with frosting from a tube. Make legs with large marshmallows, eyes with silver balls, using one Red Hot for the cheek.

CUT
CUT
CUT AWAY
CUT AWAY
CUT
MARSHMALLOWS

SUPERHEROES

(Ages 7 and up)

Is there anyone among us who has never wanted to fly through the sky, just once, like Superman, or drive off in the all-powerful Batmobile, or climb up slinky skyscrapers like Spiderman, or speed between buildings like Superwoman, or wear that slick yellow raincoat of Dick Tracy's? For those superhero addicts out there, here's a party where the magic words are Popeye and Superman, Spiderman and The Punisher, X-Men and The Flash, Batman and The Hulk, Mighty Mouse and Superwoman, Excalibur and Blackhawk, Silver Surfer and Zorro.

INVITATION

Send a comic book as an invitation to each guest. On the cover of each book, white out the words the characters are saying and fill in the following copy with a black marker:

How to Draw Cartoons and Caricatures by Judy Tatchell, and *Tex Avery, King of Cartoons,* by Joe Adamson (Avery is the man who created Bugs Bunny, Daffy Duck, and Porky Pig) are two books that young cartoonists will love. Look for others at bookstores (see Resources, page 252).

DECORATIONS

Cans of spinach (Popeye's favorite), red and blue crepe paper streamers, covers of comic books all over the table, posters of superheroes (available at all comic book stores) hanging about. On each balloon, write one action word so familiar to comic book lovers: "Vroom!" "Bam!" "Knock!" "Zoom!" "Pop!" "Crash!" "Zane!" "Pow!" "Zap!" "Crunch!" "Bang!"

GET READY!

1. Prepare the decorations listed above.

2. Prepare a three-ring binder, 30 sheets of plain, three-hole paper, and markers per child for cartooning. You will also need a video camera for putting all the children's cartoons together.

3. Locate a high-density Superball and a basket for the "Big Bounce" game.

4. Collect bean bags or old mittens and uncooked rice for the "Krypton Rock Toss."

5. Cut out at least ten different 4-panel comic strips from the newspaper for the "Striptease." Save some Sunday comic sections for "Comic Art." You will also need items that can be easily wrapped, white glue, brushes, and shellac.

6. Organize plastic liter bottles, sand, Ping-Pong balls, water pistols, and a stopwatch for the "Ping-Pong Challenge."

7. Xerox and enlarge drawing on page 197 for "Super Vision."

8. Buy different color balls for the "Superfly" game.

9. Buy trophies, magic tricks, and favors.

ACTIVITIES

STRIPTEASE

The idea is to create an original comic strip from existing comics. Gather together at least ten different 4-panel comic strips you have collected from the newspaper and cut up into squares (you should have at least 40 squares but there's no limit). Mix them all up. By picking 4 squares at random, each player makes his own strip. Provide everyone with tape and a pen for changing dialogue. If you like, allow the squares to be traded. When everyone is done you can find an area to display the panels and hand out five "Peanuts" awards for the funniest, the weirdest, etc.

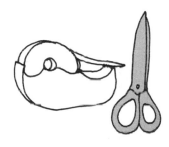

If you are comfortable with the idea, and can supervise them, you can have the children try lifting small weights to show their superhero strength.

MAKE A CARTOON FILM

Start with a three-ring binder—an "animation board"—for each child. Tape each to the floor or a table, making sure that they cannot move. Give each child 30 sheets of unlined three-hole paper. Instruct the cartoonists to draw simple images, each slightly different from the last one, in sequence. After each drawing is completed, place it under another blank sheet, allowing the picture to show through just enough to insure that the image is drawn right on top of it. It will take between 20 and 30 sheets for each child's animated cartoon. Be sure to include a title sheet and place it under all the rest (you will be putting the sheets, after they have been drawn in sequence, into the binder backwards, with the first sheet and the title sheet on the bottom of the pile).

Next, with a video camera that has been placed in a fixed position on a tripod and focused on the animation board, shoot the "title board" of the cartoon first, holding the image for about ten seconds. Then film each sheet for one second (basically you turn the camera on and off). That's it—when you play the videotape back, you have a full-fledged cartoon created by each child.

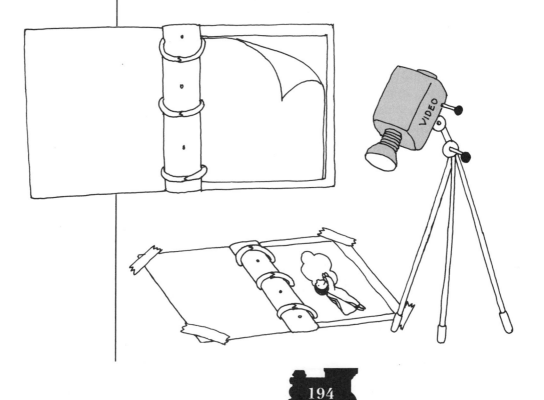

SUPER STRENGTH

Put together a few tests of strength for your various superguests:

Krypton Rock Toss

Toss bean bags; each contestant gets three tries and the one who throws the farthest wins. You can use store-bought bean bags, but we have found that these are easy to make and kids love to make them. Hand out one old mitten to each child. (You can decorate the mittens or just use them as they are.) Fill each mitten three quarters full with uncooked rice and then sew or staple shut.

The first animated cartoon was made by Winsor McCay in 1914. It was a five-minute film called *Gertie the Dinosaur*, and it took 10,000 drawings to complete.

Big Bounce

It may not be so easy to bounce high-density superballs into a container but if your "heroes" are up to the challenge, go to it. Put an empty basket on a chair. Mark a spot six feet away. Instruct each superhero to stand on the line and attempt to bounce the ball into the basket (each child should get several tries). Prizes can be awarded for each successful throw into the basket or to the person with the most baskets.

Dead Foot

Let each superhero try this trick: Ask one of your guests to stand sideways near a wall with his right foot and shoulder touching the wall. Now show everyone that you will put a dollar bill under his left foot. You then challenge him: If he can lift his left foot without moving his right shoulder or foot, he can keep the money. The trick is that *no one* can do this; when anyone stands in this manner, the center of gravity of his body will not allow him to pick up that left foot!

After the "Super Strength" contests have been completed, award the winner(s) with a trophy. The "gold-plated" plastic variety will serve the purpose!

Karen Blumberg, from Ocean, New Jersey, gave a superhero party for her six-year-old son. Her idea: She asked all the guests to wear red capes.

Jill's father was one of the cartoonists that "ghosted" Batman during the late 40s. When Remy was little, he always invited his grandfather to his parties because he could draw a perfect Batman. Jill says that it was a sad day for her Dad when Remy retired him and recruited his Uncle Andrew instead, because he could juggle fire.

X-RAY VISION AND OTHER FEATS

Magic tricks that will show the "X-ray vision" of superheroes are available at most toy stores. One manufacturer in particular, The Adams Company, makes dozens of widely available inexpensive tricks, so you'll have plenty to choose from; or you can set up your own without buying anything. Let the kids try these to show their superpowers. (Learning the inside information on how these tricks are done is the object here.) You can have the birthday superhero play one trick after another on each of the guests or each child can try each trick.

Super Vision

The drawing below has an assortment of superhero toys, clothes, and accessories. Xerox it, enlarge it, and place it in the center of a table, with all the superheroes surrounding the table so they can watch what will happen. The birthday superhero then hands a coin to any of his guests and asks him to place the coin anywhere on the superhero toy board, covering one of the pictures. He then leaves the room before he can see where the coin is placed.

When the coin is placed, everyone calls the superhero back to the room. He looks at the board, closes his eyes as if he is communicating with spirits from another world, and suddenly he tells everyone which image is under the coin. Guess what? He is always right. You can do this again and again and he will always guess the correct image covered by the coin. Here's how: When Jill drew the board, she repeated each image at every four spaces, whether it is up or down on the board.

Try it. Cover one of the pictures with the tip of your finger, count four squares after the covered image, and you'll find the exact same image as the one you covered. No matter in which direction you count to four, the same picture will be in that fourth box. It's a neat trick to teach the other superheroes—you may want to Xerox the drawing and give it out as favors so they can try this trick on their unsuspecting parents at home.

A quick fun game: Give each guest Silly Putty. Have them pick up words from the newspaper and try to read them (they will be backwards).

sew a small ball in center

Listen Carefully

Have the birthday child hold a page out of a magazine in front of the guests. "If anyone can tear this in four equal pieces," he announces to the guests, "I will give them a quarter." Eager hands will volunteer, and one smart young guest will most assuredly fold the paper in four sections and tear them just fine. When he is done, the birthday superhero takes one of the pieces of paper and hands it back to the one who tore it. "Here's a quarter!"

Magic Hanky

Take a big white handkerchief and sew a small rubber ball in the center. Tuck the handkerchief into a pocket in your shirt or pants, making sure that the white ends are hanging out. The trick is to pull the handkerchief out of your pocket and make some grand gestures with it—wave it around, wipe your forehead with it. Drop the handkerchief to the floor right in front of where you are standing. The handkerchief will immediately bounce back to you and the audience will burst into great laughter.

Balloon Magic

Before the party you will have taped Scotch tape on a couple of balloons. Now take those balloons and a safety pin and hold them up to the guests. Tell them that you will stick the pin through the balloons and they won't pop because you have superhero powers. When they challenge you to perform this feat, just stick the pin into the tape on one of the balloons. The balloon won't pop because the tape is holding it together (and no one can see the tape on the balloon so they don't know how you are accomplishing this!). You can try this again and again until one smart cookie asks to see the balloon!

PING-PONG CHALLENGE

This game takes place outside. Place eight liter plastic bottles filled with sand or water to weight them down on the ground in a row or on a picnic table. Put a Ping-Pong ball on top of each. The object is to shoot as many balls down as possible with a water gun in 15 seconds.

SUPERFLY

Ask your guests to make a circle and then divide them into couples. The couples do not stand together—they should pace themselves away from their partners in the circle. Give each team a ball of a different color. Now each player must throw his ball past all others and into the hands of his partner. As everyone is throwing the balls, players try to catch the balls of other teams. When an opponent's ball is captured, that team is out of the circle. The remaining couple is the winner.

COMIC ART

Take the colored comic sections you collected from the Sunday papers. Spread them around and let each child cover a box, a bottle, or any other item you have collected. You merely cover the object carefully and with a brush shellac it (Mod Podge or white glue work well for this as they are transparent). When done you will have a comic-covered object that is a great favor!

FAVORS

Magic tricks, comic art they made, comic books, their "animation boards"

MENU

Super-sized hero sandwich
Super ice cream sodas

SUPERHERO CAKE

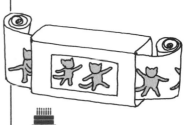

Jon Kasdan and Marc Gilbar spend a lot of time together drawing their own cartoons. Here's a quick way they found to make an instant television cartoon: Take a large matchbox and cut out a rectangle in the front (it will look like a television set). Using adding machine tape, draw your cartoon, making it as long as you want. By moving the paper quickly through the box, you get a little cartoon!

Use **The Perfect Chocolate Cake** recipe, page 224. Bake the cake in a 9×13-inch cake pan. Remove the cake from the pan and place on a large platter or piece of stiff cardboard. Cut in the form of a cartoon balloon. Frost with the **Seven-Minute Frosting**, page 229, and pipe the outline using chocolate frosting from a tube. Write "Pow!" "Zap!" "Bam!" with the chocolate frosting. Use Red Hots for the exclamation points.

SWEEPSTAKES

(Ages 8 and up)

G otten a sweepstakes entry lately? Well, here's one where each contestant is a guaranteed winner. All your guests have to do is return their entry forms (which invite them to your "Sweepstakes" party) in order to participate in contests and games, and even a talent show!

INVITATION

Xerox the invitation below, adding your child's name and each guest's name in the spaces provided.

SWEEPSTAKES ENTRY FORM

for **CAROLE'S 12th BIRTHDAY**

to: *Katie Philips*

12TH ☆ I WILL PERFORM ☐ SOLO ☐ WITH PARTNER 12TH

Fill in and mail back as a formal entry to Carole's Sweepstakes Birthday.

Drawing and games to be held July 30th at 555 Merrill Lane from 6 to 8 P.M.

CUT HERE

To be eligible for the sweepstakes you must appear in person and sign up for the following:

Pick One for the TALENT SHOW:

☐ Impersonation
☐ Singing
☐ Playing instrument
☐ Dancing
☐ Magic
☐ Joke telling
☐ Whistling
☐ Goldfish swallowing
☐ Hula-hoop
☐ Juggling
☐ Other

Pick One for the CRAZY COMPETITION:

☐ Craziest hair
☐ Silliest nail polish
☐ Outlandish dress
☐ Unusual face
☐ Extraordinary hat
☐ Off-the-wall glasses
☐ Most glittery jewelry
☐ Weirdest shoes
☐ One-color costume
☐ Celebrity look-alike
☐ Other

DECORATIONS

Hang blow-ups of entries all over the room and hang a big sign saying "Sweepstakes Hall."

GET READY!

1. Make entry forms to send as invitations.

2. Enlarge the returned RSVPs so they can be hung as decorations.

3. Cut out 25 pictures from catalogs for the "Price Is Right" game.

4. Buy prizes, certificates, or "gold cups."

5. Use two rolls of film of 36 shots each, photograph closeups of things that are familiar, both indoors and out. Have two sets of pictures developed (these will be used for "Concentration"). Here is a list of things you can photograph for this game (or for a variation, you can ask everyone to submit two photos of themselves with the sweepstakes entry and play the game with those):

Lamppost	Toothbrush
Car	Kitchen sink
Window	Painting
Flower	Piano
Movie marquee	Candy bar
For sale sign	Candles
Mailbox	Toy truck
Person	Teddy bear
Rooftop	Bookcase filled with books
Traffic light	Ice skates or roller blades
Fire hydrant	Pair of sneakers
Television set	Pair of eyeglasses or sunglasses
Sandwich	Doll
Bowl of fruit	Closeup of a patterned carpet
Clock	Lawn mower
Football or soccer ball	Garden hose curled up
Jewelry box	Stop sign

6. Cover empty milk cartons with white paper. Get white socks and roll up several pairs.

7. Prepare for the "Talent Show." You may need some extra costumes, sound effects, and seating.

8. Prepare a video camera and tape if you plan to film the "Talent Show." Gather props and choose a music tape.

9. Xerox the "What's Wrong Here?" drawing for each guest.

10. Prepare a small white bag with 20 dry white beans for "The 'I' Game," for each guest.

ACTIVITIES

THE "I" GAME

This is a game to play while waiting for all the guests to arrive. Each person receives a small white bag holding 20 dry white beans. During the next ten minutes, or until everyone has arrived, encourage conversation (you may suggest topics, if you like). Using the word "I" carries with it a penalty and the user has to give a bean to the person who calls him on it. The player having the most beans at the end of the time period wins the game. Players may ask questions or use other means to get people to say "I." (Remember, the homonyms count in this game, so "I," "aye," "eye," all work.)

THE PRICE IS RIGHT

Using mail order catalogs, cut out 25 pictures of items familiar to children. Write down the price of the item on the back of each picture; number the items from 1 to 25 on the front of each picture. Position in a visible place. Examples include a book, pin, soccer ball, cereal box, cassette tape, hair band, miniature car, large car, computer, television, watch, Nintendo game, and so on.

Each player gets a sheet of paper, numbered 1 to 25, and is allowed five minutes in which to fill in as many prices as he can. The player to get the most prices right (or closest to the actual right price) wins.

Dale Mallory and her daughter Joanna, from La Grange, Georgia, gave a "TV Show" party, with "Show Time" antics as the theme. The invitations were bright blue construction paper stars and written in silver ink was: "Come to our Show Time Antics: Dress as your favorite film or TV star." They made a mock TV set out of an 8 by 8-foot piece of foam board (and even placed card tables and chairs out front for the audience). The object of the party was for each guest or couple to stand behind the TV set and act out who they were. The results were surprising! They ranged from variety numbers to interviews with world leaders, from murder mysteries to news reports. Favors were miniature Emmys and Oscars, microwave popcorn, and discount coupons to the local video store and the movie theater. Says Dale, "Everyone wants us to do this party again!"

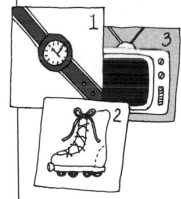

For older children who are film buffs and who can operate a video camera, have them tape their own invitation. Your child can set up the camera and perform the invitation. She can sing a song, give instructions for what to bring to the party, give a hint as to what to expect at the party, etc. She can also change outfits in the middle, add music to the background—and the performance will make an unusual and memorable invitation!

SOCK IT TO ME

Gather the milk cartons and socks you prepared. Line up the cartons in a pyramid shape (like bowling pins). Give each carton a score—you can write points on the front of each, and keep score as they fall, adding up the fallen ones. Divide into teams. One player from each team throws a pair of socks at the pyramid from across the room. The team with the highest score wins. Option: Buy an inexpensive bowling set and play this game the same way.

CONCENTRATION

Gather the photos you have taken. Choose the best 15 or 25 and their doubles. Shuffle all the pictures to mix them up. Place them face down on a large table or on the floor in rows. Each person then takes turns turning over (so you can see the photos) any two pictures at a time. If they don't match, they are turned back over. If they do match, that person keeps the two matching photos. At the end, the person with the most matched photos wins.

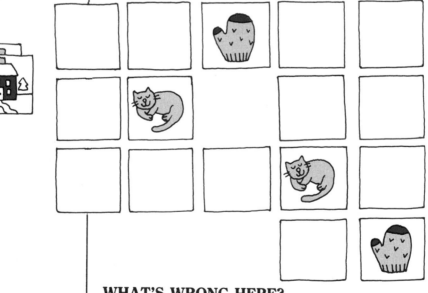

WHAT'S WRONG HERE?

Xerox the drawing on page 205. Make as many copies as you have guests. Give each child a copy of the drawing and a pencil and give him a limited amount of time to circle all the things he finds wrong. The child with the most right answers wins.

See answers on page 248.

TALENT SHOW

Organize the performers. Assign or draw for order of performance. Have a specific area set aside for the show, and don't forget audience seating. Everything will proceed more smoothly if you have a designated emcee or at least an announcer. The props and music must be gathered ahead of time. Give awards for all sorts of categories. If you can, videotape the show, for it will be shown again and again as everyone grows and remembers the fun they had!

CRAZY COMPETITION

Give out prizes for the "Crazy Competition" as listed in the invitation.

FAVORS

Plush dice, miniature trophies for prizes, inexpensive pins

MENU

Talent show buffet:
Spaghetti Pie
Green Salad
Garlic Bread
Any sparkling punch

See recipes on page 247.

SWEEPSTAKES CAKE

Use **The All-Around Birthday Cake** recipe, page 226. Bake the cake in a 9×11-inch pan. Remove the cake from the pan. Cover with green **Seven-Minute Frosting**, page 229. Pipe a huge dollar sign with chocolate frosting from a tube. Scatter gold-covered chocolate coins over the top; you can even pile some to form a mound of money.

THIS IS YOUR LIFE

The Bi...

APRIL 10th

Today is the... rest of...

(Ages 13 and up)

L isa Gilbar and other friends of Emily Deschanel planned and executed a "This Is Your Life" party for a Sweet-Sixteen birthday. Invite guests to come a half hour early as this is a surprise party. Now, surprise parties are fun for most everyone, especially teenagers, but it can be very difficult to keep such a party a *total* surprise. It is simpler (and can be more effective) to tell the birthday child that there will be a party but keep the theme a surprise. And remember, this is a party that parents and friends can give together, so enlist everyone's help and the process of creating, planning, and giving the party will be as much fun as the party itself!

INVITATION

Make a mini book of the life of the birthday child. Place one or two photographs on each page of the book and xerox. If you have 20 guests, Xerox 20 copies of each page and staple together as a book. For the outside cover, print or stencil or use a computer:

Chana Leah Friedman, age 13½, wrote us suggesting turning a birthday party into a mock charity dinner (the program had a "chairman," a "guest speaker," visiting "reporters," and a small choir). Everyone ate on a dais—but Chana Leah didn't ever tell us if they actually raised any money!

Make a collage of pictures of the birthday girl through the years, and color the cover with colored pencils for an artistic effect. On the inside back cover, write the actual invitation copy:

For an added touch, you can ask the guests to come dressed as their idea of the birthday child.

DECORATIONS

Hang everywhere:

- Blowups of pictures of the birthday girl as well as an exhibition of baby photos of the guests (these remain unidentified until the party begins).
- Blowups of the newspaper of the date of her birth.
- Balloons; try for a favorite color of the celebrant. If you plan far enough ahead of time, you can order balloons with the child's name and "Sweet Sixteen" printed on them.
- Covers of old *Life* magazines.
- Other assorted party decorations to create a festive air.

GET READY!

This party takes some planning but it is worth every minute!

1. Ask at least one friend who is the contact for all so that your phone won't be ringing off the wall! (While parents can certainly help with the planning of this party, it's best done by your child's friends.)

2. Assign someone to be the emcee at the party. A person whose job it is to run the party helps keep the pace going.

3. Cut out the cover photos of the *Life* magazines and insert Xeroxed photos of the birthday child.

4. Collect pictures of the birthday girl throughout her life. Make arrangements to get them blown up and copied so you can hang them around the room. (If you have the time and inclination, mount them on colored tagboard so they really look like framed photos.)

5. Ask friends to assemble a slide show. It is not difficult and is actually a lot of fun, but it takes some organization. Gather photos using as many pictures that include friends as possible. A "committee" of friends working together on this ahead of time is bound to come up with funny captions to read as each slide is flashed on the screen. Title cards can be made to show before a series of shots, which will help organize the production (e.g., "And Baby Makes Three," "Brat of the Year," "The Best Friend," "Soccer Champ," "Academy Award Winner"). You can also include background music. The songs

Bring somebody who means a lot to your child to the party as a surprise guest—like a favorite teacher, grandparent, camp buddy, or counselor.

should have a relationship to the photos being shown, for instance, "Baby Face," "There's No Business Like Show Business," "Itsy Bitsy Teeney Weenie Yellow Polka Dot Bikini," "California Girls," and so on.

If the kids are sophisticated video camera operators, you can videotape the slides or photos and show a complete "film."

A project like this pays off twice. While watching it together at the party is a lot of fun, the experience of producing the show could be even better!

6. Assign someone the duty of photographer who will walk around the party and take pictures. This is something you don't want to have to think about while the party is going on.

7. Ask some friends to prepare funny stories about your child—ones that can be told in public without embarrassment.

8. Make a list of a dozen phrases or titles that relate to your child or that he likes for the "Life Charades" game. You might choose phrases that will remind everyone of your child's life or titles of movies or books he loves.

9. Collect baby pictures of all the guests for the gallery display. Get another baby photograph of each guest and number it for the "Baby Exhibit." You may even want to include baby photos of the birthday girl's parents. If you can find any, throw in some baby pictures of famous people in magazines; this will just add to the fun.

10. Have on hand enough paper and pencils for "The Life and Times of . . ."

11. Prepare balloons for the "Balloon Dance."

12. Write out the "password cards" for the "Real Life" game.

13. Get prizes and favors.

ACTIVITIES

BABY EXHIBIT

This is an excellent starter to occupy each arriving guest. As the guests come in, hand out a piece of paper and a pencil on which to identify the numbered photos of everyone (including themselves) as babies in the "Baby Exhibit." The numbers on the paper correspond to the numbers on the photos, so each guest writes his guesses, folds the paper over, puts his name on the other side, and returns it to the host. Winners are announced later.

REAL LIFE

Play this guessing game using the honoree as the main subject. Write a word relating to her on each "password card." Make three copies of each password card. One card will be given to one member of each team and the third card of that word to the onlookers so they can share in the fun. The words you choose can be obvious (redhead) or more oblique (sensitive, insomniac). Divide the guests into two teams—the "Sweets" and the "Six-teens" for example. One member of each team will see the word while the other members of her team will try to guess it.

The "Sweets" go first. The person who gets the card must give her teammate a one-word clue so that she can guess the word on the password card. The teammate has 15 seconds to come up with the word. If she misses, the "Sixteens" get a turn which means that their team will have two words as clues: the first word that the "Sweets" gave, and the second word that the "Sixteens" clue giver will now offer. The play continues until the word is guessed. For example, one of the passwords used for Emily was "redhead" (because Emily is a redhead); the first clue could be "hair," to which the guessing partner might guess "short" (because Emily's hair is short), and she would be wrong. Then the next team gives a clue, which could be "color." That second player guesses "redhead" and she is right. How-ever, she could have said "red," in which case she would have been wrong; then the next clue could be "auburn" or "Lucy" (for famous redhead Lucille Ball) and that guesser could say "redhead" and she would then be right.

BALLOON DANCE

If the party is coed, music and dancing will undoubtedly work their way into the format. A good way to start is with the "Balloon Dance." Tie inflated balloons on the right wrist or ankle of every girl. While dancing, each couple must try to protect its balloon while trying to break others. A couple whose balloon is broken has to leave the dance floor. Give prizes to the last remaining couple.

For Jill's 40th birthday (that's Jill Weber, our il-lustrator), her family gave a surprise version of "This Is Your Life" that certainly sur-prised her! The invitation was a photograph of Jill as a baby, sitting in a sink having her bath and screaming her head off! Her brother An-drew Schwartz did a skit on "A Day in the Life of Jill," entirely without words, using balloon signs for Jill's voice when appropriate. "You can't imagine how hard everyone was laughing!" remembers Jill. "But what surprised me was that everyone knew all this about me!"

THIS IS YOUR LIFE

Show the slides or video tape accompanied by commentary by the emcee and background music.

LIFE CHARADES

Take your list of one dozen familiar phrases, names of films, or whatever you decided will be acted out by the teams of players. The object is for each team to guess, as quickly as possible, all the phrases on the list as they are pantomimed by their teammates.

Divide the guests into two teams and send them to opposite sides of the room. Tell the first phrase on the list to one player from each team. Each player returns to his team and pantomimes the phrase for them. The team has a certain amount of time to guess the phrase. When a team has guessed the correct phrase, the player who guessed it runs to the list keeper to get the next phrase, which he then acts out. You keep doing this like a relay race until one team completes the list—and that team wins.

When Miki Jaeger moved from New York City to North Carolina, her staff and friends gave her a never-to-be forgotten going away party. The highlight for Miki was a personalized version of TV's "Jeopardy" with categories apropos of all the years they had worked together—including Blast from the Past, Appliances, Special Times, and Adam (Miki's son). Some of the other activities included songs, skits, poems, as well as a customized version of charades played by all. As a keepsake, they presented Miki with a scrapbook filled with more memories to take with her, along with a video of the day.

THE LIFE AND TIMES OF . . .

The guests will write a story about the birthday girl together, each guest contributing a part of the story without knowing what anyone else has written.

Distribute pencil and paper to everyone. Each guest sits in a circle with his paper and pencil and writes the first sentence which is the beginning of the story on her life. When done, she folds the paper over that sentence and passes it to the person on her right, who then adds a sentence to the story. She then folds the paper over that one and passes it to her right. When the papers have made a complete circle, everyone gets to read their paper out loud.

TOASTING/ROASTING

Mealtime is the ideal moment to offer toasts or roasts of your honoree. If assignments are made ahead of time, the results will show it!

FAVORS

Photo key chains, blank books with pretty covers to write messages

MENU

12-foot-long submarine sandwich
Fruit Pizzas
Fruit punch

See recipes on pages 247–248.

Come dressed as your idea of the birthday child.

LIFE MAGAZINE CAKE

Use **The All-Around Birthday Cake** recipe, page 226. Bake the cake in a 9×11-inch pan. Remove the cake from the pan and frost on all sides with white **Seven-Minute Frosting,** page 229. Cut out the top banner from the cover of a *Life* magazine and lay across the narrower part of the cake. With tube frosting, pipe around the edges of the banner to hold it down; you can also pipe around the word "Life" in white to make it stand out. With your tube of frosting, draw the outline of a birthday cake. Place real candles on top of your pictured cake and then write "_____, This Is Your Life!"

UNDER THE BIG TOP

(Ages 5–12)

Don't wait for Barnum and Bailey's "Greatest Show on Earth" to come to town; you can organize your own backyard circus birthday party. A variety of contests and activities, wandering clowns and musicians, silly antics and surprise shows, can be a bigger hit with the kids than taking them to sit quietly under the big top. Everyone seems happier as a participant than an observer at any party, and your children and their friends should be "flying high" with this one.

This outdoor party is organized by booths, one for each activity. Guests can wander from booth to booth participating in whatever game or contest they like. Each booth is manned by a teenager or an adult helper so the activities can go on simultaneously. With a little organization and planning ahead of time, this birthday circus will be a smash.

INVITATION

On a red and white striped popcorn bag (available at many markets), write the following message with a felt-tip pen across the stripes:

> FEED the Elephants on MICHAEL'S
>
> 5th BIRTHDAY! It's a Big Top Bash
>
> MARCH 2ND, 2 to 5 pm
>
> 555 Elm Street   R.S.V.P. 555-1234
>
> Come as a circus performer

Fill each bag half full with peanuts in the shell. Fold over the top and punch two holes in the fold, side by side. Thread a red ribbon through the holes and tie in a bow. Mail the invitation in a padded envelope or hand deliver.

DECORATIONS

The big top look can be created by:

- Putting up a large tent.
- Hanging streamers, from corner to corner of tent.
- Hanging balloons everywhere.
- Making a ticket booth (buy rolls of tickets at your local stationery store).
- Hiring high school band members to march around the "circus" or do silly antics in a "march of the clowns." In fact, all the people working the party, including any teenagers or adults, can be clowns, snake charmers (with rubber snakes draped around their necks), bearded ladies, or magicians, and can show off their hidden talents with yo-yos, hula hoops, or juggling balls.
- Including pets, appropriately caged, around the area. Don't forget "tiger" cats, pet snakes, mice, gerbils, etc.

GET READY!

1. Rent a large tent from your local party supply service or decorate your backyard, carport, or arbor.

2. Prepare a shopping bag for each child with his name on it for favors. Tie a helium balloon to the handle.

3. Buy two boxes of toothpicks for the "Javelin Throw."

4. Order prizes for games.

5. Collect a wide plastic bucket, sand, wooden skewers, and red paint or nail polish for the "Bucket of Chance." Prepare ahead.

6. Buy bubble wrap from a packing-supply store.

7. Organize pennies, nickles, and drinking straws for "Shot Put."

8. Buy frogs for the "Frog Jumping."

9. Assemble an assortment of sponges for "Pie Throwing" (whipped cream and aluminum pie plates if you choose to go that route). You will also need a bucket and a large sheet of cardboard.

10. Purchase a large piece of plywood with holes cut out for heads for the "Photo Booth" plus paint and a Polaroid camera and film.

11. Organize washable decals and mini stencils for tattoos and assorted makeup for the "Funny Face Booth."

12. Locate Halloween paraphernalia for the "Freak Show."

13. Order packages of tiny prizes for the favors from Frank Stein (see Resources, page 252).

14. Arrange for adult or teenage helpers.

ACTIVITIES

The first stop for each child as he arrives at the circus is at the ticket booth. Each child receives a supply (tickets of 50 each is a good amount to start with). The tickets are used at each booth for entering the contest activity or "buying" food. It may be necessary to issue more tickets as the party progresses.

Each activity is held in a "booth." Either build a booth out of cardboard, plywood, or foam board or create one by using a card table or appliance box, or simply outline different areas with rope to set apart for the activities. It's most fun if you encourage participation in groups so that there's always a cheering section. Remember that having enthusiastic teenagers and adult guests around not only will add to the atmosphere of entertainment, but will also help you organize, lead, and explain the various activities.

CLOWN OF CLOWNS

Clowning is an art, but even amateurs can be funny if they are given a role to play. Here are a few suggestions for your clown volunteers:

- Use a broom for a prop; anytime someone comes near this clown he sweeps them away.
- Hold a leash for walking an imaginary dog.
- Blow bubbles with the large bubble wands (or with any bubble blowers).
- Ride a tiny tot bicycle or a unicycle.
- Walk on stilts or hop on a pogo stick.
- Carry a hula hoop for gyrations and for rounding up the guests. You can also cover a bunch of small hoops with tissue paper so the children can run through them and break the tissue.
- Demonstrate any gymnastic skills, such as doing cartwheels, somersaults, and flips.
- Extinguish a "fire" in a very inefficient manner.
- Play the role of a hobo clown with bandanna knapsack on a stick.

Want to walk an invisible dog? Take a chain leash with a leather collar at the end and place the collar into a bowl of white glue. As it sits in the bowl, mold it with your fingers until it is perfectly round. Take it out and let dry (it will be stiff). To stiffen the leash so it stands out in front of you, wind florist wire through the chain links.

If anyone calls to ask for suggestions for costumes they might wear at the "Under the Big Top" party, you can suggest Siamese Twins, Muscle Men, Lion Trainers, Trapeze Artists, Clowns, Wizards, and circus animals.

FROG JUMPING

First, procure your frog contestants. Nell Otto decided that a frog jumping contest would be a great addition to the circus birthday party her ten-year-old twins were planning. She thought she'd be able to scare up a couple of frogs in the backyard, but she ended up buying two frogs at the local pet store.

Next, set out a course that is measured in feet. Place the frogs at the starting line and assign ownership for each frog. The winning group of kids has the frog that gets to the finish line first. Cheering the frogs on with whistles and various yells will give the frogs great incentive (so will a dish of dead flies at the finish line).

JAVELIN THROW

Each competitor places an elbow at the edge of a table at the javelin booth. He then holds a toothpick between the thumb and forefinger and tosses the toothpick as far as possible without lifting his elbow off the table. Each ticket is worth three tries. Mark distances 2, 3, and 5 feet from the table's edge. Award a small prize for each contestant's best effort (a lollipop for 2 feet, a piece of gum for 3 feet, and a candy bar for any distance over 5 feet, for example).

HOP AND POP

Place a large supply of bubble wrap from your local packing-supply store in a large pile—or, better yet, recycle your friends' collections. This is not a contest. Players just hop in and pop to their hearts' desire.

SHOT PUT

Gather as many pennies or nickels as you have players and keep them in a bowl at the booth. As each competitor steps up to play, he picks a coin and puts it at the edge of the table. He then takes a drinking straw and, blowing hard, tries to blow the coin across the table as far as possible in 15 seconds. (He must keep the straw at the edge of the table at all times.) Measure the distance blown with a tape measure. Determine what distance merits a reward.

BUCKET OF CHANCE

Before the party, fill a rubber bucket three-quarters full of sand (you can get sand at most lumberyards and nurseries). Buy 300 bamboo skewers at the supermarket. Dip 50 skewers into red paint or nail polish, covering about 1 inch of the tip. Let dry. When you're ready to play, stick all 300 skewers into the sand, making sure they are just deep enough so that none of the red shows. Each player gets three chances to pick up one red stick. You get a prize for every red stick picked.

PIE THROWING

Collect an assortment of sponges in all colors, shapes, and sizes and place in a big bucket of water. At one end of the booth, stand a large sheet of cardboard with a hole cut in it about 4 or 5 feet from the ground. Select a willing victim or two to take turns sticking their heads through the hole and letting the guests take turns throwing wet sponges at them. Adults as targets and kids as pie throwers works best.

Another version of pie throwing is more traditional and some kids would probably say more fun—and that is aluminum pie plates full of whipped cream thrown at human targets.

Draw a whole body connected to the face for the "Pie Throwing" game.

PHOTO BOOTH

Buy a large piece of plywood or pressboard from your lumber-yard; ask them to cut out four head-sized holes at different heights. Paint different body figures under each of these holes. Place the board at one end of the photo booth and have the designated photographer take Polaroids of the guests. Tack up the photos on a wall for viewing.

FUNNY FACE BOOTH

A booth featuring face painting and tattooing (washable decals) always draws a crowd. Teenagers are often very good at this art and will have fun helping transform the whole party. They know that exaggerated makeup, such as bright blue, yellow, or green eye shadow, bright red outlined lips, eyelashes drawn on the bottom lid, all work very well. But an unbeatable treat is to offer a selection of decals that can be affixed to a forehead or cheek for the afternoon. These "tattoos" come in fantasy figures like angels, unicorns, stars, ballerinas, and the like. Some makeup artists might like to paint such figures using paper stencils as forms. They can also add glitter to the liquid makeup or body paints.

FREAK SHOW

Next to the face-painting booth, arrange a variety of eye masks and piles of materials for making monster faces and head-dresses. Feathers, plastic noses, synthetic hair (even old wigs), markers, and Halloween paraphernalia (such as plastic scars, steel wool, makeup for added "blood" or wrinkle effects) will be huge successes; the scarier, the better. Kids can make themselves into the monster of their choice.

MIME TIME

Two circus officials can be mimes. They dress all in black with white face makeup and can play Simple Simon with several children at a time.

FAVORS

Either you can award tickets at each booth and then set up a store where the children turn in tickets for prizes or you can give out tiny prizes like balls, key chains, marbles, rubber animals, plastic jewelry, eye patches, at each booth (see Resources, page 252).

MENU

One or two booths should be food stalls. "Sell" popcorn, cotton candy (easy if you buy or rent a sugar spinner), peanuts, hot dogs, lemonade, and sodas. The sale is made, of course, with the tickets you've given out. If you have decided to have all the kids eat at the same time picnic style, you might have all the adult entertainers do their tricks at the same time.

CIRCUS TRAIN BIRTHDAY CAKE

Use **The All-Around Birthday Cake** recipe, page 226. Bake the cake in six mini loaf pans (see Resources, page 249) and one regular loaf pan. Remove the cakes from the pans. Frost with the **Orange Cream Frosting,** page 229, in four different colors. All the cars of the train will have Oreo cookie wheels. Life Savers will make windows and each car can have different goodies on top—jelly beans, peanuts, animal crackers, popcorn. Decorate the engine with a graham cracker "cowcatcher" and a marshmallow chimney (or you can use a toy locomotive, either plastic or wood). Make tracks out of ice cream sticks on a piece of foam board covered with freezer paper. Place all the cakes in a row on the board.

ENGINE

pipe chocolate frosting

popsicle stick TRACKS

LIQUID AND DRY MEASURE EQUIVALENCIES

Customary	Metric
¼ teaspoon	1.25 milliliters
½ teaspoon	2.5 milliliters
1 teaspoon	5 milliliters
1 tablespoon	15 milliliters
1 fluid ounce	30 milliliters
¼ cup	60 milliliters
⅓ cup	80 milliliters
½ cup	120 milliliters
1 cup	240 milliliters
1 pint (2 cups)	480 milliliters
1 quart (4 cups, 32 ounces)	960 milliliters
1 gallon (4 quarts)	.96 liters
1 ounce (by weight)	3.84 liters
¼ pound (4 ounces)	28 grams
1 pound (16 ounces)	114 grams
2.2 pounds	454 grams
	1 kilogram (100 grams)

OVEN TEMPERATURE EQUIVALENCIES

Description	°Fahrenheit	°Celsius
Cool	200	90
Very slow	250	120
Slow	300-325	150-160
Moderately slow	325-350	160-180
Moderate	350-375	180-190
Moderately hot	375-400	190-200
Hot	400-450	200-230
Very hot	450-500	230-260

CAKE, FROSTING, AND ICING RECIPES

BIRTHDAY CAKES

For all sheet cakes: Spray the bottom and sides of your cake pan with vegetable spray and then place parchment paper on the bottom. Spray again and then dust with flour. This will insure that you will be able to remove the cake easily from any cake pan.

THE PERFECT CHOCOLATE CAKE

You can use this recipe for the **Film Strip Cake (Candid Camera)**, the **Island Cake (Shipwrecked)**, and the **Superhero Cake (Superheroes)**.

½ cup boiling water
½ cup cocoa powder
⅔ cup margarine, softened
1¾ cups sugar
1 teaspoon vanilla
2 eggs
2¼ cups all-purpose flour
1½ teaspoons baking soda
½ teaspoon salt
1⅓ cups buttermilk

Preheat the oven to 350°F. Grease and flour two 9-inch round cake pans (you can also use three 8-inch pans).

In a bowl, stir together the boiling water and cocoa until the cocoa has dissolved. In a food processor or with a mixer, cream the margarine, sugar, and vanilla until very smooth. Now add the eggs and beat again. In another bowl, mix together the flour, baking soda, and salt. Using a soup spoon, add the buttermilk and flour mixture to the creamed mixture, one spoonful at a time. Now add the chocolate mixture and stir everything together.

Pour the cake batter into the prepared cake pans. Bake for about 40 minutes (25–30 minutes for 8-inch pans). When a cake tester (or a knife or toothpick) comes out clean, the cake is ready. Let it cool before removing from the pans.

CHOCOLATE FROSTING

8 ounces semisweet baking chocolate or 1⅓ cups semisweet chocolate chips
½ cup whipping cream
1 cup sugar

In a small pan, combine the chocolate, cream, and sugar. Cook over low heat until the chocolate is melted and smooth. Stir constantly! Make sure the mixture doesn't boil. It's ready when it is thick and smooth (about 12–15 minutes).

CARROT CAKE

Adapted from *Good Enough to Eat* by Carrie Levin and Ann Nickinson; use for the **Psychedelic Cake (Flower Child)**. Children love this cake because it is so moist!

> 1 cup whole wheat flour
> 1 cup all-purpose flour
> 2 teaspoons ground cinnamon
> 1 teaspoon ground nutmeg
> ½ teaspoon salt
> 1½ teaspoons baking soda
> ½ cup sweet butter, softened
> 2 cups sugar
> ½ cup vegetable oil
> 4 large eggs
> 2 teaspoons vanilla
> 1 pound carrots, coarsely grated
> ½ cup raisins, dried cranberries, or dried cherries
> Grated rind of 1 lemon

Preheat the oven to 350°F. Grease and flour two 9-inch round cake pans.

Combine the flours, cinnamon, nutmeg, salt, and baking soda in a mixing bowl. In another bowl, cream the butter and sugar until light and fluffy (use a mixer). Now add the oil and mix well. Add the eggs, one at a time, beating well after each addition. Stir in the vanilla. Now fold in the dry ingredients, then the carrots, raisins (or other dried fruit), and lemon rind. Pour the batter evenly into the two pans.

Bake for about 25–30 minutes, or until a cake tester comes out clean. Let cool in the pan for about 10 minutes.

CREAM CHEESE FROSTING

> 8 ounces cream cheese, softened
> ½ cup butter or margarine, softened
> 2 cups powdered sugar
> ½ teaspoon vanilla
> 1 teaspoon lemon juice

Place the cream cheese and butter in a large mixing bowl and cream well. Add the sugar slowly, beating until smooth. Now add the vanilla and lemon juice and beat again until the mixture is smooth and spreadable.

ROCKY ROAD CAKE

Use this recipe for the **Dog Dish Cake (It's a Dog's Life)**.

> 3 cups all-purpose flour
> 3 cups sugar
> 6 tablespoons unsweetened cocoa
> ¾ teaspoon salt
> 3 sticks butter or margarine, cut up into small pieces
> 1½ cups cola soda pop
> 3 eggs, at room temperature
> ¾ cup buttermilk
> 1½ teaspoons baking soda
> 1½ teaspoons vanilla

Preheat the oven to 350°F. Lightly oil and flour an 8-quart metal dog dish.

Combine the flour, sugar, cocoa, and salt in a large bowl. Melt the butter in a saucepan, add the cola and bring to a boil. Pour into the flour mixture and stir. In another bowl, beat the eggs until frothy; add the buttermilk, baking soda, and vanilla. Add to the batter; stir until blended. Pour into the dog dish and bake for approximately 40 minutes.

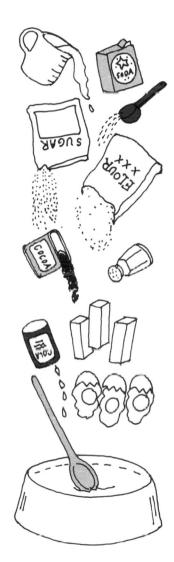

ROCKY ROAD FROSTING

3¾ cups powdered sugar
½ cup unsweetened cocoa
1 tablespoon vanilla
½ cup butter, softened
⅓ cup milk
1 cup miniature marshmallows
½ cup walnut pieces

Sift together the powdered sugar and cocoa. Beat the vanilla and butter together until light and fluffy, then add the vanilla and butter mixture alternately with the milk to the sugar and cocoa mixture. Beat at high speed for about a minute. Add the marshmallows and nuts. Spread on the cooled cake.

THE SUPER CHOCOLATE CAKE

This recipe is good for the **Corral Cake (Horsin' Around)** and the **Dice Cake (Club Casino)**.

Double the ingredient amounts for the Dice Cake; amounts below will work for any sheet cake.

3 ounces unsweetened chocolate
½ cup butter
1 cup water
2 cups all-purpose flour
1¼ teaspoons baking soda
1 teaspoon salt
2 eggs
2 cups sugar
1 teaspoon vanilla
1 cup sour cream

Preheat the oven to 350°F. Grease and flour a 9 x 11-inch or three 8-inch square cake pan(s).

Place the chocolate, butter, and water in a saucepan and melt over low heat. Let cool. In a mixing bowl, sift together the flour, baking soda, and salt. In another bowl, mix together the eggs, sugar, and vanilla with a mixer. To this bowl, add the sour cream and beat well. Now add the melted chocolate mixture. Beat again. Add the dry ingredients to this bowl and beat one more time. Pour into the cake pan(s) and bake for about 55 minutes–1 hour. Check readiness with a knife every five minutes after 45 minutes. If you are making the Dice Cake, rotate the pans once or twice while they are baking.

Frost with Chocolate Frosting or Seven-Minute Frosting.

CHOCOLATE FROSTING

½ cup butter or margarine
1½ tablespoons cocoa
3 tablespoons milk
1 teaspoon vanilla
2 cups powdered sugar

In a small saucepan, heat the butter, cocoa, milk, and vanilla until very hot but not boiling. Then add the powdered sugar and mix well.

THE ALL-AROUND BIRTHDAY CAKE

Use this recipe for the **Circus Train Birthday Cake (Under the Big Top)**, the **Dinosaur Cake (Stegosaurus & Friends)**, the **Fish Cake (Gone Fishin')**, the *Life* **Magazine Cake (This Is Your Life)**, the **Star Cake (Stargazing Party)**, and the **Sweepstakes Cake (Sweepstakes)**.

A little lemon rind and 2 tablespoons of lemon juice instead of another liquid will turn "The All-Around Birthday Cake" into a lemon cake.

226

1 cup butter, softened
2 cups sugar
4 egg yolks
1 teaspoon vanilla
3 cups sifted all-purpose flour
¼ teaspoon salt
3 teaspoons baking powder
1 cup milk
4 egg whites

Preheat the oven to 350°F. Grease and flour three 8-inch round cake pans.

Cream the butter and sugar with a mixer. Still beating, add the egg yolks and vanilla. In another bowl, sift the flour, salt, and baking powder. Add the dry ingredients to the creamed mixture, one tablespoon at a time, alternating with the milk, also one tablespoon at a time. When done, mix together with a wooden spoon.

With an electric mixer, beat the egg whites until quite stiff. Fold them gently into the cake batter.

Pour the batter into the prepared cake pans. Bake for about 30 minutes, or until a toothpick comes out clean.

SYLVIA'S WONDER CAKE

The creamy filling in this sheet cake will be a great surprise for the kids! This is good for **Chocolate House Birthday Cake (Chocolate Factory), Matisse Cake (Art Attack), Number One Cake (So What's vs. The Big Deals)**, and **Soccer Field Cake (Soccer)**.

2 cups sugar
½ cup butter or margarine, softened
2 eggs

4 ounces baking chocolate, melted
2 cups sifted all-purpose flour
1 teaspoon salt
1 teaspoon baking powder
½ teaspoon baking soda
1⅓ cups milk
1 teaspoon vanilla

FILLING
2 tablespoons butter or margarine, softened
8 ounces cream cheese, softened
¼ cup sugar
1 tablespoon cornstarch
1 egg
2 tablespoons milk
½ teaspoon vanilla

Preheat the oven to 350°F. Grease and flour a 9 x 11-inch pan.

Batter: In a mixer, cream together the sugar and butter until light and smooth. Now add the eggs, mixing continuously. Add the chocolate and continue mixing. Now add the dry ingredients, alternating with the milk and vanilla. Mix these until just smooth and blended and then stop.

Filling: In a food processor, cream together the butter, cream cheese, sugar, and cornstarch. Now add the egg, milk, and vanilla while you continue to mix.

To make the cake: Pour half the chocolate batter into the cake pan. Now pour all the filling on the batter. When done, pour the rest of the cake batter on top of the filling.

Bake for about 45 minutes. Frost with Seven-Minute Frosting.

ANGEL FOOD CAKE

This is great for the **Doll Cake (Doll Shower)** and the **Cloud Cake (Cloud 9)**.

> 1¼ cups cake flour
> ½ cup sugar
> ¼ teaspoon salt
> 1¼ teaspoons cream of tartar
> 1½ cups egg whites, at room temperature
> 1⅓ cups sugar
> 1 teaspoon vanilla
> ½ teaspoon almond extract

Preheat the oven to 375°F. Grease and flour a 10-inch tube pan.

Sift the flour. Now measure it to make sure it gives you 1¼ cups flour. Sift it together with ½ cup sugar three times to get it as pure as possible. Set aside.

Add the salt and cream of tartar to the egg whites and beat until stiff but not dry. Fold in 1⅓ cups sugar, about 2 tablespoons at a time. Now add the vanilla and almond extracts. Fold in the flour and sugar mixture, a little at a time.

Pour the mixture into the cake pan and bake for 40–45 minutes. When done, remove from the oven and turn upside down. Let it cool before you frost with Seven-Minute Frosting.

PIGLET CUPCAKES

Use also for **Caterpillar Cake (Camp-out)**.

> 2 cups sugar
> 2 cups all-purpose flour
> 4 tablespoons cocoa powder
> ½ cup butter, melted
> ½ cup milk
> ½ tablespoon vinegar
> 2 eggs
> 1 teaspoon baking soda
> 1 teaspoon baking powder
> 1 cup boiling water

Preheat the oven to 350°F. Grease a muffin or mini ball pan (see Resources, page 249). The 6-ball pan can be filled twice with this recipe.

Mix together all the ingredients in a bowl or a food processor. The mixture will look thin but don't worry! Fill the muffin pan three-quarters full. Bake for 20 minutes or until done.

ADDITIONAL FROSTINGS AND ICINGS

CHOCOLATE FROSTING

> 2 squares baking chocolate
> 2 cups powdered sugar
> ¼ cup butter or margarine
> Approximately 3 tablespoons decaffeinated coffee or milk

Mix everything together. Add as much coffee or milk as you may need to make it smooth. To frost, dip each cupcake upside down into the frosting.

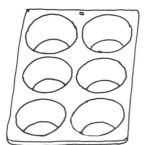

Rowaco makes a giant muffin pan (6 muffins)—each of these could be an individual mini birthday cake (see Resources, page 249).

PEANUT BUTTER ICING

½ cup sweet butter, softened
1 pound sifted powdered sugar
3 tablespoons milk
1 teaspoon vanilla
3 tablespoons peanut butter

In a food processor or a mixing bowl, beat the butter until it is smooth. Slowly add the sugar, milk, and vanilla. When totally mixed, add the peanut butter. If the mixture needs to be thicker, add more sugar.

ORANGE CREAM FROSTING

½ cup butter
4 cups sifted powdered sugar
4–6 tablespoons cream
1 teaspoon orange extract

Cream the butter and the sugar. Add the cream to spreading consistency. Add the extract. Makes enough to cover 6 mini loaf pans.

SEVEN-MINUTE FROSTING

This icing is smooth and thick and covers a cake easily and quickly. It is the perfect frosting for any cake.

2 egg whites
1½ cups sugar
3 tablespoons water
¼ teaspoon cream of tartar
2 tablespoons lemon juice
½ teaspoon grated lemon rind
1 teaspoon vanilla

Combine all the ingredients in the top of a double boiler. Set a kitchen timer for 7 minutes. When the water boils in the bottom of the boiler, beat the ingredients in the top part with an electric mixer. When done, remove from the heat and let cool for about 7 minutes.

ATECO food coloring is our favorite.

PARTY RECIPES

ART ATTACK

MATISSE CAKE

See page 50 for decorating instructions.

PEANUT-CHILI DIP

½ cup peanut butter (creamy or
crunchy)
3 tablespoons water
2 tablespoons soy sauce
2 tablespoons lemon juice
2 cloves garlic, minced
Dash of cayenne pepper

In a bowl or a food processor, mix together the peanut butter and water. Add the other ingredients while continuing to mix. (If it seems too thick, add a little more water.)

MAKES ⅔ CUP DIP

229

CAMP-OUT

CATERPILLAR CAKE
(Cupcakes)

See page 59 for decorating instructions.

BRAN MUFFINS

1¼ cups all-purpose flour
1 cup whole bran cereal
3 teaspoons sugar
3 teaspoons baking powder
⅓ cup chopped peanuts
1 egg
1 cup mashed bananas
¼ cup milk
1 cup butter or margarine, melted
1 cup raisins

Preheat the oven to 400°F. Grease muffin pans.

In a medium mixing bowl, stir the flour, bran, sugar, baking powder, and peanuts. In another bowl or in a food processor, beat the egg and then add the bananas, milk, and butter. When thoroughly mixed, add it to the flour mixture. Stir until the dry ingredients are just moistened (the batter will be lumpy). Add the raisins, mixing them in with a wooden spoon.

Pour the batter into the muffin tins about two-thirds full. Bake for 20 minutes.

MAKES 12 MUFFINS

When decorating a cake, first trace the design that you'll be piping onto your cake with a toothpick or a wooden skewer.

BREAKFAST PIZZA

For each:
2 slices Cheddar cheese
2 slices Mozzarella cheese
2 tablespoons grated Parmesan cheese
1 Boboli or pita bread

Place the cheese on the dough. Put the dough over the grill or in the oven and bake until the cheese is melted and bubbly.

Some kids may like smoked salmon on top.

CAMPGROUND STEW

Jean Brokaw, Tom's mother, gave this recipe to Meredith who has made it countless times as the girls were growing up. You can spoon the stew into individual foil packets for each child.

2 pounds lean beef stew meat
8 carrots, cut into thick coins
1 cup chopped celery
1 can whole tomatoes
½ package onion soup mix
4 ounces cooking sherry
3 tablespoons tapioca
2 slices white bread, cubed
1 tablespoon sugar
1 tablespoon salt
Dash each of pepper, thyme, marjoram, and rosemary
1 cup peas

Preheat the oven to 250°F.

Combine everything except the peas in a large greased baking dish. Bake, covered, for 6 hours. For the last 20 minutes, add the peas and then bake uncovered for the rest of the time.

SERVES 8 ADULTS OR
ABOUT 14 CHILDREN

S'MORES

For each:

  2 graham crackers
  4 squares of a plain chocolate
    bar
  2 marshmallows

On one graham cracker place four pieces of chocolate. Toast two marshmallows over a fire. When they are gooey, push them on to the chocolate. Top with a second cracker.

CANDID CAMERA

FILM STRIP CAKE

See page 65 for decorating instructions.

CHICKEN ENCHILADAS

  4 tablespoons oil
  ⅓ cup minced onion
  2½ tablespoons all-purpose flour
  1 (8-ounce) can tomato sauce
  1 tablespoon chili powder
  ¼ teaspoon oregano
  1 clove garlic, minced
  ½ teaspoon salt
  2 cups diced cooked chicken
  1 cup sour cream
  12 tortillas
  1 cup half-and-half
  ½ cup chicken broth
  1 cup shredded Cheddar cheese

Preheat the oven to 350°F.

Heat 3 tablespoons oil in a medium saucepan. Add the onion and cook for 4 minutes. Now add 1 tablespoon flour and cook until brown. Add the tomato sauce, chili powder, oregano, garlic, and salt. Simmer, uncovered, for 10 minutes. Add the chicken and sour cream, mix well, and set aside.

Heat the remaining tablespoon of oil in a large skillet. Fry the tortillas in the oil, a few at a time, about 2 minutes each, turning only once. Combine the half-and-half and the broth and heat in a saucepan. Make a paste with the remaining 1½ tablespoons flour and a small amount of the half-and-half mixture. Stir into the remaining mixture and cook and stir until thickened. Dip the fried tortillas into the cream mixture.

Spoon about ¼ cup of the filling onto each tortilla, roll, and place seam side down in a baking dish. Pour the remaining sauce over the enchiladas and sprinkle with the cheese.

Bake for 20 minutes or broil until the cheese is melted.

MAKES 12 SERVINGS

SPANISH RICE

  6 tablespoons oil
  1 cup long-grain rice
  ½ onion, chopped
  ½ green pepper, chopped
  ½ cup tomato sauce
  3 cups hot water
  Salt and pepper to taste
  ½ cup ice water

Heat the oil in the skillet. Add the rice and cook and stir until it is translucent. Add the onion and green pepper and cook for 3 minutes, stirring often. Add the tomato sauce, hot water, and salt and pepper to taste. Boil, uncovered, until almost dry. Add the ice water, cover, and simmer 20 minutes.

MAKES 14 KIDS' SERVINGS

MEXICAN BEAN DIP

½ cup butter or margarine
1 onion, chopped
1 (8-ounce) can green chilies, drained and diced
1 (15-ounce) can refried beans
2 cups grated Cheddar cheese

In a saucepan, melt the butter over medium heat. Add the onion and chilies and sauté for 5–10 minutes. Add the beans and cook until a thick bean paste is formed. When done, garnish with Cheddar cheese.

MAKES 1½ CUPS

CHOCOLATE FACTORY

CHOCOLATE HOUSE BIRTHDAY CAKE

See page 73 for decorating instructions.

PEPPERMINT ICE CREAM SODAS

For each soda:
1 cup milk
1 cup sparkling water
2 scoops peppermint ice cream

Mix the milk and water together; add the ice cream and serve. For a milk shake, place all the ingredients in a blender and mix well.

OREO SANDWICHES

For a real "Oreo" look you should use a filling like cream cheese, but you can choose your child's favorite sandwich filling (lunch meats, tuna salad, peanut butter, all work well). Cut slices of black pumpernickel with a round cookie cutter. Spread one circle with the filling and top with another circle for an instant "Oreo" cookie sandwich.

CLOUD 9

ANGEL CAKE

See page 79 for decorating instructions.

Melissa Dabilis wears her son Adam's swimming goggles when she cuts up onions. She swears it keeps away the tears.

JENNY'S PEANUT BUTTER NOODLES

This is an easy salad to make and the kids absolutely love it!

1 (8-ounce) package linguini
2–3 tablespoons creamy peanut butter
½ teaspoon salt
2 tablespoons soy sauce
1 tablespoon Oriental sesame oil
1 teaspoon sugar
½ teaspoon white wine vinegar
2 cloves garlic, crushed
1 teaspoon chopped onion

Cook the linguini according to the directions on the package. Drain. In a large mixing bowl, mix all of the remaining ingredients. Add the linguini to the sauce and coat well.

QUESADILLAS

5 jalapeño peppers, chopped
1 pound Muenster or Jack cheese, grated
1 cup chopped parsley
16 tortillas

Combine the peppers, cheese, and parsley. Place a portion of the mixture in the middle of a flat tortilla. Fold over and press the edges together. Spray a large skillet with Pam and fry the tortillas over medium heat, or toast in your toaster oven. The quesadilla is ready when the cheese has melted. Keep warm until ready to serve or reheat in the toaster oven for 5 minutes. Do not reheat in the microwave. You may want to make some without the peppers for those who don't like them hot.

MAKES 16 SERVINGS

CLUB CASINO

DICE CAKE

See page 88 for decorating instructions.

FOCACCIO

You can buy focaccio bread at the market, top it with cheese and pepperoni or other favorite toppings, and serve for an easy lunch. If you prefer to make your own focaccio from scratch, here is our recipe:

2½ teaspoons (1 package) active dry yeast or 1 small cake fresh yeast
¼ cup warm water
7½ cups unbleached all-purpose flour or half all-purpose flour and half bread flour
1 tablespoon fine sea salt or table salt
2¼ cups plus 1 to 2 tablespoons water, at room temperature
2 tablespoons olive oil

Process this dough in the food processor in two batches: Stir the yeast into the warm water in a small bowl; let stand until creamy, about 10 minutes. Place the flour and salt in a food processor fitted with the steel blade and process with 2 or 3 pulses to sift. With the machine running, pour 2¼ cups plus 1 tablespoon water, the dissolved yeast, and the oil through the feed tube and process until the dough is velvety and elastic, 2 to 3 minutes.

First Rise: Place the dough in a lightly oiled bowl, cover tightly

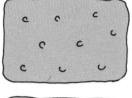

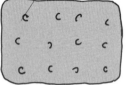

with plastic wrap, and let rise until doubled, about 1½ hours.

Shaping and Second Rise: For round focaccio, cut the dough into three equal pieces on a lightly floured surface. Shape each piece into a thick disk to a 9 or 10-inch circle and place in the bottom of an oiled 9 or 10-inch pie plate. For rectangular focaccio, cut the dough in half and shape to fit two oiled 10½ × 15½-inch pans. Cover the dough with towels and let rise for 30 minutes.

Dimpling and Third Rise: Dimple the dough vigorously with your fingertips, leaving indentations that are as deep as ½ inch (the bakers of Genoa do this to trap the little pools of oil and salt that flavor the surface). Cover the tops with moist towels and let rise until doubled, about 2 hours.

Toppings: A variety of cheese and lunch meats make easy and familiar toppings for kids. For spices, add a little kosher salt (1 teaspoon), 2–3 tablespoons olive oil, chopped fresh or dried rosemary.

Baking: Heat the oven to 400°F. Use baking stones if you have them (turn the oven on 30 minutes before baking) and place the pans directly on the preheated stones. Bake 20 to 25 minutes, spraying with water 3 times in the first 10 minutes; immediately invert the focaccio onto racks to cool so that the bottom crusts don't get soggy. Eat the focaccio warm or at room temperature the same day you bake them. No matter what,

don't refrigerate; they simply won't taste right.

MAKES ENOUGH FOR THREE 9- OR 10-INCH ROUND FOCACCIO OR TWO THINNER 10½×15½-INCH RECTANGULAR FOCACCIO

DOLL SHOWER

DOLL CAKE

See page 95 for decorating instructions.

TEA SANDWICHES

Traditional tea sandwiches are filled with cream cheese, smoked salmon, sliced cucumber and dill, chicken salad or egg salad. However, use any filling your child likes. Spread on the bread of your choice and cut with cookie cutters to make interesting shapes.

FAST ICE CREAM

1 cup whipping cream
⅓ cup sugar
12 ounces frozen solid straw-berries or blackberries (do not use a fruit in syrup—it must be fruit with no ice particles clinging to the fruit)

In a food processor, beat the whipping cream with the metal blade until very thick. Add the sugar and the frozen fruit and keep beating. This ice cream should be eaten immediately.

MAKES 2 SERVINGS

PEANUT BUTTER LADYFINGERS

8 dried figs
2 cups creamy peanut butter
4 ladyfingers, chilled

In a food processor or blender, process the figs and peanut butter to a fairly smooth paste.

If they are not already precut, slice open 4 ladyfingers. Spread one half with the peanut butter mixture and cover with the other half. Wrap in plastic wrap.

MAKES 4 SERVINGS

MICROWAVE FUDGE

1 (16-ounce) package pow-
  dered sugar, sifted
½ cup cocoa powder
¼ teaspoon salt
½ cup butter or margarine
¼ cup milk
1 tablespoon vanilla

Combine the sugar, cocoa powder, and salt in a 2-quart glass bowl. Add the butter and microwave on high, uncovered, for 2–3 minutes. Add the milk, stirring until it is well blended. Put back into the microwave at high for 1 minute. Now add the vanilla and pour the mixture into a lightly greased

8-inch square pan. Refrigerate until it is firm. Cut into squares.

KISS COOKIES (see page 94)

You have lots to do at this party, so we suggest using prepared sugar cookie dough. If you have a favorite sugar cookie recipe, you can use it instead.

FLOWER CHILD

PSYCHEDELIC CAKE

See page 107 for decorating instructions.

CHEESE FONDUE

2 cups bread crumbs
1 cup milk
¾ cup grated Cheddar cheese
4 tablespoons butter
1 teaspoon salt
Nutmeg to taste
1 loaf of French bread

Heat the bread crumbs, milk, cheese, butter, salt, and nutmeg in the top of a double boiler until the cheese is melted. Move into a fondue pot over a Sterno flame.

Cut the French bread into bite-size pieces and place in a basket. Each child spears a piece of bread with a wooden skewer and dips it into the cheese. Be sure to remind the kids to *blow* before they place the hot bread into their mouths!

You can also dip cut-up carrots, broccoli, and cauliflower into this fondue.

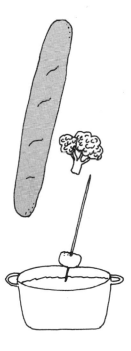

RAREBIT FONDUE

4 cups diced Cheddar cheese
2 teaspoons Worcestershire sauce
2 cloves garlic, minced
1 cup tomato puree
4 tablespoons dry sherry (the alcohol will evaporate, but leave it out if you are concerned)
Cubes of French bread

In a large saucepan, combine the cheese, Worcestershire sauce, garlic, and tomato puree. Cook over a low heat until the cheese has melted and is smooth. Now add the sherry, if you like, and continue cooking for 5 minutes. Then pour the mixture into a fondue pot.

Spear the bread on wooden skewers and dip into the mixture.

CHOCOLATE FONDUE

½ cup half-and-half
4 ounces bittersweet chocolate, finely chopped
1 ounce milk chocolate, finely chopped
¼ teaspoon vanilla
Assorted fruits to dip: strawberries, sliced bananas, slices of oranges

In a small saucepan, bring the half-and-half to a gentle boil. Remove the pan from the heat. Stir in the chocolates until melted. Add the vanilla and stir until smooth.

Pour the chocolate fondue into a fondue pot over a Sterno flame. Arrange the fruit in cups and hand out wooden skewers to each guest. Let each dip in turn, blow, and eat immediately.

GIANTLAND

GIANT COOKIES

See recipe below.

MINI SANDWICHES

Make your child's favorite sandwiches but cut them into small squares so they look like miniatures.

PEANUT BUTTER PRETZEL SNACKS

3–3½ cups all-purpose flour
1 package quick-rising active dry yeast
1 cup milk
⅓ cup creamy peanut butter
2 tablespoons sugar
1 tablespoon butter or margarine
½ tablespoon salt
1 egg
1 tablespoon water
1 egg white
1 recipe Chocolate Glaze (optional)
Chopped peanuts (optional)

In a large mixing bowl, combine 2 cups of the flour and the yeast. In a small saucepan, heat the milk, peanut butter, sugar, butter, and salt just until warm (120 to 130 °F) and butter is almost melted, stirring constantly. Add the milk mixture to the flour mixture; add the 1 whole egg. Using a wooden spoon, mix well.

Now turn out onto a lightly floured surface. Knead in enough of the remaining flour to make a moderately stiff dough that is smooth and elastic (6–8 minutes total). Divide the dough into four portions. Cover and let rest for 10 minutes. Divide each portion into six pieces. Roll each piece of dough into a rope about 16 inches long.

Shape each pretzel by crossing one end of a rope over the other to form a circle, overlapping about 4 inches from each end and leaving the ends free. Take one end of the dough in each hand and twist once at the point where the dough overlaps. Carefully lift each end across to the opposite edge of the circle. Tuck the ends under the edge to make a pretzel shape. Moisten the ends; press to seal.

Place the pretzels on greased baking sheets about ½ inch apart. Cover and let rise in a warm place until nearly doubled (about 20 minutes). Meanwhile, in a small bowl, stir together the water and the egg white. Just before baking, brush the pretzels with a little of the egg white mixture.

Bake in a preheated 375 °F oven for 10–12 minutes or until golden brown. Remove from the baking sheets. Cool on wire racks. If desired, place on waxed paper (or, on a wire rack over waxed paper). Using a teaspoon, drizzle with Chocolate Glaze. Sprinkle with chopped peanuts.

MAKES 24 PRETZEL SNACKS

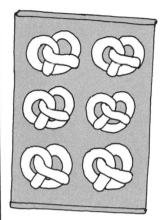

CHOCOLATE GLAZE

1 ounce semisweet chocolate
1 cup powdered sugar, sifted
1-2 tablespoons hot water

In a small saucepan, melt the chocolate over low heat (or, in a 1-cup glass, microwave the chocolate, uncovered, on 100 percent power (high) for 1–2 minutes or until soft enough to stir smooth, stirring after every minute during cooking; the chocolate will not look melted until stirred). Add the sugar and enough hot water to make glaze of drizzling consistency.

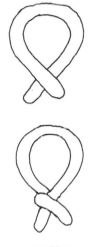

GIANT COOKIES

½ cup butter or margarine, softened
½ cup plus 2 tablespoons sugar
½ cup brown sugar
1 large egg
1 teaspoon vanilla
1 cup all-purpose flour
1 teaspoon ground cinnamon
½ teaspoon baking powder
½ teaspoon baking soda
¼ teaspoon salt
1 cup quick-cooking oats
1 cup chocolate chips
¼ cup raisins
½ cup chopped peanuts

Preheat the oven to 375 °F.

Put the butter, ½ cup sugar, brown sugar, egg, and vanilla into a large bowl. Beat with an electric mixer until creamy.

Add the flour, cinnamon, baking powder, baking soda, and salt to the bowl and beat again on low until well blended. Add the oats, chocolate chips, raisins, and nuts. Mix with a wooden spoon so the chips won't break. Now roll the dough into balls (we use about ¼ cup dough for each ball). Place four balls far apart on an ungreased cookie sheet.

Put the remaining 2 tablespoons of sugar in a small bowl. Dip the bottom of a glass in the sugar and press into one of the dough balls to flatten into a circle about ¼ inch thick. Do this with all the balls, dipping the bottom of the glass into the sugar each time.

Place the cookie sheet on the middle rack of the oven. Bake 10–12 minutes or until the cookies are light brown.

MAKES 4 LARGE COOKIES

GONE FISHIN'

FISH CAKE

See page 120 for decorating instructions.

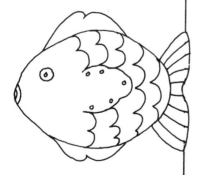

TUNA SALAD

> 3 cans (12½ ounces) tuna packed in water, drained
> 3 tablespoons low-fat mayonnaise
> ½ onion, chopped
> 2 hard-boiled eggs, chopped
> ½ teaspoon lemon juice
> ¾–1 teaspoon dill
> Dash of hickory seasoning

Combine everything in a bowl. Add more mayonnaise if the salad is too dry.

MAKES ENOUGH FOR 12–16 SMALL SANDWICHES

HORSIN' AROUND

CORRAL CAKE

See page 127 for decorating instructions.

ROAST CORN ON THE COB

Place the corncobs (with leaves intact) on the grill. Turn the ears over often while they are roasting. Baste with butter. Tip: Sylvia Gilbar soaks her corn in salted water for an hour or so before she roasts it.

SPARERIBS WITH BARBECUE SAUCE

Preheat the oven to 300°F.

Arrange 6 pounds of lean spareribs in a single layer in a roasting pan. Pour the Barbecue Sauce over the ribs, mixing well. Cover and bake for 2 hours or until the ribs are tender (test with a fork). If you want the ribs to be crisper, remove the cover and place under the broiler for a few minutes before serving.

BARBECUE SAUCE

- ½ cup wine vinegar
- 1 cup water
- ⅓ cup salad oil
- ¾ cup catsup
- 2 tablespoons Worcestershire sauce
- 2 teaspoons dry mustard
- 1 teaspoon paprika
- 1 teaspoon salt
- ¼ teaspoon pepper
- 2 slices lemon
- ⅓ cup chopped onion
- ¼ cup honey

Mix all the ingredients except the honey in a saucepan. Bring to a quick boil, stirring constantly. Turn the heat to low and simmer 20 minutes or until slightly thick. Remove from the heat and strain. Add the honey and mix well.

MAKES 2 CUPS SAUCE

IT'S A DOG'S LIFE

DOG DISH CAKE

See page 132 for decorating instructions.

CHOCOLATE DOGGIE BONE COOKIES

(For people only!)

(Adapted from the Marlene Sorosky *Seasons Greetings Cookbook*.)

- 2½ sticks butter or margarine, softened
- 1¾ cups powdered sugar, sifted
- 1 large egg, at room temperature
- 2½ cups all-purpose flour
- ½ cup unsweetened cocoa powder
- ¼ teaspoon salt

Cream the butter and sugar in a mixing bowl with an electric mixer until light and fluffy, about 2 minutes. Mix in the egg; beat another minute. Add the flour, cocoa, and salt; mix well. Divide the dough into three parts. Flatten each into a disk and wrap in plastic wrap. Refrigerate until firm, at least 1 hour. The dough will keep for up to 5 days in plastic wrap in the refrigerator.

To bake, preheat the oven to 325°F. Grease a cookie sheet. Remove one disk of dough at a time from the refrigerator. Roll until approximately ⅛ inch thick. Remove the top piece of plastic wrap and cut out your cookies using a doggie bone cookie cutter. Bake for 8–10 minutes. These cookie cutters come in four sizes. You will produce 2½ dozen cookies with the 4½ size bone.

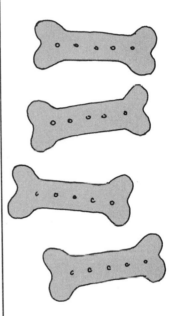

TRAIL MIX

3 cups rolled oats
1½ cups wheat germ
½ cup skim milk powder
1 cup slivered or coarsely
  chopped almonds
½ cup sesame seeds
1 cup hulled sunflower seeds
½ cup vegetable oil
¼–½ cup honey
1 cup raisins
½ cup cut-up dried apricots

Toast the oats in a shallow pan at 300°F for 15 minutes. In a large bowl, combine the wheat germ, skim milk powder, almonds, and sesame and sunflower seeds. Heat the oil and honey just until warm. Combine with the mixture in the bowl. Combine the contents of the bowl with the toasted oats and spread in several shallow pans in a thin layer. Continue toasting, stirring occasionally, for 15 minutes more, or until all the ingredients are toasted.

Place in a large container and add the raisins and apricots. Cool and store in a tightly covered container in the refrigerator.

MAKES ABOUT 10 CUPS

KIDNAPPED PARTY

The doughnuts serve as birthday "cakes."

RICOTTA PANCAKES

1 (15-ounce) container ricotta
  cheese
4 eggs
⅓ cup sifted all-purpose flour
2 tablespoons butter or margarine, melted
2 tablespoons sugar
1 teaspoon vanilla
½ cup butter or margarine
2 cups nonfat plain yogurt,
  vanilla yogurt, or sour cream

In a food processor, using the steel blade, blend all the ingredients, except the ½ cup butter and yogurt, until smooth. In a skillet, over low heat, melt 1 tablespoon butter, using the rest as needed. Use a soup spoon to ladle the batter into the skillet, making each pancake silver dollar size. When the pancake is brown on one side, turn over quickly just once to finish cooking.

As you remove each pancake from the pan, place on a hot plate to keep warm. Stack the pancakes and cover with aluminum foil to keep them warm as you are cooking. When they are all ready, serve and top with yogurt.

MAKES ABOUT 30 SILVER
DOLLAR PANCAKES

POPOVER PANCAKE

Kids love this because it is puffy.

1 cup all-purpose flour
1 cup milk
4 eggs
2 tablespoons butter or
  margarine

Preheat the oven to 425°F.

In a bowl, combine the flour, milk, and eggs. Beat by hand lightly, leaving the batter slightly lumpy. Heat the butter in a casserole or 12-inch skillet with an ovenproof handle. Pour the batter into the skillet and bake for 20 minutes, until the pancake is puffy and golden brown. Serve immediately! SERVES 4; MAKE TWO FOR 8–10 KIDS

GINGERBREAD PANCAKES

1 cup whole wheat flour
¾ teaspoon baking soda
½ teaspoon ground ginger
½ teaspoon ground cinnamon
¼ teaspoon salt
¼ teaspoon ground cloves
2 teaspoons instant chocolate powder
¼ cup hot water
1 egg, beaten
1 (6-ounce) can frozen apple juice concentrate
2 tablespoons margarine, melted

Combine the flour, baking soda, ginger, cinnamon, salt, and cloves in a large mixing bowl. In another smaller bowl, dissolve the chocolate powder in the hot water. Add the egg, apple juice concentrate, and melted margarine and mix well. Add the liquids to the dry ingredients and mix just enough to moisten (the mixture will be lumpy).

Pour the batter, ¼ cup at a time, onto a hot skillet greased with margarine or oil. Cook until each pancake is bubbly, then turn over just once and brown the other side.

PANCAKE TOPPINGS

Here are a couple of alternatives for kids who are tired of maple syrup:

ORANGE-HONEY SYRUP
¾ cup honey
1 teaspoon butter or margarine
1 tablespoon grated orange rind
¼ cup orange juice
1 teaspoon orange extract

In a saucepan, heat the honey and butter just until bubbly. Remove from the heat and stir in the orange rind, orange juice, and orange extract. Serve warm.

APPLE BUTTER
8 cups thinly sliced peeled apples
½ cup frozen apple juice concentrate
1 cup water
1 teaspoon ground cinnamon
½ teaspoon ground allspice
A pinch of ground cloves

Combine all the ingredients in a large saucepan and bring to a boil. Reduce the heat and simmer, uncovered, for 15 minutes, stirring occasionally. Remove from the heat and cool slightly. Place in a blender and mix until smooth.

SHORTCUT DOUGHNUTS

Vegetable oil as needed for frying
2 eggs
½ cup sugar
2 cups biscuit mix
½ cup milk
2 tablespoons grated orange or lemon rind

Pour 1 cup vegetable oil into a deep-sided frying pan (you will need more later) and heat to 375 °F (you can use an electric frying pan if you have one).

Beat the eggs in a mixing bowl. Add the sugar and beat again. Add the biscuit mix (don't sift it) to the egg mixture alternately with the milk, about a third at a time. Stir in the grated rind for flavor.

Grease two teaspoons by dipping them into the boiling oil. Pick up a spoonful of batter and use the other spoon to ease it into the pan. Fry until golden on one side (under 2 minutes); turn and brown on the other side. Remove and drain on paper towels.

You can sprinkle with powdered sugar or roll in a mixture of sugar and ground cinnamon.

MAKES 3 DOZEN

BREAKFAST BANANA SPLITS

Pancakes:
 1 egg
 1 cup all-purpose flour
 ¾ cup milk
 1 tablespoon sugar
 2 tablespoons vegetable oil
 3 teaspoons baking powder
 ½ teaspoon salt

Toppings:
 3 bananas, split in half and
    quartered
 1 (8-ounce) carton strawberry
    yogurt
 1 (8-ounce) carton vanilla yogurt

 1 (8-ounce) can crushed pineapple
    in its own juice, drained
 ½ cup fresh blueberries
 2 tablespoons granola
 Fresh strawberries

In a food processor, beat the egg until fluffy. Add the remaining ingredients and beat until smooth. Grease a hot skillet and drop a serving spoonful onto the skillet, one for each pancake. When each bubbles and the edges are brown, turn over just once.

To serve, place two pancakes on each serving plate; top each serving with 2 banana pieces, ⅙ each of strawberry yogurt, vanilla yogurt, pineapple, and blueberries. Sprinkle each serving with granola. Garnish with strawberries.

MAKES 6 SERVINGS

PIG-OUT BIRTHDAY

PIGLET CUPCAKES
See page 144 for decorating instructions.

SPAGHETTI MARINARA

½ cup olive oil
3 cloves garlic, chopped
*4 cups canned Italian plum
tomatoes, drained and
chopped*
½ teaspoon salt
*¼ teaspoon freshly ground
pepper*
*½ cup finely chopped fresh
parsley*
*1 teaspoon fresh oregano
(or ½ teaspoon dried)*
1 pound spaghetti
*1 cup freshly grated Parmesan
cheese*

Heat the oil in a skillet or a saucepan. Add the garlic and cook until soft, less than a minute (watch so it doesn't burn). Add the tomatoes, salt, pepper, parsley, and oregano. Simmer 2–2½ hours or until the sauce has thickened. Cook the pasta according to the package directions. Drain and add the spaghetti to the sauce. Sprinkle the Parmesan cheese on top.

SECRET AGENTS

ICE CREAM CAKE

See page 153 for decorating instructions.

For the mystery menu you can choose any of the dishes listed (we have included many of the recipes in other parties).

SHIPWRECKED

ISLAND CAKE

See page 162 for decorating instructions.

Serve the Tuna Salad (see recipe page 238) in cucumbers or pineapples that have been scooped out to resemble boats. Add a paper flag (on a toothpick) to each.

SOCCER

SOCCER FIELD CAKE

See page 167 for decorating instructions.

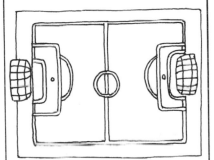

SO WHAT'S VS. BIG DEALS

THE NUMBER 1 CAKE

See page 174 for decorating instructions.

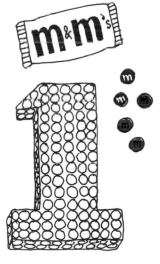

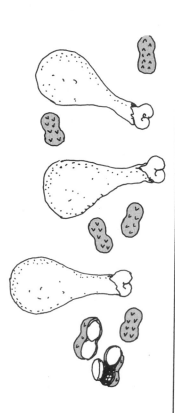

If you don't want to serve hot dogs, here's another choice:

PEANUT CHICKEN

4 tablespoons peanut butter
  (creamy or chunky)
4 tablespoons margarine, melted
1 cup apricot juice
10 chicken legs
2 cups corn flakes, crushed
Pinch of ground ginger
Pinch of ground cinnamon
Pinch of pepper

Make the marinade by mixing the peanut butter, margarine, and juice and pour over the chicken in a glass baking dish. Refrigerate at least 1 hour or overnight.

Preheat the oven to 350°F.

Mix together the corn flakes, ginger, cinnamon, and pepper. Remove each piece of chicken from the marinade with a slotted spoon and roll in the corn flake mixture, coating well. Place back in the baking dish (if you have a rack that fits in the dish, use it). Pour the rest of the marinade over the chicken. Bake for 45 minutes, basting occasionally.

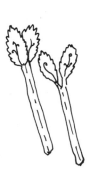

AMERICAN PICNIC POTATO SALAD

(Adapted from *The Silver Palate Cookbook* by Rosso and Lukins, our kids' favorite potato salad!)

2 pounds small red unpeeled
  potatoes, well scrubbed
¼ cup cider vinegar
¼ cup olive oil
1 cup mayonnaise, plus more if
  needed

2 tablespoons prepared Dijon-
  style mustard
4 tablespoons chopped parsley
½ cup thinly sliced red onions
½ cup diced celery, 1 inch long by
  ¼ inch wide
2 medium cucumbers, peeled,
  seeded, and sliced
Salt and pepper to taste
5 hard-boiled eggs, peeled and
  quartered

Boil the potatoes until tender; do not overcook! Drain and slice. Add the vinegar and olive oil. Add the mayonnaise, mustard, parsley, onions, celery, and cucumbers. Toss. Now add salt and pepper to taste.

Add the quartered eggs and toss again. Cool, cover, and refrigerate overnight. Before serving you may want to toss the salad again, correct the seasoning, and add more mayonnaise if needed.

SERVES 10–12

CORN MUFFINS

Our friend Suzy Kreiser, a master chef whose dishes for both grown-ups and kids alike are legendary in Los Angeles, has shared this recipe from the cookbook she put together for her mom.

¼ cup yellow cornmeal
¼ cup all-purpose flour
1 teaspoon baking powder
1 teaspoon sugar
½ teaspoon salt
2 egg whites
5 tablespoons milk
1 tablespoon vegetable oil

Preheat the oven to 400°F. Grease two 6-gem muffin tins or one 12-gem muffin tin.

In a mixing bowl, stir together all the ingredients until just combined. Divide the batter among the tins; using about ⅛ cup for each muffin.

Bake for 15 minutes. Turn the muffins out on a rack to cool. They can be made 4 days in advance and stored in airtight containers.

MAKES 12 GEM MUFFINS

STARGAZING PARTY

STAR CAKE

See page 183 for decorating instructions.

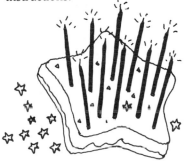

ANGEL HAIR PRIMAVERA

Believe it or not, there are some children who do love vegetables. For those who don't hold them in high regard, this recipe may change their minds!

16 thin asparagus spears
1 yellow crookneck squash
1 medium zucchini
1 red bell pepper
2 tablespoons butter or
*   margarine*
2 tablespoons olive oil
1¼ cups heavy cream

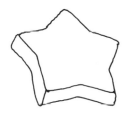

1 cup peas, fresh or frozen,
*   thawed*
12 ounces thin spaghetti
½ cup grated Parmesan cheese
1 cup thinly sliced scallions,
*   with the green tops*
¼ cup chopped fresh basil
*   (or 1 teaspoon dried)*
Salt and freshly ground pepper
*   to taste*

Heat a large pot full of water for the pasta. Add a drop of oil and 2 teaspoons of salt.

Cut the tips off the asparagus about 2 inches down the stem and slice the stalks crosswise into ¼-inch pieces. Slice the two squashes (throw away the seeds). Slice the pepper into thin slices about 1½ inches long.

In a large skillet, melt the butter and oil until hot. Add each vegetable, one at a time, and cook for about 1 minute each (add the pepper last). Then add the cream and peas and simmer for 2 minutes.

Cook the pasta about 5 minutes. While the pasta is cooking, watch the vegetables so they don't get too soft. When the pasta is done, drain, return it to the pot, and add the vegetable mixture. Sprinkle the cheese, scallions, and basil and toss together. Add the salt and pepper.

SERVES 8–10 CHILDREN

STELLAR SALAD

To your favorite green salad add sliced carrots, peppers, and mushrooms all cut into star shapes with a 1-inch star-shaped cookie cutter.

STEGOSAURUS & FRIENDS

DINOSAUR CAKE

See page 190 for decorating instructions.

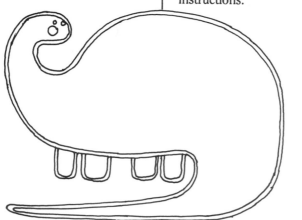

Frozen cakes are easier to cut, especially when you are trying to create unusual shapes.

CHICKEN WINGS

¼ cup soy sauce
¼ cup water
2 teaspoons brown sugar
⅛ teaspoon ground ginger
1 small clove garlic, minced
24 chicken wings
Salt and pepper
Cornstarch
Vegetable oil for frying

Mix the first five ingredients and pour over the wings to marinate. Refrigerate for at least 3 hours or overnight. Drain. Sprinkle with salt and pepper and dust with cornstarch, shaking off the excess.

Heat 1½ inches of oil in a deep frying pan to 350°F. Cook 4–5 wings at a time for 5–6 minutes or until golden brown. Remove from the skillet with a slotted spoon. Drain on paper towels and keep warm in a 150°F oven while the others are cooking.

PEANUT BUTTER BREAD

½ cup chunky peanut butter
½ cup orange or plain honey
3 tablespoons vegetable oil
2 eggs
½ cup grated carrots
2 bananas, mashed
¼ cup low-fat milk
¼ teaspoon ground cinnamon
¼ teaspoon ground cloves
¼ teaspoon ground nutmeg
1 teaspoon vanilla
Pinch of salt
1 teaspoon baking powder
1 teaspoon baking soda
1¾ cups whole wheat flour

Preheat the oven to 300°F. Butter a 9 × 5-inch loaf pan.

In a bowl, blend together the peanut butter, honey, oil, eggs, carrots, and bananas. Add the milk, spices, vanilla, salt, baking powder, baking soda, and flour. Blend together well.

Pour the batter into the prepared pan. Bake for 1 hour and 15 minutes, or until a toothpick inserted in the center comes out clean. Cool the bread on a wire rack.

Use plain or top with a spread.

EGG BOWLS

Choose your child's favorite fillings (tuna fish, salmon salad, cream cheese, etc.) and fill the white halves of hard-boiled eggs. Figure two halves (one egg) per child.

SUPERHEROES

THE SUPERHERO CAKE

See page 199 for decorating instructions.

SWEEPSTAKES

THE SWEEPSTAKES CAKE

See page 206 for decorating instructions.

SPAGHETTI PIE

6 ounces spaghetti
2 tablespoons butter
⅓ cup grated Parmesan cheese
2 eggs, well beaten
1 pound ground beef or pork sausage
½ cup chopped onion
¼ cup chopped green pepper
1 cup canned tomatoes, un-drained and cut up
1 (6-ounce) can tomato paste
1 teaspoon sugar
1 teaspoon dried oregano
½ teaspoon garlic salt
1 cup cottage cheese
½ cup shredded mozzarella cheese

Cook the spaghetti as per package instructions and drain. Stir in the butter, Parmesan, and eggs. Form the spaghetti mixture into a crust in a buttered 10-inch pie plate.

Cook the ground beef, onion, and pepper until the vegetables are tender and the meat is brown. Drain off the excess fat. Stir in the undrained tomatoes, tomato paste, sugar, oregano, and garlic salt. Heat through. Spread the cottage cheese over the bottom of the spaghetti crust. Fill the pie with the beef mixture. Sprinkle mozzarella cheese on the top.

Bake for 5 minutes or longer, until the cheese melts.

SERVES 6–8 CHILDREN; MAKE TWO PIES FOR MORE OR IF YOUR KIDS ARE BIG EATERS

THIS IS YOUR LIFE

LIFE MAGAZINE CAKE

See page 213 for decorating instructions.

Cassie Dabilis makes colored sugars for decorating by adding liquid food coloring a drop at a time to regular sugar.

FRUIT PIZZAS

1 (20-ounce) package refrigerated sugar cookie dough
1 (8-ounce) package cream cheese, softened
2 tablespoons milk
1 teaspoon grated orange or lemon zest
2 teaspoons sugar
¼ cup sliced strawberries
¼ cup sliced bananas, dipped in lemon juice
¼ cup sliced and peeled peaches
¼ cup halved seedless grapes
6 melon balls

Preheat the oven to 300°F.
Press the dough into six 4-inch tart pans. Bake for 25–30 minutes or until lightly browned. Let cool. Meanwhile, combine the cream cheese, milk, orange zest, and sugar in a small mixing bowl. Beat until smooth. Now spread the cream cheese mixture over the cooled cookie tarts. Top with the fruit.

MAKES 6 TARTS

UNDER THE BIG TOP

THE CIRCUS TRAIN CAKE

See page 221 for decorating instructions.

Answer to puzzle on page 205.

Answer to puzzle on page 138.

RESOURCES

GENERAL

The Penny Whistle Toy Store: (212) 925-2088. If you can't find the toys, games, or crafts materials listed in the book locally, call Penny Whistle.

Wilton Cake Decorating Yearbook, 1992,
  2240 West 75th Street, Woodridge, IL 60517-0750.
  (708) 963-7100.

  Star pan 2105-Y-2512
  Superhero pan 503-Y-857; 2105-Y-8507
  Mini loaf pan 2105-Y-9791
  Twelve-inch round pan 2105-Y-2215
  Mini ball pan 2105-Y-1760
  For individual mini birthday cakes, use jumbo muffin pan 2105-Y-1820
  Crayon candles 2811-Y-227

Personalized pencils and gifts may be ordered through Seastrom Associates, 133 West 19th Street, New York, NY 10011. (212) 243-1488. Plan to order at least six weeks in advance.

Birthday Flipbook by Jill Weber can be found at Penny Whistle™ Toys or order directly from Frajil Farms, Inc., Box 13, Mont Vernon, NH 03057.

The Oriental Trading Company, Inc., P.O. Box 3047, Omaha, Nebraska 68103-0407. 1-800-228-2269.

Call us at Penny Whistle and we'll try to help.

ART ATTACK

Fimo clay is available at all toy stores, as is Night Glow Fimo which glows in the dark. If you have trouble getting it, call Flax Co., (800) 547-7778.

Masterpiece: 60 Famous Paintings and Their Stories, from the Start Exploring Series by Mary Martin and Steven Zorn, published by Running Press. This is a coloring book of reproductions with stories about each painting.

Pads of paper with paint in the paper are available at Peerless Paints, 11 Diamond Place, Rochester, NY 14609. (716) 288-7460.

Art posters and postcards are available through Metropolitan Museum of Art, Fifth Avenue and 82nd Street, New York, NY 10028. (212) 535-7710.

How to Draw Cartoons and Caricatures by Judy Tatchell (Tulsa, OK: EDC Publishing, 1987).

Tex Avery, King of Cartoons, by Joe Adamson (New York: Da Capo, 1985).

CAMP-OUT

Tents and camping gear are available at Adventure 16, Outdoor and Travel Outfitters, Los Angeles, CA. (310) 473-4574.

For camping accessories contact The Nature Company, 750 First Avenue, Berkeley, CA 94710. Catalog telephone (800) 227-1114.

Wilton Cake Decorating Yearbook (see General Resources, above) mini ball pan 2105-Y-1760.

CHOCOLATE FACTORY

Set for painting your own candy bars is available from Flax Co. catalog, (800) 547-7778, item #1164H.

CLUB CASINO

Contact Beistle Company, Shippensburg, PA 17257, for oversized playing cards, dice, and posters of roulette wheels and one-armed bandits, etc.

Plush dice and other casino items are available at Frank Stein Novelty Co., 1969 South Los Angeles Street, Los Angeles, CA 90011, (213) 747-9585 (see General Resources above for further information).

KIDNAPPED

Wilton Cake Decorating Yearbook (see General Resources, above): superhero pan 2105-Y-8507 or twelve-inch round pan 2105-Y-2215.

PIG-OUT BIRTHDAY

Robinson's Racing Pigs, a coloring book, is available at 5809 20th Avenue South, Tampa, FL 33619. (813) 628-4770.

Wilton Cake Decorating Yearbook (see General Resources, above): mini ball pan 2105-Y-1760.

SOCCER

Offsides Sports Service, 11710 Santa Monica Boulevard, Los Angeles, CA 90025. (310) 473-5192. Soccer accessories including T-shirts, posters, miniature balls, and cones.

STARGAZING PARTY

StarWriters and astronomical paraphernalia can be purchased at The Nature Company, 750 First Avenue, Berkeley, CA 94710. Catalog telephone (800) 227-1114.

Planetarium books:
> Hayden Planetarium, 81st Street and Central Park West, New York, NY 10024. (212) 769-5920.
> Griffith Observatory, Los Angeles, CA 90027. (213) 663-8171.

Wilton Cake Decorating Yearbook (see General Resources, above): star pan 2105-Y-2512.

Night sky and stargazing maps are available at Museum of Natural History, 79th Street and Central Park West, New York, NY 10024, and at Griffith Observatory, Los Angeles, CA, 90027. (213) 663-8171.

"Starry Night" Glow in the Dark Stick-On Vinyl Stars. Package of 150 self-adhesive stars, moons, and comets: #1832. Made by Romar Enterprises, Ltd., P.O. Box 616, Pomona, NY 10970. Retail price, $4.35; available at toy stores and nature stores.

Tasco Telescopes. Available at toy stores and planetariums.

Super Star Machine (a portable planetarium) by Bushnell, Bausch & Lomb. Available at toy stores and planetariums.

Solar System Mobile is made by Geo Systems, DeMer & Co., San Teandro, CA.

Inflatable Celestial Globe is made by Small Wonder Toys. Available at toy stores.

Glow in the Dark Stargazer Constellation and Solar System is available through Schulling, P.O. Box 233, Peabody, MA 01960.

Glow in the Dark Planetarium (500 self-adhesive stars, planets, comets, and meteors) and Glow in the Dark Moon, Earth, Saturn are made by Illuminations, Cambridge, MA. Available at toy stores or through The Nature Company Catalog. (800) 227-1114.

Find the Constellations, by H. A. Rey (Boston: Houghton Mifflin, Co., 1988).

Glow in the Dark Constellations: A Field Guide for Young Stargazers, by C.E. Thompson (New York: Grosset & Dunlap, 1989).

The Young Astronomer, an Usborne Guide by Sheila Snowden (Tulsa, OK: EDC Publishing, 1983).

Astronomy Activity Book, by Dennis Schatz (New York: Simon & Schuster, Little Simon, 1991).

Sun, Stars & Planets, by Tom Stacy (New York: Random House, 1990).

STEGOSAURUS & FRIENDS

Inflatable dinosaurs and "Make Your Own Dinosaurs" models are available through The Nature Company, 750 First Avenue, Berkeley, CA 94710. Catalog telephone (800) 227-1114.

Dinosaurs Punchout Stencils Book, A. G. Smith (New York: Dover Publishing, 1987).

Colossal Fossils: Dinosaur Riddles, ed. by Charles Keller (New York: Simon & Schuster, Little Simon, 1987). A good book for party favors.

Dinosaur Bob, by William Joyce (New York: HarperCollins, 1988).

Did the Comets Kill the Dinosaurs?, by Isaac Asimov (New York: Dell Yearling, 1990).

Dinosaurs and Things, a board game by Aristoplay, available at toy stores.

Dinosaurs and Prehistoric Life, made by Educational Insights, available at toy stores.

Dino Dominoes, made by Ravensburger, available at toy stores.

SUPERHEROES (Cloud 9)

How to Draw Cartoons and Caricatures, by Judy Tatchell (Tulsa, OK: EDC Publishing, 1987).

Tex Avery, King of Cartoons, by Joe Adamson (New York: Da Capo, 1985).

Wilton Cake Decorating Yearbook (see General Resources, page 249): superhero pan 503-Y-857; 2105-Y-8507.

UNDER THE BIG TOP

Prizes and favors can be ordered from Frank Stein (see General Resources, page 249).

Wilton Cake Decorating Yearbook (see General Resources, page 249): mini loaf pan 2105-Y-9791.

INDEX